Pennsylvania

Douglas Root, Gwen Shaffer, and Caroline Tiger
Photography by Jerry Irwin

COMPASS AMERICAN GUIDES
An imprint of Fodor's Travel Publications

Compass American Guides: Pennsylvania

Compass Editorial Director: Jennifer Paull
Editor: Emmanuelle Alspaugh
Design: Tigist Getachew, Nora Rosansky
Creative Director: Fabrizio La Rocca
Photo Editor and Archival Researcher: Melanie Marin
Desktop Production Support: Siobhan O'Hare
Editorial Production: Astrid deRidder
Map Design: Mark Stroud, Moon Street Cartography
Manufacturing/Production: Angela L. McLean

Cover photo, Jerry Irwin: Country road near Sugar Grove

Third Edition
ISBN 978-1-4000-0739-4
ISSN 1543-1665

The content of this book is based on information supplied to us at press time, but changes occur all the time, and the publisher cannot accept responsibility for facts that become outdated or for inadvertent errors or omissions.

Compass American Guides, 1745 Broadway, New York, NY 10019
PRINTED IN CHINA
10 9 8 7 6 5 4 3 2 1

The Brandywine Valley, site of
a key Revolutionary battle.

CONTENTS

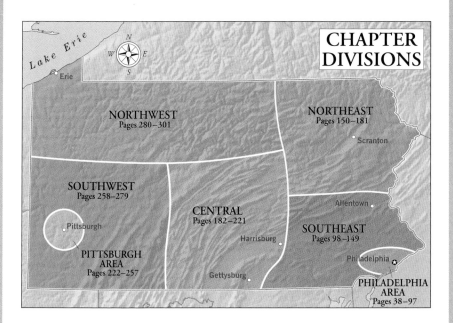

TOPICAL ESSAYS & SIDEBARS

LITERARY EXTRACTS

MAPS

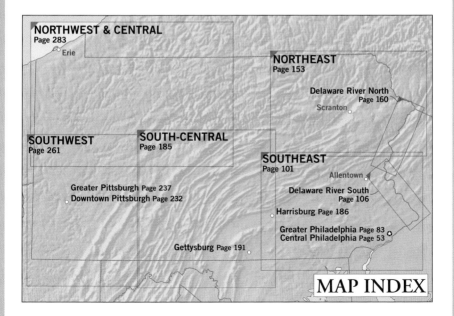

NORTHWEST & CENTRAL
Page 283

Erie

NORTHEAST
Page 153

Delaware River North
Page 160

Scranton

SOUTHWEST
Page 261

SOUTH-CENTRAL
Page 185

SOUTHEAST
Page 101

Allentown

Greater Pittsburgh Page 237
Downtown Pittsburgh Page 232

Delaware River South
Page 106

Harrisburg Page 186

Greater Philadelphia Page 83
Central Philadelphia Page 53

Gettysburg Page 191

MAP INDEX

AVERAGE JANUARY TEMPERATURES

Celsius	Fahrenheit
-1.1	30
-2.2	28
-3.3	26
-4.4	24

AVERAGE JULY TEMPERATURES

Celsius	Fahrenheit
23.3	74
22.2	72
21.1	70
20.0	68

Lake Erie

North East
90

NEW YORK

Erie
86 17

Lake City   Avonia   20
5   90

Jamestown   Olean

Waterford   19   Allegheny Reservoir   Bradford   44

Albion   6N
18   6   Union City   62
79   19   Cambridge Springs   Pittsfield   Warren   Smethport   Port Allegany   Coudersport
59   6
Pymatuning Reservoir   Sheffield   6   Lantz Corners
9   6   Conneaut Lake   Meadville   Titusville   Tidioute   Kane   219
285   27   Allegheny   62
322   322   Emporium   144
Jamestown   Oil City   Tionesta   Ridgway   St Marys   120   Kettle Creek State Park
Greenville   Franklin   Driftwood
Shenango River Lake   8   322   Shippenville   Brockway
9   18   62   Clarion   28   219
Mercer   80   Brookville   153
60   Slippery Rock   Dubois   80
422   Mayport   Reynoldsville   322
224   New Castle   New Bethlehem   219   Clearfield   322   Bellefonte
76   60   422   28   Punxsutawney   879   Philipsburg
19   Butler   422   119   Port Matilda   220   State College
79   356   Kittanning   85   Home   219   Barnesboro
Rochester   28   Allegheny   Indiana   422
68   65   Freeport   Tarentum   Altoona   22   Huntingdon
60   Ambridge   119   Ebensburg   22   Mt Union
30   51   279   Pittsburgh   Murrysville   Blairsville   22   522
22   Carnegie   376   30   76   Greensburg   Latrobe   Johnstown   220   Shade
Paris   79   19   51   Ligonier   30
Washington   70   Jennerstown   219
40   Scenery Hill   119   Kanter   Bedford   76
70   40   Youghiogheny   220   30   Chambersbu
Brownsville   51   Berlin   70   76
Waynesburg   21   Uniontown   Garrett   70   522
21   Mt Davis 3,213   Meyersdale   220   Mercersburg
Farmington   (highest point in Pennsylvania)   219   522
250   119   43   40
WEST VIRGINIA   79   68   MARYLAND   68   WV

OHIO

Ohio

N
W   E
S

AVERAGE ANNUAL PRECIPITATION

Centimeters	Inches
116	46
111	44
106	42
101	40

AVERAGE ANNUAL SNOWFALL

Centimeters	Inches
202	70
177	60
152	50
127	40
101	30

PENNSYLVANIA

0   20   40 Miles

0   20   40   60 Kilometers

Elevation
in feet

| 3,213 |
| 2,200 |
| 1,800 |
| 1,400 |
| 1,000 |
| 600 |
| 100 |

NEW YORK

Elmira   Binghamton

Elkland   Sayre   Hallstead   Susquehanna   N Y   Delaware

Mansfield   Montrose

Wellsboro   Towanda   Kingsley   Union Dale

Grand Canyon of Pennsylvania   Wyalusing   Honesdale   White Mills

Liberty   Dushore   Tunkhannock   Carbondale   Hawley

Trout Run   Muncy Valley   Dunmore   River

Williamsport   West Pittston   Scranton   Milford

Jersey Shore   Wilkes-Barre

Lock Haven   Mt Pocono   Bushkill

Berwick   Stroudsburg   Delaware Water Gap

Lewisburg   Milton   Hiskory Run   Hazleton   Kresgeville   Mt Bethel

Sunbury   Shenandoah   Palmerton   NEW JERSEY

Potters Mills   Middleburg   Shamokin

Wagner   Pottsville   Allentown   Bethlehem   Easton

Lewistown   Kintnersville

Elizabethville   Hamburg   Kutztown   Point Pleasant

Duncannon   Millersburg   Quakertown

HARRISBURG   Hershey   Lebanon   Reading   Doylestown   New Hope

Carlisle   Ephrata   Pottstown   Trenton

Shippensburg   Columbia   Lancaster   Valley Forge

York   Paradise   Chatwood

Gettysburg   Quarryville   Philadelphia

Chadds Ford

DE   Wilmington

MARYLAND   Conowingo   NEW JERSEY

Performers reenact the first reading of
the Declaration of Independence.

CULTURE & HISTORY

[Pennsylvania] is a clear and just thing, and my God that has given it me through many difficulties, will, I believe, bless and make it the seed of a nation. I shall have a tender care for the government, that it be well laid at first.... I purpose that which is extraordinary and to leave myself and successors no power of doing mischief, that the will of one man may not hinder the good of an whole country.

—William Penn's letter to a friend in 1681

LANDSCAPE AND EARLY HISTORY

Long before the King of England bequeathed Pennsylvania to the good-hearted English aristocrat William Penn, its lands had been home to tribal nations that reaped the bounty of its forested mountains, rushing rivers, and fine valleys. When the first European explorers arrived in Pennsylvania in the early 17th century, they found the peaceful Lenni Lenape tribe, the Susquehannocks, and the Eries. These tribes were by that time vassals to the powerful and warlike Five Nations of Iroquois, which had expanded from what is now New York during the previous century. Weakened by war, Pennsylvania's tribes had lost most of their population to measles and smallpox, diseases that had made their way inland from European coastal settlements during the previous half-century. Despite the terrible difficulties of the Indian, writes Sylvester Stevens in *Pennsylvania, Birthplace of a Nation:*

> He was living in an advanced Stone Age culture, which included settled life in villages and farming. He was making pottery vessels for his cooking and for the storage of food ... even decorating his pottery in the later years of this era.... He was growing corn, along with tobacco. He lived in semipermanent bark houses and they were grouped into villages ... Penn described those [native people] he saw as "generally tall, straight, well built, and of singular proportion; they tread strong and clever, and mostly walk with a lofty chin."... In councils he found them very well able to conceal their true feelings in a certain impassive attitude.... He noted their "Liberality" and that "Nothing is too good for their friend."

Swedish and Finnish explorers began a fur and tobacco trade with the Indians and by the middle of the 17th century had established a few scattered forts—near New Castle in the southwest and around present-day Wilmington, Chester, and Philadelphia in the southeast. However, Dutch settlers in New Amsterdam (now New York City), who feared their lucrative trade with the Iroquois would be siphoned off at the source, weren't pleased. Their soldiers marched on the settlements and, with little resistance, won control.

Native American Man of the Northeast Woodlands (ca. 1820), artist unknown. (Philadelphia Museum of Art)

The Dutch made a half-hearted effort to colonize the territory, changing the name of the Scandinavian fort near New Castle to New Amstel, and resettling other areas. But in 1664, the Dutch were driven out when the English dispatched hundreds of troops to claim the territory.

ENGLISH SETTLEMENT

By the 1680s, British control had thrown the territory wide open to European colonists—ragtaggers of every sort, some from Great Britain, some from Germany fleeing wars in the Rhineland. Most newcomers favored the lower Delaware River area and its nearby countryside, but there was no plan to the settlements and the territory was sorely in need of a strong governor.

Into this unsettled landscape came the aristocratic English idealist William Penn, granted title to Pennsylvania by Charles II of England. Penn was a Quaker, a follower of theologian and Society of Friends founder George Fox, who preached that individuals have a direct relationship with God and did not need the priests or ministers of religious institutions to mediate their faith. Civil hierarchies were similarly discredited: Fox's followers did not recognize titles, to the consternation of the titled British, nor would they take oaths. Religious persecution took the form of civil prosecution: William Penn himself was imprisoned four times, once for refusing to swear allegiance to the crown.

Charles II's gift to William Penn can be seen as a brilliant solution to an intractable problem. Penn's beliefs, along with his status, eloquence, and charm, made him a disruptive force in England. His father, Admiral William Penn, had been a distinguished naval officer, the holder of various government posts, a wealthy landowner, and, most important, the king's friend and creditor. After Admiral Penn died, his son requested and accepted the land in payment of the king's debt.

The only land available to Penn was territory inland from the coveted North American seacoast, though what England's rulers considered undesirable hinterland would quickly turn out to be one of the richest and the most strategically located of all the new American colonies. The difficult young aristocrat, who arrived in his new territory in 1682, stayed only two years before he sailed home again.

TOLERANT, WELL-GOVERNED SOCIETY

Penn's Quaker faith informed his new passion, the planning of government and the laying out of cities in the new colony. When Penn arrived to enact his vision of a free and tolerant society, about a thousand Europeans were living near the

Delaware River, many of whom had risked everything for an opportunity to make their fortunes unfettered by government interference. They awaited the first address of their new lord with apprehension. Penn's public proclamation to these people, written in Quaker style, began as follows:

Dear Friends,

You are now fixed at the mercy of no governor who comes to make his fortune great. You shall be governed by laws of your own making, and live a free, and if you will, a sober and industrious people.

For the populace, it was as if the King of England himself had removed his crown and thrown it into the crowd. Penn's beliefs pleased the people of his new colony, although it wouldn't be long before some of his "citizen friends" took advantage of their governor's haphazard way of surveying land.

In the 1840s, sign painter Edward Hicks painted several idealized versions of Penn's treaty with the Indians, including the one shown here. (Shelburne Museum)

Although William Penn lacked business acumen, he made up for it in his promotion of his colony to immigrants and investors and in his "urban planning." He took advantage of some of the progressive thinking of the time, including the notion that cities and towns be located to serve as trading and supply centers for farming areas. For Philadelphia, the capital of the new colony and, eventually, the de facto capital of all the American colonies, Penn envisioned a "greene Countrie Towne" of straight, wide streets, with orchards and gardens interspersed with buildings. Although the vision only partly materialized, it served to inspire the planning of hundreds of other cities in the new nation.

By the time of his death in 1718, the most important legacy Penn had left to his province was a genuinely tolerant and self-governing democracy—an extraordinary legacy in a world ruled by autocrats.

Penn's sons, less idealistic than their father, hoped to profit from the sale of land he had promised to the Indians, and they promoted Philadelphia in European newspapers and journals as the best place to set up a business in the colonies. Penn's middle son, Thomas, even advertised in the *English Bristol Journal* that any craftsman willing to "go over to the most flourishing city of Philadelphia" would be given a new suit of clothes.

PROSPERITY AND TAXES: RECIPE FOR A REVOLUTION

In 1700, Philadelphia's population was about 6,000 and that of the outlying territory totaled 20,000. By the beginning of the Revolutionary War, 75 years later, Pennsylvania's population was estimated at 300,000. Most of the new settlers came as indentured workers, obliged to work off their ship passage and supply costs to businessmen in Great Britain and other parts of Europe. Promotional advertising by the Penn family and letters from settlers back to family and friends were well timed. Opportunity abounded in the brisk trade with the West Indies, especially in the grain, meat, and lumber that Pennsylvania possessed in abundance. As treaties with the Indians were broken and settlements spread inland, the city became a point of internal transshipment for produce and animal furs.

A powerful, literate, and worldly merchant class—most of them Quaker—soon emerged in Philadelphia. It was the taxes these wealthy men paid that made possible the military adventures of the British Empire, such as the French and Indian War. The merchant classes were furious at the taxes levied upon them to support these campaigns, and eventually they would use their wealth to finance the Continental Army in the War of Independence.

WILLIAM PENN: THE FOUNDER

William Penn (1644–1718) had made every effort to correct England's ills before he decided to start from scratch in the New World. He had preached and protested. He had railed against the excess and luxury of the church. He had refused to take off his hat or swear allegiance to the crown, and he had championed human rights. He had written tracts with titles like "No Cross, No Crown" and "The Great Case of Liberty of Conscience." He had defended not only his right to practice his Quaker faith, but also the right of all citizens to follow their own beliefs. But in England, he had not been persuasive enough to bring about the changes he sought.

Penn had another reason for founding his colony. His father died in 1670, leaving him an uncollectible debt from King Charles II. The Crown was land-rich and cash-poor, a condition Penn himself would one day know all too well. He took Pennsylvania in payment.

The new colony was vast, making Penn the largest landholder in the kingdom aside from the king. Penn owned the lands outright with "free, full and absolute power." Remarkably, he did not take advantage of his power but instead wrote liberal charters, allowing more and more representative government. He and his Council proposed laws that were then approved by the Assembly.

He did not grow rich. The people who ran the colony were far more conscientious about billing him for their salaries than they were about collecting rents for him. His land did not bring him wealth but cost him an estimated 75,000 pounds. His trusted Quaker agent in London defrauded him, and a debt owed to the agent's widow landed Penn in prison for several months. Finally, insolvent and in despair, Penn made plans to return the colony to the Crown, but he suffered a stroke before he could sign the transfer documents.

Penn wrote prolifically on religious, philosophical, and political subjects. In Pennsylvania, he thought he could put some of his most cherished ideas to the test. That they did not entirely succeed is not the fault of his plan of government. As he himself wrote, "Governments, like clocks, go from the motion men give them; and as governments are made and moved by men, so by them are they ruined too."

Penn made only two visits to his colony, the first from 1682 to 1684, and the second from 1699 to 1701. One of Penn's unrealized dreams was that colonists and Indians would live side by side in harmony. In the words of one historian, "He seems to have been one of the few genuine Christians Christianity has ever produced."

Pennsylvania's founder, the idealist-aristocrat William Penn, at the age of 22.
(Atwater Kent Museum, Historical Society of Pennsylvania Collection)

One of the most prosperous of these early businessmen was Robert Morris, in whose house on High (Market) Street, below Sixth Street, George Washington would live as president from 1790 to 1797. At the start of the American Revolution, Robert Morris was reluctant to break with England, but he finally gave in and raised the money necessary for George Washington to move his army to Yorktown in 1781.

The most famous of Philadelphia's businessman-politicians was Benjamin Franklin, who at age 17 had arrived from Boston and, at 23, had established his own newspaper, the *Pennsylvania Gazette*. He pursued elective and appointive offices, including that of deputy postmaster general of Philadelphia.

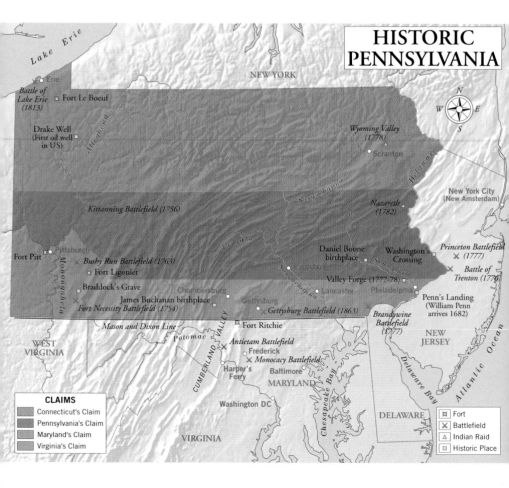

HISTORIC
PENNSYLVANIA

Second Street North from Market (ca. 1799), by William Birch. Christ Church is visible in the center of Birch's painting, which depicts a bustling and orderly Philadelphia. (Free Library of Philadelphia)

DISSENTERS, SEEKERS, AND PLAIN PEOPLE

The liberal and tolerant principles of William Penn's government did not go unnoticed in Europe, with the result that Pennsylvania attracted a steady flow of immigrants. Some were dissenters desiring religious freedom; some were from the lower classes wanting economic opportunity. In Pennsylvania, they had heard, a person might easily accumulate enough land to be able to vote and even become an elected official. There was no compulsory military service, and civil liberties were guaranteed, even to native peoples.

Between 1680 and 1710, most settlers who followed William Penn were, like him, Quakers from England, Wales, and Germany. Their numbers and wealth made them the dominant force in the Pennsylvania Assembly until 1756, when

PATCHWORK OF FAITHS

As a tolerant Quaker, William Penn vowed to form a colony where all could worship freely. He succeeded. A visitor to Penn's colony reported finding "Lutherans, Reformed, Catholics, Quakers, Menninists or Anabaptists, Herrnhuters or Moravian Brethren, Pietists, Seventh-Day Baptists, Dunkers.... In one house and one family four, five and even six sects may be found...."

QUAKERS

In England, these followers of the theologian George Fox had been persecuted because they believed in neither churches nor creeds but in the "inward light" by which they could sense God's presence. At meetings they meditated silently or testified to their faith. To this day, they practice tolerance and pacifism and demonstrate simplicity and honesty by adopting plain dress and manners.

MENNONITES

Mennonites, who emerged in Europe well before the Society of Friends was founded by George Fox in 1650, first reached Pennsylvania in 1683. Mennonites were Anabaptists, believers in baptism only for those who have chosen the faith. They sought to live separately from the rest of society, but in time showed a willingness to mingle in the non-Mennonite world, where their social concerns have led them into the helping professions and even politics.

AMISH

Jakob Ammann was a Mennonite leader who preached that church members who had left the fold should be shunned. After he and his followers broke away from the Mennonites in 1693, they became known as the Amish. Like the Mennonites, the Amish are Anabaptists and pacifists, but they have remained more strictly apart from the world, true to their chief tenet: "Be ye not conformed to the world." Whether to enforce their separation from society or to demonstrate it, they maintain an archaic style of dress and speech and avoid the use of cars, telephones, and electric lights.

MORAVIANS

Predating the Reformation, the Moravian Church is an outgrowth of the teachings of John Hus, a heretical Catholic priest from Prague burned at the stake in 1415. The church was founded in Bohemia in 1457 and claims to be the oldest organized Protestant church. It was nearly wiped out after the Thirty Years War and was renewed by Count Nicholas Von Zinzendorf of Saxony in 1722. The influence of German Pietism, which sought a more personal, less intellectual faith than that prevailing at the time, shows in the Moravian love feast and in the church's strong missionary tradition.

Mennonite girls waiting to enter school in Hinkletown, 1942.
(Library of Congress)

their pacifism lost them the support of frontier settlers who wanted armed protection against Indians.

Along with the Quakers came the first of the Germans from the Rhineland, beginning with Francis Daniel Pastorius, the Mennonite founder of Germantown, now a part of Philadelphia. The early German settlers were mostly members of smaller religious sects who settled as groups—Mennonites, Amish, Dunkers (German Baptists), German Quakers, and Moravians—though sometimes the immigrants converted from one religion to another after their arrival. Pastorius, for instance, left Germany as a Mennonite but converted to Quakerism after meeting William Penn.

After 1727, German immigrants were mostly members of the larger Lutheran and Reformed churches. With their farming methods, they transformed the region they settled into a rich agricultural area. By the time of the American Revolution, the Germans numbered about 100,000, more than a third of Pennsylvania's population. German farmers provided food for the Revolutionary Army and German craftsmen made the legendary "Pennsylvania long rifle," used

This 1757 engraving depicts Bethlehem, a communal religious settlement about 50 miles northwest of Philadelphia that eventually became an industrial city. (New York Public Library)

by George Washington's soldiers in many battles. The Germans' skill in the decorative arts added to the beauty of the area, now known as "Dutch" country, a derivation of the German word *Deutsch* ("German").

Between 1717 and 1776, about 250,000 Scots-Irish emigrated from Ulster to America. These were Presbyterians whom the English had moved into northern Ireland to thwart the Catholic Irish, but the economic hardship they faced was so severe that many signed on as indentured servants to pay their way to Pennsylvania. At first they settled in the Dutch country, farming without much success. From 1730 on, they led the movement west and north, to the frontiers. The Scots-Irish were a stern and self-sufficient group, too independent to settle into the agrarian communities envisioned by Penn but devoted to education and to the founding of schools. Eventually they became leaders in the revolutionary movement.

WESTWARD EXPANSION

Settlement was far from orderly. William Penn had envisioned a land of townships of 5,000 acres, each consisting of farms and a central village. Lands were offered to "first purchasers" in England at a uniform price, to be resold as farms, with 10 percent retained by the proprietors as manors. That plan was undermined after a decade or two by speculation on the part of the proprietors, by additional purchases from Indian tribes, and by the refusal of settlers to live in villages.

Until 1730, most expansion beyond Philadelphia followed the Schuylkill and Delaware rivers. But the landlocked farm region to the west of Penn's original three counties had a population sufficient to justify the creation of Lancaster County in 1729. By the middle of the 18th century, new waves of immigrants, border disputes with other colonies, and the colonial government's consequent encouragement of settlers pushed the boundaries beyond the Susquehanna into southwestern Pennsylvania. As Stevens describes in *Pennsylvania, Birthplace of a Nation:*

> The first stage in the growth of the farming frontier was the true wilderness of the typical frontiersman. He usually squatted upon the land for a time and lived in a crude cabin or lean-to. He was the man with the leather jacket and breeches, the fur cap, and the long Pennsylvania rifle with which he shot game, or Indians. He came on foot, or at best with a pack horse or mule. He was not apt to own any livestock and lived from hunting, fishing, and crude cultivation of the soil in a small clearing on which he raised corn and vegetables. This type of pioneer was restless and did not wish to be crowded.

As settlement continued, towns were laid out, and some emerged as cities in the wilderness. Between 1768 and 1788, two-thirds of the total area of Pennsylvania was wrested from Indians.

REVOLUTIONARY ERA

In Boston in 1773, a group of anti-tax demonstrators disguised as "Indians" threw a shipload of tea into Boston Harbor, while in Philadelphia, protesters invited the captain of a British tea ship to their own more polite protest. As all this was happening, new ideas were coursing through the land. Quakers and other Protestant sects had long stressed the importance of individual conscience, free of the dictates of traditional institutions and guided by a sense of civic responsibility. One aspect of this notion was the Protestant belief that all people should be able to read the

A drawing of John Nixon reading the Declaration of Independence on July 8, 1776. (Library of Congress)

Bible, and the high concentration of Protestants living in the northern colonies created one of the highest literacy rates in the world. The spirit of freedom of individual expression encouraged the writing of ideas and opinions, especially in the fields of religion and politics. Philadelphia, the publishing center of the colonies, was the place where many of the books and pamphlets by political thinkers such as Thomas Paine were published and distributed.

These literate, forward-thinking individuals were 4,000 miles from Great Britain, a distance sufficient to encourage rebellion against the monarchy. Democratic government did not lack precedent—models came from the ancient world, from Athens and early republican Rome. But though many of the colonists were willing to take the bold step into self-government, some knew there would be more than a few bumps in the road. The institution of slavery tarnished America's democratic idealism, and more than a few free thinkers in the colonies had said so, Paine among them. At the time of the Revolution, this injustice seemed beyond remedy and at any rate secondary to maintaining a united front against Britain. Moreover, though Jefferson himself owned slaves, apologists for slavery were a source of frustration to him. The original draft of the Declaration of Independence included condemnation of the slave trade, but Southerners and some New England politicians insisted on its deletion.

GREAT MEN CORRESPOND

By 1774, the men who would become the patriots of the American Revolution and the founders of the United States were in correspondence. In Philadelphia, City Tavern was the center of social, business, and political activities. Informal debates held there laid the groundwork for the Declaration of Independence and later for the Revolution.

The Philadelphia Committee of Observation, Inspection, and Correspondence, operating out of its tavern headquarters, proposed that a Congress of the Thirteen Colonies convene in September 1774 to discuss grievances with Britain. This first meeting of the Congress in Philadelphia adjourned without a demand for independence, but after the British marched on Lexington and Concord the following April, the voices of those advocating rebellion grew louder. By May, Paul Revere was galloping toward Philadelphia. When he arrived, he made straight for City Tavern seeking support for the city of Boston. A second Continental Congress convened, and the few Pennsylvania conservatives in attendance were no match for the fiery oratory of Philadelphians like Thomas Paine.

Virginian Richard Henry Lee offered a resolution declaring "That these United Colonies are, and of right ought to be, free and independent States," and that a plan of confederation be created. A committee that included Thomas Jefferson, John Adams, Benjamin Franklin, Roger Sherman, and Robert R. Livingston was formed to draft a declaration "setting forth the causes which impelled us to this mighty resolution." Working at a desk in the home of a young bricklayer and drawing on the political thought of the Enlightenment, Jefferson wrote the Declaration of Independence in two weeks. On July 2, 1776, Lee's resolution was adopted after a heated debate, and two days later the Congress formalized this act by adopting the Declaration of Independence.

The course of armed struggle for independence was set. When the Congress met in July 1776, at what is now known as Independence Hall, to adopt the document, the few remaining Pennsylvania conservatives reluctantly added their signatures. The English monarch, King George III, was not amused. From his point of view, the insurgents were traitors and deserved a traitor's punishment. The British army consulted with colonial representatives, after which war was declared.

Washington reviews his troops at Valley Forge in this 1883 painting by William B. T. Trego. (National Center for the American Revolution/Valley Forge Historical Society)

REVOLUTIONARY WAR

The early years of the war did not go well for the Americans. The circumspect and soft-spoken general from Virginia, George Washington, led an inexperienced and poorly supplied army. The government that was to support him barely existed and had almost no money. Having lost several early campaigns in New York, he was forced to retreat across New Jersey to Pennsylvania.

The tide began to turn—and popular support for Washington rallied—the day after Christmas 1776, when he ordered a successful surprise attack on a garrison of German mercenaries camped on the east bank of the Delaware River, in Trenton. A month later, he captured another contingent of British soldiers at Princeton.

The British commander who had taken New York City, Major Gen. William Howe, struck back, defeating the forces of the Continental Army at Brandywine Creek in Pennsylvania in September 1777. Howe then settled into Philadelphia, forcing the Congress into exile and the patriots to flee. George Washington and his farmer-soldiers did not give up. Digging in at nearby Valley Forge through what turned out to be a brutal winter, they suffered disease, hunger, and cruel cold. More than 2,000 of the 12,000 soldiers perished, and Washington reported that others were deserting. Morale was at an all-time low. Meanwhile Howe and the occupying Brits lived in warmth and comfort, enjoying parties, the theater, and the loyalist women of Philadelphia.

Two things happened that would contribute to the turning point in the war. First, even as Washington suffered in Pennsylvania, armies he had sent north to New York and Vermont were winning victories at Saratoga, Bennington, and Oriskany. The outcome of these battles helped to convince the French to recognize and support the Americans. Friedrich von Steuben, a German baron who had served as a lieutenant in the Prussian Army, was hired by the French Minister of War to help train the ragtag American soldiers. Steuben arrived in Pennsylvania in February 1778. Steuben's involvement and French backing gave heart to the Continental Congress, still on the run.

FRENCH ASSISTANCE

The fledgling United States government, lacking funds and allies, looked to France for help against Britain, their common antagonist. In late 1776, Benjamin Franklin sailed to France for a meeting with King Louis XVI. Self-interest had

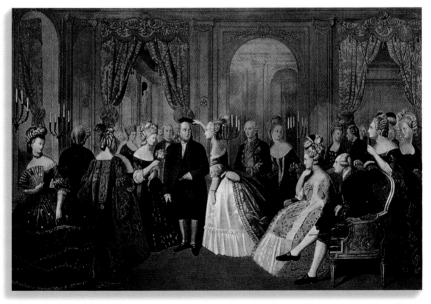

Benjamin Franklin meets Marie Antoinette (shown seated, in a yellow gown) at Versailles in 1776. Franklin had been sent to Paris to seek aid from the French government for the Revolutionary War effort. (Library of Congress)

already prompted the king to offer help, but Franklin's enormous popularity in France may have increased the king's generosity. Louis immediately ordered secret assistance to the revolutionaries, and in 1778, after treaties had been signed promising favorable trade status, the French declared war on Britain and sent their fleet of warships in open support. (The financial assistance they offered the colonies, to the tune of more than one billion *livres tournois,* compounded France's already heavy debts and would later come back to haunt Louis XVI and his wife, Marie Antoinette.) Howe raced out of Philadelphia to reinforce his troops in New York.

In 1781, the highest-ranking British commander, Lord Cornwallis, settled in the Virginia seaport town of Yorktown after failing to capture Thomas Jefferson in a chase through the Piedmont region of the colony. George Washington saw another opportunity for surprise attack and forced the Continental Army— 16,000 strong—on a horrendous march south from New York. Aided by French

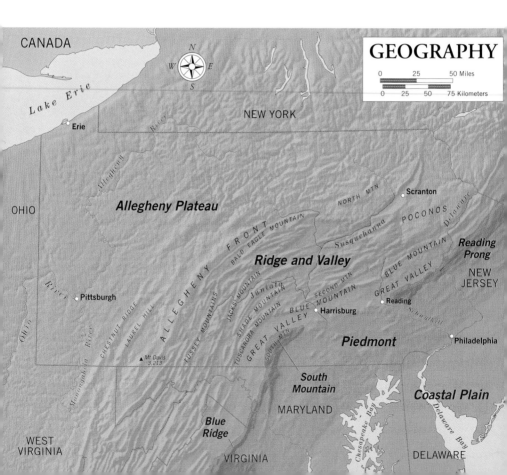

soldiers, Washington's forces cornered the British troops, who waited in vain for reinforcements to come by sea. After a three-week standoff, the vastly outnumbered Cornwallis surrendered.

Though several battles continued in New York during the next 18 months, General Washington's stunning defeat of the British at Yorktown secured victory for the American forces. The captured British colors were sent to Philadelphia by Washington and presented to the Continental Congress in a formal ceremony in Independence Hall. Philadelphia, and Pennsylvania with it, had been the staging ground for a revolution. Benjamin Franklin and peace commissioners John Adams and John Jay negotiated with a representative from the British government in Paris for two months: the Americans wanted recognition for their independent state and its boundaries, while Great Britain wanted simply to grant Americans more autonomy under the crown. The ensuing Treaty of Paris was signed (bitterly by George III) in 1783, granting the new American government international recognition. When the Constitutional Convention met at Independence Hall after a few years of an unsatisfactory confederation, Philadelphia further fulfilled William Penn's dream of "planting the seed of a nation." In December 1787, Pennsylvania became the second state, after Delaware, to ratify the United States Constitution.

PROGRESS IN PENNSYLVANIA

Pennsylvania was in the vanguard of states that took advantage of the economic freedoms guaranteed by the new central government. In the decade after independence, both Philadelphia and Pittsburgh began developing the infrastructure required for an economy with the capacity to trade with the world.

From the 1780s through the 1820s, the state experienced an expansion of roads, bridges, and canals. And by 1850, Pennsylvania's economy had reached the level of many of Europe's powerhouses. The key was the state's abundant natural resources—among them the largest anthracite coal deposits in the world, lumber to meet the building demands of an expanding nation, and waterways to transport these products.

CAN SUCH A UNION LONG ENDURE?

If Pennsylvania was central to the founding of the nation, it was also intensely involved in the moral and emotional debates that preceded the Civil War. Quaker-dominated Pennsylvania had abolished slavery in 1780, the first state to do so, and it had long been a stop on the Underground Railroad, which directed

A memorial to General Robert E. Lee at Gettysburg National Military Park.

escaped slaves north. Its people were sympathetic to the abolitionist cause. Yet as the place where the union of the states had first begun, it did not take national dissolution lightly.

Pennsylvanians reacted angrily to the United States Supreme Court's infamous Dred Scott decision of 1856, invalidating an act of Congress—the Missouri Compromise—and permitting the spread of slavery into the American territories. In 1860, Pennsylvania's vote was pivotal to Abraham Lincoln's election as president. Powerful Southern leaders had declared their region would secede from the Union if Lincoln were elected, and when he was, Southern states began to carry out that threat.

When Lincoln called for troops to support the Union in 1861, no other state was as ready as Pennsylvania to go to arms. The president requested 14 regiments; volunteers filled 25 regiments almost immediately.

Pennsylvania also became the site of the war's most devastating battle when Confederates led by Gen. Robert E. Lee crossed the narrow sliver of Maryland that separates Virginia from Pennsylvania and brought the war to the sleepy farming community of Gettysburg. The ferocious Battle of Gettysburg, which lasted from July 1 through 3, 1863, caused more than 51,000 Confederate and Union casualties, almost all under the age of 21.

CAPITALISTS AND UNION MEN

The Civil War had stimulated Pennsylvania's industrial might. With the end of the war came an era of industrial expansion led by entrepreneurs who built the mills, mines, and factories of the late 19th century. Businessmen like Andrew Carnegie, Henry Clay Frick, Robert Hunt, Joseph Wharton, and William Scranton saw fortunes to be made in steel production and coal mining, and they set about building enormous empires. Along with them came some of the country's most innovative financiers—the Mellons of Pittsburgh and the Cookes of Philadelphia.

Factories need laborers, and they came to Pennsylvania by the thousands: blacks from the South, Irish Catholics, the Welsh and the Scots-Irish, Russian Jews and Eastern Europeans. Pennsylvania owes much of its cultural wealth and economic

In these "beehive ovens," coal was baked into coke, which burns at the high heat necessary to produce steel. (Library of Congress)

Ironworkers at a factory in Sharon. (Carnegie Library of Pittsburgh)

success to these people, who did all the heavy lifting—mining coal and laying track, stoking the coke furnaces and pouring the molten iron ore into ingots.

As the titans of industry exercised largely unfettered control over their workers, Pennsylvania became the testing ground for the American trade union movement. Several important labor struggles took place among the burgeoning semi-skilled labor forces of railroad, mining, and steel manufacture, most notably the Homestead Steel Strike of 1892.

LOOKING TO THE FUTURE

Pennsylvania followed an almost predictable course for an industrial state in the first half of the 20th century. Economic slumps were devastating, and wars were financially invigorating. The Great Depression brought unemployment as high as 80 percent in the steel and railroad industries. World War II eliminated unemployment with a vengeance: factories ran around the clock and women were recruited into the workforce.

So much is said about the "Rust Belt" in the post-industrial age that it is surprising to learn there are still steel mills and coal mines in Pennsylvania. But steelmaking and other heavy manufacturing have declined steeply in the past three or four decades, and services now play a much larger role in a diversified economy. Government initiatives encourage growth in such high-technology industries as electronics and biotechnology.

The decline of heavy industry made it possible to undo some of the environmental damage wrought by mining and manufacturing. As a result, agriculture and tourism, now two of the state's major industries, have benefited from improvements in air and water quality.

Pennsylvania grapples with problems that vex every state—public safety, race relations, and educational opportunities. An additional problem for Pennsylvania has been the "brain drain" of talented people who move away from its urban areas or out of the state altogether. Several world-class research universities, including the University of Pennsylvania and Pennsylvania State University, are in Philadelphia and Pittsburgh, but graduates tend to leave post-commencement.

Revitalization may take several decades to fully unfold, but both cities show evidence that the most difficult parts of the process are behind them. The construction of sports stadiums and arts centers have attracted new business, which in turn has brought hotels, restaurants, and housing to previously blighted areas. And both cities have emerged as key players in the new economy. Pittsburgh is among the largest software employers in the nation, and both Pittsburgh and Philadelphia have become hotbeds of activity in the budding biotechnology industry. Revenues from tourism are similarly building,

A promotional piece for the Pennsylvania Railroad.

A dramatic sunset over Lake Erie, as viewed from Presque Isle.

and Philadelphia and Pittsburgh are increasingly seen as desirable places to live. In 2005 a *New York Times* article deigned to call Philadelphia, "New York City's sixth borough," a designation that caused much local ire but which clearly expresses Philly's rising profile in the arts, culture, shopping, and overall hip factor. Pittsburgh was ranked America's Most Livable City in the 2007 edition of the *Places Rated Almanac,* for the first time in 22 years. The rankings are based on cost of living, transportation, jobs, education, climate, crime, health care, recreation, and ambience. (Philadelphia came in at number five.)

Philadelphia and Pittsburgh's ability to adapt to industrial and demographic changes is indicative of the resilience and creativity of Pennsylvanians as a whole. That's an assertion with some basis in historical truth. The citizenry of this state did, after all, play a key role in creating the United States and an equally pivotal one later in the development of the nation's industrial might. At the start of the 21st century, new challenges loom, but if the past is a road map to the future, there can be little doubt that Pennsylvanians have what it takes to meet them.

HISTORICAL AND CULTURAL TIME LINE

1643 Governor Johan Printz of New Sweden establishes his capital at Tinicum Island within the present limits of Pennsylvania.

1654 British seize control of New Sweden.

1681 Charles II of England grants land to William Penn.

1683 Penn purchases land from Indians in the Delaware Valley.

1701 Penn grants charter to the city of Philadelphia.

1731 Richard Allen founds the Mother Bethel African Methodist Episcopal Church in Philadelphia.

1774 The first Continental Congress convenes at Carpenter's Hall in Philadelphia in response to new taxes imposed on colonists by the Crown.

1776 Commonwealth of Pennsylvania is established in June during conference at Carpenter's Hall.

1776 On July 4, Declaration of Independence is signed at Independence Hall in Philadelphia.

1777 The British occupy Philadelphia. News of the French alliance with the colonies, negotiated by Benjamin Franklin, leads to withdrawal of British forces from the city in the spring of 1778.

1784 Treaty of peace with England ratified by Congress in Philadelphia.

1787 The Constitution of the United States is adopted at Independence Hall in Philadelphia.

1793 Yellow fever kills 4,000 in Philadelphia. The health crisis results in improved sanitation and the opening of a hospital, in 1810, devoted to the study of infectious disease.

1814 Domestic use of anthracite coal begins, resulting in the organization of important mining companies throughout the state.

1850 Women's Medical College is founded, opening the medical profession to women.

The Johnsons, pacifist Quakers, turn their Philadelphia home into an Underground Railroad station, and it becomes a crucial stopover for runaways en route to freedom in upstate New York and Canada.

1860 Republicans dominate in the state and nation with the elections of Gov. Andrew Gregg Curtin and President Abraham Lincoln.

1863 Battle of Gettysburg marks a change in fortune for the Union.

1868 Women in Philadelphia organize the Pennsylvania Women's Suffrage Association.

1876 In Philadelphia, on July 4, Susan B. Anthony reads her "Declaration of Rights for Women" at Independence Hall.

1877 Strikes and bloody flare-ups lead to the creation of the United Mine Workers union in 1890.

1892 Carnegie Steel Company chairman Henry Clay Frick orders 300 armed Pinkerton guards to repel strikers at the Homestead Steel Works. Sixteen workers are killed.

1940 The Commonwealth is the second-most populous state in the nation, after New York.

1948 In Donora, 20 people are asphyxiated and 7,000 are hospitalized because of severe pollution from zinc factories. Public outcry results in federal and state laws to control air pollution.

1952 Jonas Salk develops a vaccine against polio in the Virus Research Lab at the University of Pittsburgh.

Bob Horn's Bandstand begins as a local program on WFIL-TV (now WPVI), Channel 6, in Philadelphia. In 1956 the show gets a new host, a clean-cut 26-year-old Dick Clark, and a new name: *American Bandstand*.

1954 WQED in Pittsburgh pioneers community-sponsored educational television.

1959 Steel strike puts many Pennsylvanians out of work; President Eisenhower invokes Taft-Hartley Act to end 116-day walkout.

Twelve workers die in the Knox Mine flood disaster, marking the end of deep mining in the anthracite region.

1962 Pennsylvania-born Rachel Carson publishes *Silent Spring,* which challenges the widespread use of pesticides in agriculture and calls for increased government action against pollution.

1968 Pittsburgh-based *Mr. Roger's Neighborhood,* the longest-running PBS series, premieres.

1979 Reactor 2 at the Three Mile Island nuclear facility experiences a partial meltdown, beginning an ongoing debate about the safety of nuclear energy.

1985 A city block in West Philadelphia burns after city officials bomb a house in an attempt to dislodge the radical MOVE group.

1990 Pittsburgher August Wilson wins Pulitzer Prize for Drama for *The Piano Lesson,* one year after winning the same prize for *Fences.*

The 1990 census indicates the state's population increased only 0.1% since 1980.

1991 Philadelphia architect Robert Venturi wins the prestigious Pritzker Prize in recognition of his career accomplishments.

2000 Republican Convention meets in Philadelphia, the sixth time in a century and half that the party has met in the city.

A fence in Shanksville becomes a memorial to those who died aboard Flight 93 on September 11, 2001.

2001 On September 11, United Airlines Flight 93 takes off from Newark, New Jersey, and is hijacked by terrorists. The plane crashes near Shanksville.

The $265 million Kimmel Center for the Performing Arts opens to great acclaim on Philadelphia's Avenue of the Arts, up the street from the 1857 Academy of Music.

2002 Nine miners assumed dead after an accident at the Saxman Mine, in Somerset County, are saved after three days underground.

2006 A gunman kills five girls, ages 7 to 13, in a one-room schoolhouse in an Old Order Amish community in Nickel Mines, before shooting himself. The Amish respond with forgiveness.

2007 The 57-story Comcast Center is completed, becoming Philadelphia's newest highest skyscraper.

PHILADELPHIA
AMERICA'S FIRST CAPITAL

Philadelphia has undergone some dramatic transformations in the past 300 years, from the seat of a rebel government to industrial powerhouse to economic slump to revitalized tourist hub. Once as proper and upright as its English Quaker founders, the city has diversified under the influence of immigrants from all over Europe, African-Americans who migrated from the South before and after the Civil War, and more recently, people from Asia, Mexico, and former Soviet countries. A center of revolutionary fervor in the late 18th century, by the late 19th, Philadelphia was basking in the prosperity of the Gilded Age. In the 1920s, the city was known in movies and novels for its "Main Line" (suburban upper-crust) society, but by the 1980s Philadelphia was down at the heels. The city's upswing hit its stride in the mid-'90s under Mayor Ed Rendell, who vowed to reverse the city's so-called second-class status. Since then the city has seen millions invested in reviving its urban landscape by buffing up its many fine, historic buildings and building new ones.

Boathouse Row, at the southern end of Fairmount Park.

The printmakers Currier and Ives created this city map in 1875. (Library of Congress)

HISTORY

WILLIAM PENN'S VISION

When William Penn arrived aboard the *Welcome* at a quay along the Delaware River in 1682, he found 10 small houses along a wooded shore and a settlement that had foundered for 44 years, first as a Swedish trading post and later as the Dutch outpost of New Amsterdam. Penn, then 38, a devoutly religious and idealistic aristocrat, stepped ashore possessed of a powerful humanitarian vision: he wished to build a society based on trust in man's better instincts. He stated his goals in a letter written a year earlier:

> I purpose that which is extraordinary and leave to myself and successors no power of doing mischief, that the will of one man may not hinder the good of an whole country.

That he did not falter in this purpose was remarkable, given his aristocratic background and the potential for abuse inherent in authority. Penn held to a vision of mankind as essentially good and deserving of dignity, a vision that would sustain his spirits as he struggled to apply high principles to real life.

Penn laid out detailed plans for his town, one in which commerce would prosper, all religions would be tolerated, and order and Christian rectitude would prevail. Philadelphia (Greek for "brotherly love") was also to be, if not fireproof, fire resistant. Heeding the advice given by Sir Christopher Wren after the great London fire of 1666, Penn designed a city with straight streets intersecting at right angles—considered an improvement on the curving lanes of European cities. Houses were to be placed at the center of their lots, with open space between them, for it was to be "a greene Country Towne, which will never be burnt, and always be wholesome." To that end he also proposed public parks for the commercial center, something unknown in English cities at the time.

PROSPERITY AND IDEALISM

With its access to shipping routes through the Chesapeake Bay and its proximity to trappers, hunters, and wheat farmers in the surrounding countryside, Philadelphia began to flourish. The city exported lumber and furs from the western forests, wheat from what are now Lancaster and Bucks Counties, and cast iron and flour from city mills.

By 1700, Philadelphia's population had reached 6,000, and the pastor of Old Swedes' Church was writing proudly: "All the houses are built of brick, three or four hundred of them, and in every house a shop, so that whatever one wants at any time he can have, for money."

This high chest, made in Philadelphia around 1770, is a fine example of the sophistication of both craftsman and merchant in the city at that time. (Philadelphia Museum of Art)

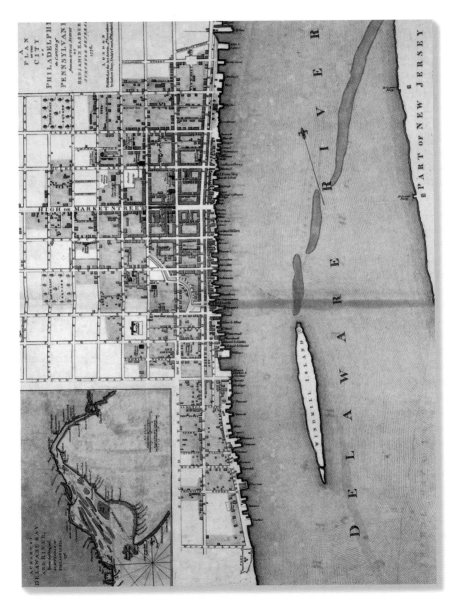

Penn's right-angled streets and green spaces remain visible in this 1776 map.
(Library of Congress)

The city skyline, reflected in the Schuylkill River. On the left are a house in Fairmount Park (outlined in lights), the Philadelphia Museum of Art, the PSFS Building (with its letters in neon), and, to its right, City Hall.

NOT SO PLAIN PEOPLE

English and French visitors were amazed by the luxury displayed in the city. President Washington's splendid coach and his liveried footmen; staid Quakers carrying gold canes and gold snuffboxes, and wearing great silver buttons and buckles; ladies with sky-high coiffures, in costumes of costly brocades and velvets, silks, and satins; the grand wigs and queues, new buckles and silk stockings, worn by the men. "Ladies paid their French maids no less than two hundred pounds a year; and there were statesmen like Gouverneur Morris who had his two French valets and a man to buckle his hair in paillots." So long as the capital was in Philadelphia and the Federalists were in power, social life was luxurious and stately.

—**Clarence P. Hornung,**
The Way It Was, **1978**

If Quakers were the backbone of the early city, their tolerance brought in their wake Anglicans, Catholics, Jews, and "Plain People"—including Mennonites and Pennsylvania Germans, or "Deutsch." Newly prosperous merchants patronized equally prospering craftsmen: silversmiths, cabinetmakers, and coach makers. (If the Quakers' philosophy of simplicity led them to avoid ostentation, the Anglicans had no such scruples.)

Philadelphians were well abreast of the egalitarian and democratic ideas circulating during the mid-18th century. By the time of the Revolutionary War, theirs was the wealthiest city in the colonies and, with 24,000 residents, the most populous. These residents were by some accounts the most outspoken and opinionated on the continent. The Rev. Jacob Duche wrote in 1772:

> The poorest labourer upon the shore of the Delaware thinks himself entitled to deliver his sentiments in matters of religion and politics with as much freedom as the gentleman or the scholar. Indeed there is less distinction among the citizens of Philadelphia than among those of any civilized city in the world. … For every man expects one day or another to be upon a footing with his wealthiest neighbor.

The first federal bank in the United States opened in Philadelphia in 1791, though the need for such an institution was a matter of great debate. (New York Public Library)

These self-confident people established libraries and discussion clubs; patronized societies studying science, painting, and music; undertook reform and civic improvement; and, as they drank ale in pubs, talked politics. Why shouldn't they govern themselves, and establish a democracy?

So the character of the city, and not just its location, helped to make it the birthplace of the American republic, beginning with the First Continental Congress in 1774. During the hot, sticky July of 1776, Benjamin Franklin, Thomas Jefferson, George Washington, John Adams, John Hancock, and other representatives from 12 of the 13 colonies composed and signed the document we know as the Declaration of Independence.

On July 8, their declaration was read to an enthusiastic group of citizens. A year later, when General Howe led the British Army into Philadelphia, the active patriots fled, and the city's thousands of loyalists welcomed the British with open arms. Yet the occupation of Philadelphia served no strategic purpose for Britain, and when Howe was dismissed from his command in May 1778 for "inactivity," it was widely said that Philadelphia had captured him rather than the reverse.

EPIDEMICS AND GAMESMANSHIP

Centrally located among the 13 colonies, Philadelphia became the new nation's capital in 1779. The city's reputation was so positive that immigrants sailed in by the shipload, disembarking at Water and Market Streets. Many of the new arrivals were willing to indenture themselves for years in order to live here.

As businesses mushroomed and skilled workers were enticed to make their fortunes, the city struggled to keep pace. Housing was scarce, and crowding favored the spread of disease and fire. Outbreaks of yellow fever occurred frequently, with each epidemic killing thousands. Still, the city managed to move ahead.

After the U.S. Constitution was ratified in 1789, New York briefly became the country's capital, but by 1790 Philadelphia had regained the title. The city's return to political prominence, though, was fleeting. The new U.S. government decided to move the nation's capital 144 miles south, to a marshy site where the Potomac and Anacostia Rivers converged. By 1800, Philadelphia was no longer the capital, and by 1823 it was no longer the country's most populous city, either. New York had edged out Philadelphia in population.

But though it had lost these distinctions, William Penn's town retained its reputation for innovation and was known as the City of Firsts—in health, public safety, education, the arts, and business. The Pennsylvania Academy of Fine Arts, the country's first art school, opened here in 1805, and during the 19th century, Philadelphia became a leading center for the manufacture of textiles, apparel, shoes, machinery, tools, iron, steel locomotives, and ships. Philadelphians formed the Anti-Slavery Society in 1833, and Philadelphia regiments answered the Union call to arms.

After the Civil War the city continued to thrive. The telephone and the

Pennsylvania Academy of Fine Arts.

automated building elevator accelerated the pace of commerce, and the first medical college for women in the United States was founded.

THE MODERN ERA

As a major manufacturing area, Philadelphia drew thousands of immigrants, each group settling into its own neighborhood: Italians in South Philly, Chinese in part of Center City, African-Americans in North Philly, Irish in Olney, Jews in the Northeast, and, much later, the Vietnamese in West Philly. Old-time Philadelphians—those who traced their lineage directly to the city's founders and prominent early leaders—were already well established in Chestnut Hill.

Mayors Richardson Dilworth and Joseph Clark presided over something of a golden age between 1951 and 1962, when the city was flush and civic pride ran high. The 1970s and 1980s proved a depressing contrast, as the politics of race and the reality of crime and poverty divided the city, especially during the tenure of police commissioner-turned-mayor Frank Rizzo, whose admirers cheered his tough-guy approach to politics and crime.

Replacing Rizzo in the 1980s was Wilson Goode, an African-American former city manager who enjoyed the support of the city's black community. That support survived the bombing by the police department of the headquarters of the radical black MOVE organization in 1985. The explosion accidentally destroyed an entire city block of 60 houses, earning Philadelphia the sobriquet "The City That Bombed Itself."

By the end of the century the city had rebounded once more. Much of the credit is given to the administration of Ed Rendell, a Democrat known for an aggressive style and a knack for getting things done. Under Rendell, Philadelphia, which has been steadily losing population—from 1.95 million people within the city limits in 1970 to about 1.5 million in 2000—began encouraging economic growth in fields such as warehousing and distribution, education, health care, and tourism. The Rendell administration breathed new life into Center City, creating the Avenue of the Arts along South Broad Street to support an emerging arts district of theaters and performance centers. Hundreds of millions of dollars, both private and public funds, were invested in sports stadiums and other building projects.

Part of the city's turnaround from the mid-'90s into the early 21st century involved a major attitude adjustment. In a 1996 *Philadelphia Inquirer* op-ed outlining his hopes for a region that is "sitting on gold," Rendell pleaded with Philadelphians to stop putting themselves down. "Baltimore and Cleveland used

The Kimmel Center and the Avenue of the Arts.

to be the national brunt of jokes," he reasoned. "Nobody makes fun of them anymore." An influx of new residents and a wealth of great press, such as a 2005 *National Geographic Traveler* article titled "Next Great City: Philly, Really", has done wonders for the city's self-image.

Rendell went on to become governor of Pennsylvania, and he was succeeded as mayor by Democrat John Street, who turned his focus away from Center City and toward the blighted, low-income neighborhoods outside its boundaries. Among his goals: to fence vacant lots, clean up abandoned cars and homes, and curtail drug activity. Also on Street's watch, two new stadiums, two office towers, and many residential developments were built. Casinos were also approved, leading to intense citizen opposition—a thorny conflict for the current mayor, Democrat Michael Nutter, to tackle.

INDEPENDENCE NATIONAL HISTORICAL PARK
map page 53, E/F-3

Perhaps no place in the country has more of an emotional grip on America's historical psyche than Independence National Historical Park in Center City. The place where some of the greatest events in American history occurred is where any tour of Philadelphia should begin.

In the 1940s, the 55 acres comprising Independence Park, Old City, and Society Hill were turned over to the National Park Service, and modern architecture was encouraged to contrast with the historic, colonial buildings. Amazingly enough, history is still being made at Independence Mall. In 2007, an archaeological dig at the President's House uncovered artifacts tied to the existence of nine enslaved Africans who worked and lived in George Washington's household. A permanent installation here set to open in 2009 will explore this paradox at the heart of the American independence movement. Also in progress on the Mall is a major expansion of the National Museum of American Jewish History, to open in 2010.

TOURING THE PARK

INDEPENDENCE VISITOR CENTER   *map page 53, E-3*

The visitors' center contains historical exhibits and provides information about tourist activities in the Philadelphia area. Two short films play continuously to orient you to Old City's sights. Maps include historical tidbits and directions.

DECLARATION OF INDEPENDENCE

When, in the course of human events, it becomes necessary for one people to dissolve the political bands which have connected them with another, and to assume, among the powers of the earth, the separate and equal station to which the laws of nature and of nature's God entitle them, a decent respect to the opinions of mankind requires that they should declare the causes which impel them to the separation.

We hold these truths to be self-evident, that all men are created equal, that they are endowed by their Creator with certain unalienable rights, that among these are life, liberty, and the pursuit of happiness. That, to secure these rights, governments are instituted among men, deriving their just powers from the consent of the governed. That, whenever any form of government becomes destructive of these ends, it is the right of the people to alter or to abolish it, and to institute new government, laying its foundation on such principles, and organizing its powers in such form, as to them shall seem most likely to effect their safety and happiness.

—Thomas Jefferson, 1776

There are also restrooms, a café, free wireless access, a bookstore, and, frequently, a knowledgeable Ben Franklin impersonator. *Sixth and Market Sts.; 800/537–7676.*

INDEPENDENCE HALL   *map page 53, E-3*

The centerpiece of the park is Independence Hall, where the Continental Congress met from 1775 to 1783 (except for the winter of 1777–78 when the city was occupied by the British). Startling in its simplicity, the structure, built between 1732 and 1756, was originally called the State House of the Province of Pennsylvania. Planned and designed by Andrew Hamilton, it is considered a fine example of Georgian architecture. A square tower and octagonal steeple at one end were added in 1753 to hold the Liberty Bell.

It was in the assembly room of this building that George Washington was appointed Commander-in-Chief of the Continental Army in 1775 and the Declaration of Independence was adopted on July 4, 1776, stating that the

Throughout its history the Liberty Bell has been a touchstone for patriotic expression.

colonies would no longer abide by the laws of England. (In the nearby National Constitution Center, life-size bronze statues of the signers really bring this scene to life.) The Articles of Confederation were ratified here in 1781.

The room is also where, between May and September of 1787, delegates from 12 states (Rhode Island did not send a representative) met to frame a thoroughly original instrument of government: the Constitution of the United States of America. In closed sessions, during long, hot days, delegates argued over and agreed upon the basic tenets of government, the balance of powers between branches of the government, and the civil protections accorded citizens.

The 55 men who met here included Alexander Hamilton of New York, Bostonian John Adams, Virginians Thomas Jefferson and James Madison, and Pennsylvania delegates James Wilson, Robert Morris, and Benjamin Franklin, then 70 years old. They constituted an intellectual elite astonishing even at the time. Louis Otto, the French *chargé d'affaires*, commented to his superiors at home:

> If all the delegates named for this Convention at Philadelphia are present, we will never have seen, even in Europe, an assembly more

CENTRAL PHILADELPHIA

1,000 Feet

300 Meters

OLD CITY

CHINATOWN

SOCIETY HILL

WASHINGTON SQUARE

CITY CENTER

LOGAN CIRCLE

S Penn Square

Independence Mall

Franklin Square

Penn's Landing

Columbus Blvd

Labeled locations

Rodin Museum
The Free Library of Philadelphia
State Office Building
Franklin Institute Science Museum
Fels Planetarium
Academy of Natural Sciences Museum
Moore College of Art and Design
Comcast Center
Tourist Center
Hahnemann University
Museum of American Art
Pennsylvania Academy of Fine Arts
Pennsylvania Convention Center
Masonic Temple
City Hall
Reading Terminal Market
Chinese Cultural Center
PSFS Building
Ritz-Carlton of Philadelphia
Doll Museum
Historical Society of Pennsylvania
Academy of Music
Avenue of the Arts
Kimmel Center for the Performing Arts
University of the Arts
Curtis Insitute of Music
Rittenhouse Square
Civil War Library & Museum
Mutter Museum
African-American Museum
US Mint
National Constitution Center
Federal Court House
President's House
Atwater Kent Museum
Liberty Bell Pavilion
Independence Hall
Congress Hall
Curtis Center
Walnut St Theater
Morris Mansion
National Archives Branch
Jefferson Hospital
Thomas Jefferson University
Forest Theater
Benjamin Franklin Grove
Christ Church Cemetery
Free Quaker Meeting House
American Jewish History
Nat'l Historic Park
Independence Visitor Center
Old City Hall
Library Bank
Penn Mutual Tower
Philadelphia Athenaeum
St Marys Church
Washington Square
Holy Trinity Church
Jeweler's Row
St George Church
Betsy Ross House
Christ Church
Elfreth's Alley
US Custom House
Visitors Center
City Tavern
Independence Seaport Museum
Man Full of Trouble Tavern
Philadelphia Exchange
Powell House
Todd House
Bishop White House
Second Bank of US
First Bank of US
Franklin Court
Physick House
Rose Garden
Society Hill Synagogue
To Mummers Museum

Fairmount Park
The Benjamin Franklin Parkway
Philadelphia Museum of Art,
Mann Center for the Performing Arts,
Sweetbriar Mansion
To Zoo

Benjamin Franklin Bridge

Antique Row

The straightforward architecture of Independence Hall echoed the urgency and forthrightness with which the American Revolution was undertaken.

respectable for the talents, knowledge, disinterestedness, and patriotism of those who compose it.

The "rising-sun" chair used by Washington during the Convention is the original. (After the Constitution was adopted, Benjamin Franklin said about the chair, "I have the happiness to know that it is a rising and not a setting sun.") That and the nicks and warping in the floor of the assembly room will help you to visualize the likes of Thomas Jefferson and Benjamin Franklin pacing back and forth between their desks and conferring with supporters while James Madison, seated at the main table, tried to move delegates toward consensus. Tours start every 15 or 20 minutes. Pick up a free timed ticket at the Visitors' Center. *Chestnut St. between Fifth and Sixth Sts.; 215/597-8974.*

Independence Hall connects with Congress Hall, the meeting place of the country's fledgling legislative body between 1790 and 1800. Two presidents were inaugurated here: George Washington (for his second term) and his successor, John Adams.

LIBERTY BELL *map page 53, E-3*

Just north of Independence Hall is one of our nation's most significant icons, the Liberty Bell. Since the terrorist attacks against the United States in 2001, the Liberty Bell has become even more of a touchstone for patriotic expression than it already was.

The bell's history is a nearly impenetrable blend of fact and fiction. We know that it was originally called the State House Bell and that it was cast in England in 1752 to commemorate the 50th anniversary of the Charter of Privileges, the democratic constitution granted by William Penn to his colony in 1701. Its famous inscription: "Proclaim liberty throughout all the land, unto all the inhabitants thereof" (Leviticus 25:10) is meant to pay homage to the freedom Penn afforded his citizens. It first cracked soon after it arrived in Philadelphia and was recast by local craftsmen John Pass and John Stow using metal from the original bell. The second crack is up for dispute—some say it happened in 1835 when it tolled at the funeral of Chief Justice John Marshall. A more likely, albeit less dramatic, story is that it cracked slowly over a period of years. In 1835 it was repaired, but then it cracked once more in 1846, after which it was silenced.

The recast bell was hung in the tower of the State House and rang on July 8, 1776, to beckon the citizens of Philadelphia to a public reading of the Declaration of Independence. Shortly after noon, Col. John Nixon climbed up onto a wooden platform and read to the crowd, "The unanimous declaration of the 13 United States of America." Later that afternoon, at the green-covered tables in the Assembly Room, the delegates signed a parchment copy of the Declaration of Independence.

During the Revolutionary War, the bell was moved to Allentown and hidden in a cellar until the British evacuated Philadelphia. By the 1830s, when abolitionists inspired by its inscription began calling it the Liberty Bell, it had begun to crack again. It is long believed the crack occurred while the bell tolled during the funeral of Chief Justice John Marshall in 1835, but this is considered apocryphal. It rang for the last time in 1846, in celebration of George Washington's birthday. In 1852, the bell was placed in the "Declaration Chamber" of Independence Hall. Occasionally it was trucked out to expositions and fairs around the country to remind Americans of their earlier days when they fought and worked together for independence and to help heal the divisions of the Civil War. Since 1915, the bell has been on display here in Independence Mall. *Market St., between Fifth and Sixth Sts.*

NATIONAL CONSTITUTION CENTER *map page 53, E-2*

This enormous, highly interactive museum on the northernmost quadrant of Independence Mall brings the U.S. Constitution to life through dynamic permanent exhibits. A highlight is "Freedom Rising," a multimedia performance staged throughout the day in a theater-in-the-round style. The combination of a live actors, swelling music, and dramatic film and video projections can masterfully manipulate even the least sentimental person into a patriot bursting with pride. Hours can be spent in "The American Experience," learning of each U.S. president's strengths and weaknesses (and voting for your favorite), then pretending to be signed in as the next leader of the free world. In Signers Hall, walk amongst the

"Ghost" structure in Franklin Court.

Inside the printing office at Franklin Court.

life-sized bronze statues of the 42 signers of the Declaration, peer into their alternately hopeful and wizened faces, and remark upon how Washington truly towered above the rest. *Arch St., between Fifth and Sixth Sts. 215/409–6600.*

FRANKLIN COURT   *map page 53, F-3*

East of Liberty Bell Pavilion on Market Street is Franklin Court, the site of the three-story, 10-room house that Benjamin Franklin shared with his wife, Deborah, and their two children. The original home was torn down in 1812, but for the U.S. bicentennial in 1976, Pritzker Prize–winning architect Robert Venturi re-created in white steel the outline of the house and two nearby structures from Franklin's era. Carved on slate tiles placed where the house's wood flooring would have been are quotations by and about Franklin and selections from his correspondence with Deborah about the furnishings and maintenance of the house. (Franklin spent a good deal of time in London as a representative of Pennsylvania and several other colonies, but wrote frequently to Deborah about the house.)

Glass sections interspersed among the rectangles of slate provide views into Franklin's privy pits and wells. Venturi's "ghost" structure, as it is called, stands

RENAISSANCE MAN

Benjamin Franklin (1706–90) arrived in Philadelphia from Boston in 1723 at age 17, stopped at a baker's shop, and bought "three great Puffy Rolls." With a roll under each arm and munching on the third, he made his way up Market Street, where he passed his future wife, Deborah Read, at the door of her family's home. She watched him "& thought I made as I certainly did a most awkward ridiculous Appearance."

Franklin moved into Deborah's father's house and courted the young woman, but when he left for London, she married John Rogers, who, as it turned out, already had a wife. Eventually Rogers deserted Deborah and Franklin took her as his common-law wife. Their marriage lasted until her death in 1774, although they were frequently apart.

Franklin's versatility and long life defy summary. He did everything it is possible to do on the printed page, as writer, editor, publisher, and printer. He served his city, colony, and new nation as postmaster, assembly delegate, and foreign envoy. He founded a library, a fire insurance company, and a university. He was as versatile and accomplished as a scientist as he was as a writer and statesman. He was also the life of the party, to judge from all accounts, as well as from this lyric he wrote:

There's but one Reason I can Think
Why People ever cease to Drink
Sobriety the Cause is not
Nor Fear of being deam'd a Sot,

But if Liquor can't be got.
If on my Theme I rightly think
There are Five Reasons why Men drink:
Good Wine, a Friend, because I'm dry,
Or least I should be by and by
Or any other Reason why.

The list of Franklin's innovations includes not just bifocals and the Franklin stove, but also shuttle diplomacy and international superstardom. He commuted between England and the colonies during the decade before the American Revolution. Once that conflict was under way he spent his time in France, seeking aid for the war effort. That the French gave generously testifies both to their animosity toward the British and their infatuation with the American envoy. As the historian Page Smith writes in his history of the American Revolution, *A New Age Now Begins*:

Franklin, a man as subtle and devious
as a French diplomat, as sophisticated
in his tastes as the most decadent
aristocrat, was nonetheless cast by the
French in the role of a simple American
agriculturalist. And Franklin—editor,
author, courtier, scientist, inventor,

sensualist, and roué—played the role with zest. He even wore a beaver cap, which was more enchanting to his admirers than the most bejeweled crown could have been. Everywhere in Paris he was honored, admired, and acclaimed. His picture was reproduced on snuffboxes, plates, vases, and commodes and sold by the thousands. Enterprising businessmen sold seats at places where the people of Paris could watch him ride by in his coach. Elegant ladies vied for his favors.

At Franklin's death in 1790, the French National Assembly took time out from its own tumultuous affairs to observe three days of mourning for a man they praised for "the simplicity and sweetness of his manners … the purity of his principles, the extent of his knowledge, and the charms of his mind."

—Jessica Fisher

Benjamin Franklin, whose accomplishments included being named the first Postmaster General of the United States, was honored by having his portrait adorn the nation's first official postage stamp, in 1847. Less official likenesses of Franklin appeared on more pedestrian objects abroad.

in the middle of a garden. Through the courtyard to the north, on Market Street, are row houses whose ground floors contain a post office, a postal museum, and a printing office and bindery with period equipment.

Below the courtyard in the **Underground Museum** are paintings, objects, and various Franklin inventions, including what he said was the invention that gave him his "greatest personal satisfaction," the armonica, a musical instrument composed of glass bowls. An 18-minute film sketches Franklin's life, and on a bank of telephones the testimonials of famous historical figures, read by actors, can be heard. *314–322 Market St., between Third and Fourth Sts. (additional entrance on Chestnut St.); 215/597–8974.*

NATIONAL MUSEUM OF AMERICAN JEWISH HISTORY
map page 53, E-2

A 1930s steamer trunk belonging to an immigrant family, an early-20th-century glass seltzer bottle sold by a Jewish merchant, and a 1901 Yiddish translation of Benjamin Franklin's autobiography are among the 40,000-plus artifacts in this museum illustrating the history of Jewish-American life. A $150 million expansion, opening in 2010, will include five new floors of interactive exhibits. Also located on the museum site is the Congregation Mikveh Israel, founded in 1740, which makes it the second oldest Jewish congregation in the country. Nathan Levy, the merchant whose ship brought the Liberty Bell to America, helped found the congregation. *Independence Mall East, 55 North Fifth St; 215/923–3811.*

OLD CITY

Aptly named Old City is one of the Philadelphia's oldest and most historic neighborhoods. The city's first homes, markets, churches, banks, and synagogues were erected right here on the banks of the Delaware River. In the 18th century, Old City was a commercial district, filled with wharves, warehouses, taverns, and the modest homes of craftsmen and artisans. In addition to Independence National Historic Park, it's where you'll find Christchurch, where George Washington and John Adams worshipped and Ben Franklin is buried, and Elfreth's Alley, the oldest continuously residential street in the country. Set yourself loose in Old City and you'll wind up on other tiny streets that are the result of initial land-owners ruining Penn's plan for a "green countrie towne" by subdividing their plots and packing them with two- and three-story row houses to rent to newer settlers.

Elfreth's Alley is the oldest continuously occupied residential street in the United States.

Today's Old City is a mix of residential, arts district, and nightlife mecca. It's drawn comparisons to New York's SoHo, and it has followed the same sort of path, from the '80s, when artists could afford to live loft-style and work in the old buildings, to today when the artists have been priced out and the old buildings developed into condos for well-to-do professionals. On weekend evenings, people from all over Philadelphia and its suburbs flock here to gallery- and bar-hop. A good time to visit is early evening, when the sidewalks are relatively empty, the boutiques are still open, and you can appreciate the colonial architecture in the waning light.

OLD CITY SIGHTS

BETSY ROSS HOUSE   *map page 53, F-2*

Historians can neither confirm nor deny that Betsy Ross sewed America's first flag, and they are equally unsure whether George Washington came secretly to her house just before he went to war and gave her his roughly sketched design. Whatever the truth about Ross's flag-making, she was well known to 18th-century Philadelphians as a tough-minded, thrice-married draper's widow who appeared regularly at patriot rallies.

RICHARD ALLEN'S CALLING

The **Mother Bethel Church** (419 South Sixth St., between Pine and Lombard; 215/925–0616), and the land it occupies is the oldest African-American-owned land in the nation. Reverend Richard Allen founded this branch of the African Methodist Episcopal Church after buying his freedom and finding his calling in the late 1700s. Once he'd purchased the land, he bought a blacksmith's shop and had it pulled here by his own team of horses. The structure was the first to house the Bethel church, dedicated here in 1794.

At Mother Bethel, Reverend Allen and Reverend Absalom Jones founded the Free Africa Society, the very first civil rights organization established in this country. Allen didn't live to see the current incarnation of the church. He preached his last sermon from the second church on this site, called the Roughcast Church because it was built from crude cinder blocks. Security against occasional angry mobs was a priority when choosing building materials. A brick-and-stone church came next, followed by the current church built in 1889. Today it doubles as a museum, exhibiting Allen's original pulpit, among many other early artifacts.

Betsy Ross liked to tell friends and family of the day in 1776 when three members of a secret committee from the Continental Congress—George Washington, Robert Morris, and George Ross—came to her home and asked her to sew a flag for the colonies.

On June 14, 1777, members of the Continental Congress, in Philadelphia, officially recognized the flag design that is said to be Ross's. Thus: "the flag of the thirteen United States be thirteen stripes, alternate red and white; that the union be thirteen stars, white, in a blue field representing a new constellation."

Even if the eight-room Ross house, built in the Georgian style around 1740, is not Betsy's confirmed place of residence, she did live in a home much like it. With few furnishings, the place telegraphs a Quaker work ethic more than comfort. The contrast between these spartan digs and the fine homes of the local gentry is startling. It's fun to see Ross's personal belongings, like the family Bible and her reading glasses, and the Upholstery Shop, where Ross and her husband,

John, managed the family business. There is also a Musket Ball Room, where Ross sewed soldiers' uniforms and other clothing. *239 Arch St., between Third and Broad Sts.; 215/686–1252.*

ELFRETH'S ALLEY
map page 53, F-2

Cobblestone-paved Elfreth's Alley, the oldest residential street in America, dates back to 1702. Back then, the modest two-story houses were mostly rented by tradespeople who'd work on the ground floor and live in the back parlor and upstairs. Today, all are owned by private individuals save for Nos. 124 and 126, museum homes restored by the Elfreth's Alley Association. These can be toured year-round, but you can tour more of the 30 homes if you're visiting in early

Pennsylvania's first Episcopal bishop lived in this house for half a century.

June, during Fête Days, or during Deck the Alley day in December, when guides dress up in period costumes and host house tours (both events require advance tickets). *Second St., between Arch and Race Sts.; 215/574–0560.*

CHRIST CHURCH   *map page 53, F-2*

Christ Church was built between 1724 and 1744 to replace a rickety wooden structure modeled after the post-Baroque style of English architect Sir Christopher Wren. Look for the brass plaques that mark the pews of George and Martha, Benjamin and Deborah, and Betsy Ross. Benjamin Franklin was an active member of the church, and a series of lotteries he ran helped pay for the 196-foot steeple and its bells. *Second St., ½ block north of Market St.*

A handful of signers of the Declaration of Independence and other Colonial patriots lie in **Christ Church Burial Ground.** The most famous is Benjamin Franklin who, with his wife Deborah, is buried near the fence on Arch Street next to a son, Francis, who died at age four. Visitors toss pennies on Franklin's marker for good luck. *Fifth and Arch Sts.*

AFRICAN-AMERICAN MUSEUM IN PHILADELPHIA   *map page 53, E-2*

The African-American Museum is the first of its kind to be funded and built by a city. The museum's collection contains more than a half-million items, and its vibrant, creative exhibits might focus on anything from breakout black films to the Negro baseball league to the fabled Philly sound, i.e. Philadelphia soul of the 1970s. A permanent exhibit on the life of African-Americans in Colonial America will open in 2009 in conjunction with the findings at the President's House site on Independence Mall. *701 Arch St.; 215/574–0380.*

BISHOP WHITE HOUSE   *map page 53, F-3*

Pennsylvania's first Episcopal bishop, William White, lived in this Georgian-style abode for half a century, beginning in 1786. The three-story house, with dormered attic and fine carvings around the windows, is typical of Philadelphia's upper-class residences in the late 1700s. The bishop hosted many famous statesmen here, holding forth in a beautifully appointed parlor that has been restored by the National Park Service. White was known for keeping a tight rein on his priests—it was not unusual to see several of them fidgeting in hardback chairs in the second-floor hallway outside his library, waiting to face him.

Free tickets for one-hour tours of the house, which is generally considered the most historically accurate re-creation of all the historic residences in Old City, are available the day of your visit at the Independence Visitor Center. The ticket also includes a tour of the Todd house (343 Walnut St.), a more modest home once occupied by Dolley Madison, whose second husband, James, was the nation's fourth president. *309 Walnut St., between Third and Fourth Sts.; 215/597–8974.*

CITY TAVERN   *map page 53, F-3*

Built in 1773 by the "principal gentlemen" of Philadelphia, City Tavern was for three decades a social, political, and economic center with several large meeting rooms, lodgings, two kitchens, and a bar. John Adams called it "The most genteel tavern in America." At a famous meeting here in May 1774, radicals pushed the heretofore moderate colony of Pennsylvania into the forefront of the dispute with England. The tavern was a gathering place for members of the Continental Congresses, the Constitutional Convention, and officials of the federal government from 1790 to 1800. In 1834, it was partially destroyed by fire, and in 1854 the original structure was demolished.

A replica of the original tavern was completed in 1976. Furnished with period reproductions and staffed with servers in period dress, the tavern serves lunch and dinner on ceramic creamware and ales made to Washington's and Adam's specs in pewter tankards. The menu successfully re-creates the cuisine of 18th-century America. *138 South Second St., at Walnut St.; 215/413–1443.*

SOCIETY HILL   *map page 53, F-3/4*

In the 18th century, wealthy merchants, sea captains, politicians, and other masters of the universe inhabited the elegant Colonial- and Federal-style townhouses that still line the streets of Society Hill. The neighborhood is named after the Free Society of Traders, a stock-exchange precursor whose offices and warehouses were located on Front Street. Starting in the mid-1800s, the wealthy began moving west toward Rittenhouse Square and the once-gracious homes here became flophouses and tenements. A major urban renewal effort beginning in the 1960s restored Society Hill to its initial stature. Walk around the meticulously preserved neighborhood today, and it's hard to believe it was once a slum.

The area has the largest concentration of original 18th-century architecture of any place in the United States. Stroll along side lanes like **Delancey Street** to view its colonial and contemporary structures. Other streets worth investigating are **American, Cypress,** and **Philip.** Peer down these lanes to note copper roofs, hidden courtyards, and remnants of Colonial life including boot-scrapers, hitching posts, and chimney pots. Within its streets is also the only surviving pre-Revolutionary tavern in Philadelphia, **Man Full of Trouble** (127 Spruce St.), which is closed to the public but still fun to see, especially as it's juxtaposed with the **Society Hill Towers,** a trio of condo towers designed in 1963 by I. M. Pei at the crest of the neighborhood's restoration.

There are also several historically significant houses of worship in the area, including **Old St. Mary's Church** (252 South Fourth St.; 215/923–7931), **Old St. Joseph's** (321 Willings Alley; 215/923–1733), and the **Society Hill Synagogue** (418 Spruce St.; 215/922–6590).

PHYSICK HOUSE   *map page 53, E-4*

The Physick House is one of only two freestanding Federal-style mansions left in Society Hill. The square three-story house, built in 1786 by wine merchant Henry Hill, reflects London architecture at the time. Philip Syng Physick, the father of American surgery—the stomach pump and catgut sutures are among his innovations still in use today—lived here from 1815 to 1837 and saw patients that included Dolley Madison and the future president Andrew Jackson. Restored

The father of American surgery lived and worked in the Physick House.

in the 1960s, the Physick House contains some of the finest period antiques in historic Philadelphia. *321 South Fourth St.; 215/925–7866.*

HEADHOUSE SQUARE AND MARKET SHED   *map page 53, F-4*

The city's original food markets were makeshift operations beneath open-air sheds. A wealthy merchant named Joseph Wharton built this one in 1745 to serve the residents of Society Hill. Farmers set up their carts beneath and around the shed's gable roof and brick piers. In its heyday the market snaked all the way to South Street; today it stretches from Pine to Lombard and serves as a site for craft fairs and a regular farmer's market. *Second and Pine Sts.; 215/790–0782.*

POWEL HOUSE   *map page 53, F-4*

Samuel Powel, dubbed the "Patriot Mayor," was the last mayor under the Crown and the first in the new republic. He and his bride, Elizabeth Willing, moved into this elegant 1765 Georgian brick mansion in 1769 and created a lavish home that reflected his seven-year "Grand Tour" of the Continent and his wife's knack for gracious entertaining. A mahogany staircase from Santo Domingo adorns the front hall, and a Gilbert Stuart portrait hangs in the parlor. Martha and George

Washington celebrated their 20th anniversary in the second-floor ballroom where the Powels also hosted John Adams, Benjamin Franklin, and General Lafayette. *244 South Third St.; 215/627–0364.*

PENN'S LANDING   *map page 53, F-3*

Society Hill's waterfront along the Delaware River is known as Penn's Landing, a 37-acre river park east of Christopher Columbus Boulevard between Spring Garden and Lombard Streets. This is where William Penn stepped ashore from the *Welcome* in 1682 and took possession of Pennsylvania.

Penn's Landing has been sliced out of the working waterfront. If you look north toward the magnificent Ben Franklin Bridge, you'll see cargo ships and tankers loading and unloading. Looking across the granite-blue Delaware River, you can see Camden, New Jersey's waterfront about ½ mile away. Its Adventure Aquarium, the Battleship *New Jersey,* and Campbell's Field, a minor-league ballpark that's home to the Camden Riversharks, are accessible via the 12-min-

Exhibits at the Independence Seaport Museum tell the story of Philadelphia's waterfront.

ute (one-way) **RiverLink Ferry,** which leaves from the Independence Seaport Museum. The fare is $6 round-trip.

Back on the Pennsylvania side of the river, you'll see the masts of fine old sailing vessels, some of which can be toured. Among these is the 394-foot-long *Moshulu* (Columbus Boulevard, Pier 34). Built in 1904, the vessel is among the world's biggest and oldest four-masted ships. Other boats you can board include the *Spirit of Philadelphia* (Pier 3) and, when in port, the 177-foot-long *Gazela,* built in 1883.

Exhibits at the **Independence Seaport Museum** illuminate the Philadelphia waterfront's place in American history. Admiral George Dewey's 1892 cruiser *Olympia* is berthed directly behind the museum in the Delaware River. One of the first ships to be made of steel, the *Olympia* served as an escort ship in the Atlantic Ocean during World War I. The vessel's last assignment, in 1921, was to carry home from Europe the body of the Unknown Soldier, which rests now in Arlington National Cemetery.

Alongside the *Olympia* floats the *Becuna,* a 308-foot-long submarine that was part of the Pacific fleet during World War II. The sub destroyed many Japanese naval ships during the war, after which it was redesigned to carry nuclear warheads. The sub was decommissioned in 1969. On the tour you'll get a feel for the cramped conditions sailors endured. *211 South Columbus Blvd., at the foot of Walnut St.; 215/925–5439.*

The **Great Plaza** amphitheater hosts events from May through September, including multicultural festivals, children's theater, concerts, and Philadelphia's Fourth of July celebration. In good weather, it's a popular spot for picnicking.

Columbus Boulevard has been in a state of transition since the late 1990s. The 3-mile stretch is the site of a Hyatt Regency and a few luxury apartment buildings plus nightclubs and more than a dozen restaurants—a few decent, most less so. In 2006, the Pennsylvania Gaming Control Board green-lighted the development of a casino on the riverfront to the consternation of a vocal faction of residents who are trying their best to prevent this. At press time, construction had not started.

WASHINGTON SQUARE DISTRICT *map page 53, D/E-3/4*

Washington Square, one of Philadelphia's original five squares, is a large park at Walnut and Sixth Streets. Though not far from the hubbub of Independence Hall, the park is often quite serene. The Tomb of the Unknown Soldier, the only such monument to Revolutionary War soldiers, is here.

Stop by the Curtis Center to see a stunning Tiffany mosaic.

The Washington Square District, bounded by Market, Sixth, Lombard, and Broad streets, connects the historic and commercial sections of Center City. Curtis Publishing, responsible for the *Saturday Evening Post, Ladies Home Journal,* and other popular magazines of the 19th and 20th centuries, had its headquarters in what is now the **Curtis Center** (Sixth and Walnut Sts.). In the center's Sixth Street lobby is *The Dream Garden,* a 15-by-49-foot glass mosaic by Louis Comfort Tiffany based on a Maxfield Parrish painting. The lobby is accessible during business hours and on Saturday until mid-afternoon.

West of Seventh Street on Sansom Street is **Jeweler's Row,** where jewelers and importers have been doing business since 1852. **Antique Row** between Ninth and 12th Streets along Pine Street is now a mix of new boutiques and longtime antique shops like **M. Finkel and Daughter,** established here in 1947 and known for its unparalleled collection of antique samplers.

A short detour north nearly to Market Street brings you to the quirky **Atwater Kent Museum,** in an 1826 Greek Revival–style building designed by John Haviland. The museum's namesake, who made his fortune manufacturing radios, collected all sorts of Philadelphia-related items, from Stetson hats to souvenirs from Philadelphia's Centennial Celebration in 1876. The museum's entire second floor is given over to a gallery of Norman Rockwell images that graced *Saturday Evening Post* covers. *15 South Seventh St.; 215/685–4830.*

The **Walnut Street Theatre,** opened in 1809, is a National Historic Landmark and the oldest theater in America. It continues to thrive as a nonprofit regional theater with some 20 productions per season on a stage that has hosted actors including Marlon Brando, Jack Lemmon, and Lily Tomlin. *825 Walnut St.; 215/574–3550.*

SOUTH STREET   *map page 53, A/F-4*

The shift in tone can be downright jarring when you pass from Old City's sedate colonial-era enclaves into the antic South Street area, the closest thing Philadelphia has to New York's Greenwich Village or San Francisco's Haight-Ashbury. In 1963, the Orlons song, "South Street" ("Where do all the hippies meet?"), reached number three on the Billboard charts. Since then the vibe has gone from hippie to trashy. Tattoo parlors and cheap clothing shops now fill the stretch between Front Street and Ninth Street. There are a few gems—mostly holdouts—among the ever-changing roster of restaurants, bars, and shops. These

The Mummers Parade, held in Philadelphia every New Year's Day, might best be described as the city's version of Mardi Gras.

JFK Plaza, across from City Hall, is known as Love Park thanks to this sculpture.

range from **The Eyes Gallery** (402 South St.), with two floors of Latin American crafts and folk art, to **Jim's Steaks** (400 South St.), many locals' favorite source for cheesesteaks. The area gets rowdy with revelers on weekend evenings.

CENTER CITY

The completion of One Liberty Place (1650 Market St.) in 1987 changed the character of the downtown area forever. At 960 feet tall, it was the first Philadelphia building to violate the long-standing gentleman's agreement among architects and engineers not to exceed the height of the William Penn statue (548 feet) atop City Hall's clock tower. Since then, about 10 buildings have surpassed Penn's topper, the latest being the Comcast Center (1701 JFK Blvd.), which towers above all others at 975 feet.

CITY HALL AREA

CITY HALL   *map page 53, C-3*

The impressive granite and white marble City Hall, adorned with a not entirely coherent mix of columns, pilasters, pediments, dormers, and sculptures, was built between 1871 and 1901. The visual centerpiece of downtown Philadelphia boasts no shortage of superlatives. The 491-foot tower is the tallest masonry structure in the world. The 27-ton cast-iron statue of William Penn by Alexander Milne Calder is the largest single piece of sculpture on any building in the world. (Penn is fitted with oversized baseball caps and hockey jerseys, depending on which team has made it to a championship that year.) And the building itself is the largest municipal building in the country. Free tours are offered at 12:30 PM on weekdays. *Broad and Market Sts.; 215/686–2840.*

MASONIC TEMPLE   *map page 53, C-2*

Membership in the Philadelphia Free and Accepted Masons, a fraternal society founded in the Middle Ages, was coveted in colonial times. Many statesmen of the Revolution, including George Washington, belonged to the Philadelphia Guild and supported building the temple as a statewide meeting place. The temple is divided into seven lodge halls, all ornately decorated in the styles of various cultures, including Egyptian, Asian, and Gothic. On display in the building's museum is a Masonic apron embroidered for George Washington by the wife of the Marquis de Lafayette. *One North Broad St.; 215/988–1900.*

PENNSYLVANIA ACADEMY OF FINE ARTS   *map page 53, C-2*

America's first art museum and art school was founded in 1805 by a group of artists and entrepreneurs that included the painter Charles Willson Peale and the sculptor William Rush. The academy had several addresses during the 19th century, but in 1876 architects George Hewitt and Frank Furness designed the school's current home, a stunning example of Victorian Gothic, complete with a mahogany and bronze staircase, Gothic arches trimmed in gold, and a blue vaulted ceiling with painted stars. So taken with the academy was the modernist architect Louis I. Kahn that he called the building "life-giving and life-inspired."

The academy's permanent collection is a survey of American art from the 1760s to the present and includes work by former faculty including Thomas Eakins, whose masterful *The Gross Clinic* brings the viewer front and center in a skylit hall to watch a 19th-century surgeon preside over an operation. Other highlights of the collection are urban scenes by members of the Ashcan school, portraits by Cecilia Beaux and Gilbert Stuart, and Winslow Homer's menacing *Fox Hunt*. *118 and 128 North Broad St.; 215/972–7600.*

Bright lights, big City Hall tower.

HISTORICAL SOCIETY OF PENNSYLVANIA *map page 53, C-4*

Following a merger with the Balch Institute of Ethnic Studies in 2002, this special-collections library established in 1824 contains some 600,000 books, 19 million manuscripts, and 300,000 graphic items, like architectural drawings and the earliest surviving American photograph. Other highlights include a first draft of the Constitution and a printer's proof of the Declaration of Independence. The emphasis is on Pennsylvania and regional history from the 17th century onward; family history; and since the merger, the immigrant and ethnic experience in Philadelphia and America. This is the place to go to trace your family roots. *1300 Locust St.; 215/732–6200.*

READING TERMINAL MARKET *map page 53, D-2*

This vibrant, eclectic, indoor market is one of Philadelphia's treasures. Back when the Reading Railroad rumbled overhead in the early 1900s, the trains both brought in and carted out goods sold here. Today the train shed is part of the convention center, but the market is still very much alive and buzzing with more than 80 stalls serving everything from chicken mole tacos, artisanal cheese, soft pretzels, and hoagies to Bassett's ice cream, shoofly pie, and much more. There's plenty of seating if you want to eat here, though chefs and locals also shop for fresh produce, meat, seafood, and spices to take away. The market contains a few restaurants, including the Dutch Eating Place, known for its fluffy blueberry pancakes, authentic scrapple, and long breakfast lines. *Reading Terminal Market entrance, 12th and Arch Sts.; 215/922–2317.*

PSFS BUILDING *map page 53, C-3*

Diagonally across from the Reading Terminal and in nearly every way its antithesis, the PSFS Building, completed in 1932, was designed by the firm of Howe & Lescaze. With its spare vocabulary of glass and glazed brick, the structure, one of the country's earliest examples of the International style, made perhaps too stark a statement. A critic in 1985 described Howe & Lescaze's creation as being "too coolly self-possessed to start a trend," and indeed there is nothing quite like it in Philadelphia. Originally the headquarters of the Philadelphia Savings Fund Society, it was restored in 2000 and converted into a hotel. Still coolly self-possessed, with crisp art deco interior detailing and austere lines, the building is well worth investigating. *1200 Market St., at 12th St.*

Reading Terminal Market, another magical downtown space, attracts food lovers from all over Philadelphia and beyond.

★ RITTENHOUSE SQUARE
map page 53, A-4

In 1840 Rittenhouse Square was slated to become the site of an observatory named for prominent astronomer David Rittenhouse. Thankfully it remained a park. In 1913, Paul Cret, the architect behind the Ben Franklin Parkway and Ben Franklin Bridge, designed this park's gracious entrances, central plaza, pool, and fountain. One of the city's most well-loved public areas, the place is packed on warm spring days. Its immediate perimeter is lined with swanky condo buildings of all architectural styles, a historic church, hotels, and restaurants with al fresco dining. Magnificent mansions on the perimeter of the square were once home to the city's wealthiest citizens and now live on in many incarnations including the prestigious Curtis Institute of Music, which emits sounds of violins and voices in warmer months; the Philadelphia Art Alliance; and the sprawling flagship shop for local brand Anthropologie. *Walnut St., between 18th and 19th Sts.*

The Kimmel Center's glass-enclosed atrium is one of Philadelphia's great public spaces.

CIVIL WAR AND UNDERGROUND RAILROAD MUSEUM
map page 53, A-4

In a 19th-century row home, this museum houses more than 12,000 volumes pertaining to the Civil War, along with 5,000 photographs documenting the war's battlefields, generals, and soldiers. Among the artifacts on display are the stuffed and mounted head of General Meade's horse, "Old Baldy"; a frock coat worn by General William T. Sherman; and, in a room entirely devoted to Abraham Lincoln, casts of the president's hands and a death mask. *1805 Pine St.; 215/735–8196.*

MUTTER MUSEUM   *map page 53, C-4*

Founded in 1856 to display medical rarities for the edification of medical students and physicians, the Mutter Museum is well-known for curiosities like skeletons demonstrating genetic disorders, trepanned skulls, and the life-sized plaster model of conjoined twins Change and Eng. Antique surgical equipment and an iron lung will give you new appreciation for modern science. It's not a place for young children; even tough cookies can start to feel woozy among these exhibits. *19 South 22nd St.; 215/563–3737.*

KIMMEL CENTER FOR THE PERFORMING ARTS   *map page 53, C-4*

The New York–based architect Rafael Viñoly designed this $250 million structure, named after local philanthropist Sidney Kimmel. The center has two concert halls: 2,500-seat Verizon Hall, where the Philadelphia Orchestra and Philly Pops perform; and 650-seat Perelman Theater, which hosts performances by smaller ensembles, among them the Chamber Orchestra of Philadelphia and the Philadelphia Chamber Music Society. The Kimmel's atrium, whose most dynamic feature is a vaulted glass roof reminiscent of European train depots, instantly became one of the city's great public spaces. *260 South Broad St.; 215/790–5800.*

ACADEMY OF MUSIC
map page 53, C-4

The former home of the Philadelphia Orchestra is a block from the Kimmel Center. The 2,900-seat hall, built in 1857 and the oldest opera house in America, takes its architectural cues from Milan's La Scala opera house. Richly detailed murals by Karl Heinrich Schmolze and an impressive chandelier are among the hall's noteworthy features, but equally impressive is the list of American premieres that have taken place here, among them Verdi's opera *Il Trovatore,* Gounod's

Verizon Hall.

Faust, Strauss's *Ariadne auf Naxos,* and Wagner's *The Flying Dutchman.* Many of the world's greatest musicians and singers have graced this stage, including Maria Callas, Vladimir Horowitz, and Luciano Pavarotti. The Academy of Music is currently home to the Opera Company of Philadelphia and the Pennsylvania Ballet, and it also presents touring Broadway shows and other productions. *1420 Locust St.; 215/893-1955.*

CHINATOWN
map page 53, D-2

People have been coming to Chinatown to eat since the first Chinese restaurant, Mei-Hsian Lou (913 Race St.), opened in 1870. A plaque on the building pays homage to the eatery and to the first Chinese immigrants to America. Chinatown is loaded with small shops and restaurants, and in recent years a few bars here have been taken up by college students, lending the neighborhood a zippier feel. The dining scene here is also more eclectic these days, including inexpensive Vietnamese, Thai, and Chinese restaurants. *From Ninth St. to 12th St., between Vine and Arch Sts.*

BENJAMIN FRANKLIN PARKWAY   *map page 83, B-4*

Stretching from City Hall northwest to the Philadelphia Museum of Art, scenic Ben Franklin Parkway was meant to be the city's Champs Élysées. The plan for the parkway was drawn up in the early 1900s by French architects Paul Cret and Jacques Greber, who modeled Logan Circle after the Place de la Concorde. Today the 250-foot-wide boulevard is lined with the city's most venerable museums and institutions, as well as apartments, office buildings, and hotels. The renowned Barnes Foundation (*see below*) is slated to join the art collections here, although at this writing the date had not been set.

FRANKLIN INSTITUTE SCIENCE MUSEUM   *map page 83, B-4*

Founded nearly two centuries ago, this largely interactive science museum has well-loved longtime exhibits like the giant Foucault pendulum that hangs in the museum's grand marble stairwell. Newer additions include a roof-top observatory renovated in 2006; Space Command, an "research station" where you can check out authentic U.S. and Russian spacesuits; and a 350-ton Baldwin steam locomotive. The museum's Fels Planetarium has a state-of-the-art aluminum dome, lighting, and sound systems; and the Mandell Center houses the Tuttleman IMAX theater. *222 North 20th St.; 215/448–1200.*

PHILADELPHIA MUSEUM OF ART   *map page 83, A/B-4*

The vast holdings of this world-class museum, founded in 1876, include more than 300,000 works encompassing 300 years of European and East Asian decorative arts, paintings, and sculpture. The painting collections alone, with works by Fra Angelico, Van Eyck, Rubens, and van Gogh, could swallow up several days of concentrated viewing. Thanks to the museum director who oversaw collections in the first half of the 20th century, there are some 30 architectural interiors—whole buildings and rooms moved from around the world, from a 15th-century

A lion dance during the Chinese New Year's parade.

A sculler on the Schuylkill River below the Philadelphia Museum of Art.

Japanese teahouse to an 18th-century grand salon from a French chateau—all of which are positively transporting. The museum's modern, Pop, and postmodern holdings include pivotal works by Brancusi, Duchamp, Twombly, Picasso, and many more. The Perelman Building (Fairmount and Pennsylvania Aves.), opened in 2007 in a renovated and expanded art deco former office building across the Parkway, has allowed for the museum to excavate from storage their works on paper, contemporary decorative arts, and textiles. *2600 Benjamin Franklin Pkwy., at 26th St.; 215/763–8100.*

RODIN MUSEUM   *map page 83, B-4 and map page 55, A-1*

Four blocks east of the Philadelphia Museum of Art on Benjamin Franklin Parkway, the Rodin Museum has the largest collection of the sculptor's oeuvre outside Paris. All the classics—*The Kiss, The Burghers of Calais, The Thinker,* and *The Gates of Hell*—are displayed inside this elegant jewel box of a museum and in its gardens. Designed by French architects Paul Philippe Cret and Jacques Greber, the museum was a gift to the city from movie magnate and art collector, Jules Mastbaum, who commissioned it in the 1920s and, sadly, did not live to see it completed. *2151 Benjamin Franklin Pkwy., at 22nd St.; 215/763–8100.*

A Calder mobile graces the airy interior of the Philadelphia Museum of Art—appropriate, because Alexander Calder was a Philadelphia native.

FAIRMOUNT PARK   *map page 83, A-2/4*

On land purchased by the city in the mid-1800s, Fairmount Park provides Philadelphians with 14 square miles of space to run, stroll, bicycle, or picnic. The **Philadelphia Zoo** (3400 West Girard Ave.) is here, as is the **Philadelphia Museum of Art.** Open-air concerts take place in summer at the **Mann Center for the Performing Arts** (52nd St. and Parkside Ave.), and 10 Victorian structures, known as **Boathouse Row,** front Kelly Drive. These are the headquarters of the city's popular rowing clubs, whose members can be seen slicing through the glass-like river water on many early mornings. You can rent bicycles along Kelly Drive. Ask for directions to the Forbidden Trail—it's so undeveloped you'll swear you're in central Pennsylvania rather than a major metropolis. Along Kelly and West River Drives are more 18th- and early-19th-century houses, "rural" retreats for well-to-do families. Most of these 90 historic homes are open for tours. **Lemon Hill, Cedar Grove, Mount Pleasant,** and the fanciful **Strawberry Mansion** are among the most famous.

Typical of the upper-class homes is **Sweetbriar Mansion** (Sweetbriar Hill, off Lansdowne Dr.; 215/222–1333), now a popular house museum. It was built on the Schuylkill River's west bank by Samuel Breck, a wealthy merchant who served in the state legislature, where he wrote the bill calling for the emancipation of the state's slaves. Many of Sweetbriar's rooms were decorated in 18th-century French style, probably due to Breck's friendship with Lafayette, Talleyrand, and other French notables. The house's south parlor is supremely elegant, with floor-to-ceiling windows framing views of the exterior gardens. For park information, call 215/685–0000.

UNIVERSITY CITY   *map page 83, A-4*

The brainpower concentrated in this relatively small section of the city west of the Schuylkill River seems astonishing when you consider what's here: the University of Pennsylvania, Drexel University, the Philadelphia College of Pharmacy and Science, and offshoots like the City Science Center (a leading think tank). The cultural offerings that have sprung up around the universities attract audiences from around the region.

The **Institute of Contemporary Art** (118 South 35th St.; 215/898–7108) is known for its exhibits of cutting-edge emerging artists. The boxy modern building on U. of Penn's campus has four exhibit spaces. The **University Museum of Archaeology and Anthropology** (3260 South St.; 215/898–4000), also affiliated with U. of Penn, has nearly a million objects collected during field excavations and research in ancient lands including a 12-ton sphinx from Egypt and a crystal ball once owned by China's Dowager Empress. The **Annenberg Performing Arts Center** (3680 Walnut St.; 215/898–3900) is a performance venue with a full schedule comprised of dance, music and theater series that showcase up-and-coming to world-renowned artists.

SOUTH PHILADELPHIA   *map page 83, A-5*

The oldest district in Philadelphia County was settled by Swedish immigrants in the mid-17th century. Today, South Philadelphia—or South Philly as it is more often called—consists of small city blocks lined with row houses. The area is best known for the Italian Market, Italian restaurants, and genuine Philly cheesesteaks. What's in a cheesesteak, you ask? Here's the high-calorie recipe: take a thinly sliced steak, top it with grilled onions and smother it with Cheez Whiz (the authentic choice) or provolone; add lettuce, tomato, mayonnaise, and pizza sauce and place the whole thing inside a bun.

South Philadelphia is famous for its sports stadiums, Italian restaurants, and the engaging Italian Market, pictured above.

ITALIAN MARKET   *map page 83, B-5*

Still in business after 100 years, this market along Ninth Street offers the cuisines of many cultures to locals and tourists. Over the years, waves of immigrants— Greek, Vietnamese, Korean, Cambodian, Mexican, and more have added new flavors and different sorts of clatter to the market's soundtrack. In recent years vendors selling dollar-store bargains have leeched some of the charm from the market, but it's still the best place in the city to buy a superlative cup of espresso, and pick up some homemade pasta, imported cheese, and olives. *Ninth St., between Washington Ave. and Christian St.*

MUMMERS MUSEUM   *map page 83, B-5*

This museum celebrates Philadelphia's Mummers and the unique parade they put on each New Year's Day along Center City's usually freezing streets. Mummery is a way of life for participants, who begin work on next year's event the day after. If you can't make the parade—which so far is televised only locally—this diverting museum is worth a visit. These days they also stage a July 4th parade plus an annual February performance at the Spectrum. The city officially began sponsoring the parade in 1901, but the Mummers' history goes back well into the 19th century. The museum is a taxi ride from Old City but just a few blocks from the Italian Market. *1100 South Second St., at Washington St.; 215/336–3050.*

SPORTS STADIUMS

South Philly is also where professional sports are played. Since 2004, major-league baseball's Philadelphia Phillies have played in **Citizens Bank Park** (11th St. at Pattison Ave.). The 76ers basketball team and Flyers hockey team play at the **Wachovia Center** (3601 South Broad St.). The Philadelphia Eagles take on the rest of the National Football League at the 55,000-seat **Lincoln Financial Field** (11th St. at Pattison Ave.).

MANAYUNK   *map page 83, A-3*

Taken from a phrase of the Lenni Lenape Indians for "where we go to drink," Manayunk, on the Schuylkill River, was once connected to the Pennsylvania canal system built in 1819. Manayunk's factories have all closed, but the former mill town has become a hip neighborhood, with boutiques, restaurants, and bars all concentrated along Main Street. (With those bars, the area still lives up to its

At Citizens Bank Park, a neon "Liberty Bell" rings for every Phillies home run.

South Philadelphia row houses.

name.) The community hosts a well-attended arts festival on the last weekend in June each year. Area restaurants supply the edibles and local artists and crafstpeople display their works. The Tow Path along the Schuykill River is popular with bikers and walkers.

GERMANTOWN AND CHESTNUT HILL   *map page 83, B-3*

When it was settled in 1683, Germantown was a separate village from Philadelphia, its citizens a mix of German Quakers and Mennonite farmers who proved to be even more progressive and welcoming than many mainstream Philadelphians. European immigrants with differing religious beliefs and cultural mores settled here and prospered. Residents of Germantown were quietly supportive of the Revolution, although as Quakers they were pacifists.

Because of the village's industrial facilities, the British army made a beeline for Germantown after routing George Washington's army and occupying Philadelphia in 1777. The Battle of Germantown, actually a series of attacks on the British troops by Washington, was a bitter early defeat for the revolutionaries. A reenactment complete with firing muskets and uniformed troops takes place here each year on the first Saturday in October.

Many fine house museums in Germantown reflect the influence of German architecture on American residential design before and after the Revolutionary War. **Cliveden** (6401 Germantown Ave.; 215/848–1777), at the north end of Germantown, is a 1763 country house occupied by the British during the Revolutionary War. The amusingly named **Grumblethorpe** (5267 Germantown Ave.; 215/843–4820) has a fairy tale–like quality amplified by its stone exterior and dark-red trim. George Washington lived in the **Deshler-Morris House** (5442 Germantown Ave.; 215/596–1748) for a spell, supposedly to avoid the dampness of sea-level Philadelphia.

Stenton (4601 North 18th St.; 215/329–7312), an early Georgian-style brick house, was built by James Logan in 1727 when he found himself "no longer in love with life." Sparsely ornamented, with light-filled parlors and a capacious library, the house makes a convincing case for the healing powers of solitude. For more information about house museums, contact the **Germantown Historical Society** (215/844–0514).

Farther northwest is Chestnut Hill, a first-ring suburb that sprang up in the late 1800s with the development of a Chestnut Hill railroad line. This quaint, charming neighborhood has more in common with some of the ritzier Main Line suburbs than it does with Germantown, parts of which are much worse for the wear and tear of urban decay. Not so Chestnut Hill's cobblestoned Germantown Avenue, which is lined with restaurants, galleries, and boutiques. The **Chestnut Hill Visitors Center** (215/247–6696) is on this strip. Walk off the avenue and you'll find well-maintained examples of Colonial Revival and Queen Anne homes.

★ BARNES FOUNDATION   *map page 83, A-4*

The Barnes Foundation has a reputation for creating circumstances that make visiting the collection more difficult than the average art museum. So why do people make a special effort to call two months in advance to reserve a ticket? They're drawn by the dazzling artworks and by the promise of a place unlike any other in the world. Critic Peter Schjeldahl believes, "You don't view the installation so much as live it, undergoing an experience that will persist in your memory like a love affair".

Nothing here is hung according to period or chronology. Instead, walls are crammed from floor to ceiling with masterworks by blue-chip artists including Renoir, Cezanne, Matisse, and Tintoretto. And alongside and in between these

The art installations at the Barnes Foundation are unlike any others in the world.

paintings are everything from New Mexico folk icons and household tools to African masks and antique door latches.

Dr. Albert C. Barnes, the inventor of Argyrol, an antiseptic widely used prior to the introduction of antibiotics, used his fortune to fuel his passions for art collecting and art education. He arranged these "wall ensembles," as he referred to them, by selecting objects and paintings that shared a single quality or a particular set of qualities. The students at his Foundation were asked to notice how a door hinge, for instance, shared a certain expressiveness of line with a Renoir form or how a color in a painting of an Amish chest was similar to a pigment used in a Courbet painting.

Barnes spelled out detailed instructions in his will, including limiting public admission to the collection to two days a week to preserve its integrity as an educational institution. (He insisted that the Foundation was not a museum but a school.) Mismanaged finances led to necessary violations of this and many more conditions. In 2004, after a two-year legal battle and impassioned public debate, a judge ruled that the Foundation could relocate to Center City. The Foundation has pledged to reproduce Barnes's idiosyncratic installation of artworks in the new location, on the Benjamin Franklin Parkway between 21st and 22nd streets. At this writing, an opening date has not yet been set. Do all you can to see it in its original location. *300 Latches La., Merion; 610/667–0290.*

BRANDYWINE VALLEY   *map page 101, D-4*

Twenty-five miles southwest of Center City, the urban landscape gives way to the verdant farm and horse country of the Brandywine Valley. In spring, when the air is thick with the fragrance of honeysuckle and mowed grass, it is difficult to imagine that this landscape once witnessed the deaths of thousands of soldiers fighting in the War of Independence. It's not surprising that the gorgeous scenery led artist N.C. Wyeth and ensuing generations of Wyeths to live and paint here for much of the 20th century.

To find this rural beauty, turn north off U.S. 1 on Route 100 at Chadds Ford and drive along Creek Road toward West Chester. This is also the exit for the Brandywine Battlefield State Park, the site of the largest engagement of the Revolutionary War.

Mill on the Brandywine (ca. 1830), by John Rubens Smith. (Library of Congress)

The interior of the tropical plants conservatory at Longwood Gardens.

Just about any turn off U.S. 1 west of I–476 will put you on a rural road. Take the exit at Route 82, for example, 6 miles from the Brandywine River Museum, and you will be in the heart of a mushroom-growing region.

CHADDS FORD   *map page 101, D-4*

In 1967, a group of residents, many of whom could trace their family histories in the area back to Colonial times, succeeded in putting a cap on development in this region. To defray costs of their efforts, they enlisted the talents of valley artists and opened the **Brandywine River Museum** in a converted 1880s gristmill. The glass-wall lobby frames views of the river and surrounding woods. On exhibit are paintings by Andrew Wyeth, his son Jamie, and others of the Wyeth clan, in addition to landscapes and portraits by other noted American artists. Tickets can also be bought here to tour the nearby **N. C. Wyeth House and Studio** as well as the farm of Karl and Anna Kuerner, from whom Andrew Wyeth drew constant inspiration. *U.S. 1 and Creek Rd. (formerly Rte. 100); 610/388–2700.*

On September 11, 1777, on the site that is now the **Brandywine Battlefield Park,** George Washington, with half his army off defending Manhattan, faced a well-equipped British force and lost, forcing his retreat to Lancaster and then to Valley Forge. Without Washington's army to protect the city, the British captured Philadelphia, dealing the revolutionary cause an enormous blow. At the 50-acre park are reproductions of the farmhouses that Washington and Lafayette used as headquarters. *U.S. 1; 610/459–3342.*

Operating out of a renovated 17th-century barn, **Chaddsford Winery** produces about 30,000 cases of wine each year. Known for its cabernets and chardonnays, the winery, established in 1982, presents outdoor concerts in summer. *632 Baltimore Pike or U.S. 1, 5 miles south of Rte. 202; 610/388–6221.*

LONGWOOD GARDENS   *map page 101, D-4*

The 1,050-acre country estate of industrialist Pierre S. du Pont encompasses 20 outdoor gardens, 20 indoor gardens, 11,000 different types of plants, elaborate fountains, two lakes, and several large heated conservatories of exotic tropical vegetation. Du Pont began creating Longwood Gardens as it is today around 1907. The Main Garden Fountain is epic, to say the least, spurting 10,000 gallons of water per minute as high as 130 feet.

In spring, the azaleas and rhododendrons are especially beautiful; in fall the blooms of chrysanthemums and the changing foliage steal the show. Water lilies with huge upturned leaves and large flowers flourish in the lakes. In the formal gardens are topiaries, and as you wander the paths you'll come upon sculptures that blend perfectly with the plantings. *1001 Longwood Rd., Kennett Square, off U.S. 1; 610/388–1000.*

★ WINTERTHUR   *map page 101, D-4*

A few miles from U.S. 1 across the Pennsylvania border in Delaware is the Brandywine Valley's most famous attraction: Winterthur Garden and Museum, the country estate of Henry Francis du Pont. H.F. du Pont, whose interests included antiques and horticulture. His father, Henry Algernon du Pont, based the design of the nearly 1,000-acre estate on English country manors of the 18th and 19th centuries. A man of exceedingly particular tastes, H.F. du Pont owned hundreds of sets of china. He expected fresh flowers from his gardens to bedeck his dinner tables and dictated that the china match the flowers and that the food complement the plates.

Winterthur contains one of the world's finest collections of early American decorative arts; beautiful Wedgwood originals; paintings by John Singleton Copley, Rembrandt Peale, and Gilbert Stuart; and no end of glittering antiques from France, Germany, England, and elsewhere. As at Longwood Gardens, something

George Washington's headquarters at Valley Forge.

is always in bloom. Many people time their visits for May, when the dogwoods and azaleas are in full flower. *Rte. 52; 800/448–3883.*

VALLEY FORGE   *map page 101, D-3*

After his defeat by the British at Brandywine, George Washington regrouped his forces briefly at Lancaster and then set up headquarters with 16 brigades across the Schuylkill River from Philadelphia at Valley Forge. A sculpture at one end of **Valley Forge National Historic Park,** the National Memorial Arch, honors the soldiers who endured the terrible winter encampment of 1777–78. Conditions were so debilitating that many soldiers deserted camp, and more than 2,000 soldiers died from malnutrition and disease. One officer, who spent the winter with them and trained in the cold, helped many find the will to survive. He was not an American, but a Prussian drillmaster, Friedrich von Steuben, and much of the tour material in the park is devoted to the role that foreign officers and soldiers played at this crucial point in the War of Independence.

Among the park's sites open for touring are several simple homes Washington and his officers used during that winter. The park also has picnic areas and a

6-mile hiking and biking trail. You can pick up audio driving tours on cassette ($10) or CD ($12) at the visitors center, or you can use your cell phone to hear the tour for free by calling 484/396–1018. *Off I–76, Exit 26B; take Rte. 422 West for 1 mile to Rte. 23 West; 610/783–1077.*

KING OF PRUSSIA MALL   *map page 101, E-3*

It's hard to miss this mall, one of the nation's largest shopping complexes, if you're headed west of the city on the Schuylkill Expressway. The gargantuan complex is anchored by seven department stores including Bloomingdales, Nordstrom, and Neiman Marcus, and contains pretty much every other store you'd expect to find in a luxury mall (Louis Vuitton, Hermès, Versace, etc.). Some shops even appear twice. *U.S. 202 at Schuylkill Expressway, 160 North Gulph Rd.; 610/265–5727.*

GETTING HERE

BY PLANE

Philadelphia International Airport is 6.5 miles south of City Hall. The SEPTA (Southeastern Pennsylvania Transportation Authority) airport rail line—the R1—runs every half hour from 6 AM until midnight from each terminal to three destinations in Center City, including 30th Street Station. A one-way ride costs $6. A taxi from the airport into Center City costs a flat rate of $26.25, plus tip.

BY TRAIN

Amtrak serves Philadelphia from New York City and Washington, D.C. Arriving by train at the beautiful **30th Street Station,** the main train terminal, puts you right downtown—an easy cab, bus, or subway ride to most hotels and attractions.

GETTING AROUND

BY CAR

Laid out in a grid pattern by its founder William Penn, you would think that Center City is relatively easy to navigate. However, many streets are one-way, and the main thoroughfares are often congested with traffic. The many squares and circles, such as Rittenhouse Square and Logan Circle, can confuse you by interrupting the grid pattern. Your best bet in Center City and the Historic District

FAVORITE PLACES TO EAT

Ansill. 627 South Third St., at South St., Society Hill; 215/627–2485. $$

Foodie-approved fare is served small-plate style in this sleek and cozy dining room. Try the feathery shirred eggs; the pork belly pieces on a bed of spaetzle twists; and the tender grilled octopus with a tang of sherry vinaigrette. For dessert, pick the dark-chocolate panini on a buttery brioche served with a mound of mascarpone.

Lolita. 106 South 13th St., City Hall area; 215/546–7100. $$–$$$

In a town where liquor licenses are hard to come by, lots of restaurants are BYOB. Lolita's genius twist is BYOT, or bring your own tequila. They'll blend a pitcher of fresh strawberry and purple basil margaritas. And the food— nouveau Mexican prepared with local ingredients—is pretty remarkable, too.

Continental Midtown. 1801 Chestnut St., Rittenhouse Sq.; 215/567–1800. $–$$$

Line up for a spot on the popular rooftop lounge or sit inside, in a swinging wicker chair or a baby-blue vinyl booth. The global tapas menu includes shoestring fries drizzled with Chinese mustard, a gargantuan crispy calamari salad, and a cheeseteak egg roll.

Amada. 217–219 Chestnut St., Old City; 215/625–2450. $–$$$

Each of the 60-plus tapas dishes here, including Parmesan-dusted baby artichokes and flatbread topped with fig jam, Spanish blue cheese, and shredded duck, is worth trying. Many ingredients, plus the glorious cheeses and wines, are sourced from northern Spain. The large, festive front room tends to be loud; for a quieter meal, ask for a table in the second dining room, beyond the open kitchen.

Jim's Steaks. 400 South St., South St.; 215/928–1911. $

Big, juicy, Philly steaks—shaved beef piled high on long crusty rolls—come off the grill with amazing speed when the counter workers hit their stride. Jim's is mostly takeout, but there are some tables and chairs upstairs.

Horizons. 611 South Seventh St., South Philly/South St.; 215/923–6117; $–$$$

Specialties at this popular vegetarian restaurant include hummus made from edamame and tempeh with tamarind. No mock meat on this menu—chef/ owner Rich Landau is coaxing a cheesesteak town into eating, and liking, unabashed vegetarian fare.

Fork. 306 Market St., Old City; 215/625–9425. $$–$$$

Tasty, attractively served bistro-style food integrates exotic and down-home tastes. Next door, Fork:etc is a great place to sit and peruse the provided newspapers and magazines while eating a muffin, some flavorful ginger–sweet-potato soup; or a turkey sandwich with cranberry compote, Brie, and caramelized onions. Their breads and baked goods are all made on the premises.

Capogiro Gelato Artisans. 119 South 13th St., City Hall area; 215/351–0900. 117 South 20th St., Rittenhouse Sq.; 215/636–9250. $

Capogiro (Italian for "giddy") is even busy in the middle of winter. Batches of unusually flavored gelato— mascarpone and fig, honey cumin, persimmon, and lemon opal basil—are displayed alongside classics like coffee and pistachio, made fresh each morning.

Morimoto. 723 Chestnut St., Old City; 215/413–9070; $$–$$$$

A glowing dining room and white leather benches set the scene for melt-in-your-mouth sushi. Like butter, but better. The <u>omakase</u> (chef's tasting menu) is the ultimate splurge, but after indulging in the series of tiny, flavorful courses studded with unusual ingredients like kobe beef and black truffles, it'll feel worth it.

FAVORITE PLACES TO STAY

Rittenhouse 1715. 1715 Rittenhouse St., Rittenhouse Sq.; 215/546–6500. $$$

This refined boutique hotel is in two adjoining circa-1911 mansions. Each room has a different set of antiques and reproductions, including neoclassical rugs, Chippendale-style tables and Louis XVI-style chairs. A few have gas fireplaces. The breakfast includes buttery pastries from nearby Le Bus Bakery, and there's a daily wine reception in the lobby.

The Rittenhouse. 210 West Rittenhouse Sq., Rittenhouse Sq.; 215/546–9000. $$$–$$$$

The staff greets you with Champagne and chocolate-covered strawberries at this small luxury hotel known for its exemplary service. Many rooms and the highly acclaimed on-site restaurant, Lacroix, overlook the park.

Park Hyatt Philadelphia at the Bellevue. 1415 Chancellor Ct., at Broad and Walnut Sts., City Hall/Ave. of the Arts; 215/893–1234. $$$–$$$$

The grand dame of Broad Street began its life in 1904 as the most luxurious hotel in the country. Its current incarnation as a Park Hyatt took hold in 1996. You can't beat its location in the middle of the Avenue of the Arts and midway between Rittenhouse Square and Independence Hall. Restaurant XIX on the 19th floor has great views of the city and a busy bar.

---

is to park and walk or use public transportation and taxis. Street meters typically charge $1 per hour. There are parking garages in key locations, including Fifth and Market streets (near Independence Mall).

BY PUBLIC TRANSIT

Philadelphia has excellent mass transit. In the summer, purple PHLASH vans follow a Center City route to all main downtown sights; you can buy a hop-on, hop-off all-day pass for $4 at the Independence Visitor Center. The SEPTA subway trains come regularly, but the underground stations are rather dank, and the two lines are limited. You're better off walking or riding the SEPTA buses, which provide good coverage of Old City and the Historic District, Center City, and University

Penn's View Inn. 14 North Front St., Old City; 215/922–7600. $$

This small hotel on the fringe of the Old City has homey rooms with character—20 of 53 have fireplaces; some have exposed brick walls; and all have hardwood floors with area rugs. Downstairs is Panorama, a well-regarded Italian restaurant, and Il Bar, with 120 wines by the glass.

Sheraton Society Hill. 1 Dock St. Society Hill/Old City; 215/922–2709. $$$–$$$$

This low-slung brick building lies at the foot of the Society Hill Towers and is walking-distance from all the Old City sights. The generic but comfortable rooms done in warm shades of taupe and burgundy were renovated in 2007, and some have great views of the Ben Franklin Bridge.

Hotel Sofitel. 120 South 17th St., Rittenhouse Sq./Center City; 215/569–8300. $$–$$$

The luxury chain's Philly location feels especially chic and modern in contrast to city's focus on the historic. Modern rooms done in tones of gold, brown, and blue are warm, tranquil, and flooded with light. Large desks, Wi-Fi access, flat-screen TVs, and large bathtubs make the hotel a popular choice for business travelers, and the lobby bar has comfy banquettes and huge windows facing the street for people-watching.

City. One ride costs $2 and buses take cash in exact change. Catch commuter trains to travel to nearby counties at 30th Street Station. Find fares, maps, and schedules at the Independence Visitor Center and online at www.septa.org.

SOUTHEAST
DUTCH COUNTRY

In Pennsylvania Dutch Country, about an hour's drive from Philadelphia, a modern couple in a convertible BMW, fleeing the city for a posh country inn, breezes by an Amish family in horse and buggy as it clings to the berm. In the more rural sections of Bucks County, also about an hour's drive from the city, stone farmhouses older than the Declaration of Independence stand near pricey new gated housing developments. Near Reading, a town founded by William Penn's sons, the old iron furnace that produced cannons and shot for the Continental Army sits peacefully just a mile away from one of the most monstrous and bustling outlet malls in the country.

Throughout this bucolic region of rolling hills, farmland, and quaint little towns that work hard to stay that way, rich pockets of early American history coexist with the trappings of modern life. In some places, the pairings seem oddly contradictory, but in others the conjoining of the American past and present provides you with a harmonious blend of creature comforts and fascinating historical sites.

The understated beauty of southeastern Pennsylvania's landscape—the earthy browns and dark greens of the hills interrupted by huge swaths of neatly tilled farmland—has a mesmerizing effect on those who pass through. Many artists have been drawn here by the quality of the light, the magical way it dances upon the Delaware River and weaves through the branches of the bankside trees. Bucks County has been especially attractive to the artistic set since the 1930s. The Pulitzer Prize–winning authors Pearl S. Buck and James A. Michener had homes here, as did the composer Oscar Hammerstein. More recently the placid country towns of the southeast are seeing more and more urbanites from Philadelphia, New York, and New Jersey snatching up homes and property.

HISTORY

Southeastern Pennsylvania lies within the fertile Piedmont Plateau, between the Delaware River in the east and the Susquehanna River in the west. Between 1682 and 1684, William Penn purchased several major tracts of land here, including most of present-day York County, from local Native Americans, primarily the Lenni Lenape. The immigrants who first settled here bought their land from William Penn's sons, whose advertisements promised rich harvests on pastures that extended as far as the eye could see.

Mennonite girls pose for a picture along the Appalachian Trail at the Blue Rocks overlook, in Berks County.

Among the settlers who poured into southeastern Pennsylvania and spread out over Berks, Bucks, Lancaster, Lebanon, Lehigh, and York Counties were German Protestants—they and their descendants have come to be known as Pennsylvania "Dutch," derived from Deutsch, the German word for Germans. Quakers, Mennonites, Amish, and members of other religious sects were attracted to the area by a spirit of tolerance that allowed them to practice their beliefs in the open. In Lancaster County, the epicenter of Pennsylvania Dutch Country, there are many descendants of the Amish and Old Order Mennonites, the plainest of the Plain People who came to Penn's woods seeking refuge from religious persecution. Their agricultural methods to this day are not far removed from those they employed in colonial times.

During the French and Indian War and, later, the Revolutionary War, some of the Quakers and others with pacifist beliefs refused to join the war effort, although they did supply food and clothing to the Continental Army. Other religious communities openly supported the British. The southeast figured prominently in several of the Revolution's key military encounters, supplying fresh frontiersmen-soldiers and supplies to counteract British gains in New York and New England.

The only significant inroad the British made into Pennsylvania territory during the war occurred two months after the signing of the Declaration of Independence, when British forces landed on the upper Chesapeake Bay and marched 57 miles north to capture Philadelphia. George Washington's attempt to stave off the invasion failed; after hours of fighting at Brandywine Creek, he withdrew to Valley Forge and the Continental Congress fled to York.

The regrouping and retraining of troops at Valley Forge and France's decision to side with the Americans led to several key American victories and forced the British to negotiate peace. After the war ended, southeastern Pennsylvania's farmers and craftsmen returned to their homes to enjoy relative prosperity. In the 1820s, a wave of immigration pushed the Pennsylvania frontier farther west, and a new railroad system spurred economic growth.

In the years leading up to the Civil War, the region's economy grew steadily, and so, too, did the political and religious movements that aimed to set a moral compass for the country. The Quakers and other local pacifist sects were abolitionists, instrumental in keeping Pennsylvania an antislavery state. Many farm communities and small towns along the Delaware River became part of the Underground Railroad, establishing networks of safe houses to help slaves from the Southern states make their way to freedom in New England and Canada.

After the Civil War, during which Quaker and Amish farmers once again supplied food for an army—the Union Army this time—southeastern Pennsylvania played a leading role in the industrialization of the nation. Although farming continued to dominate the economy, steel mills, iron works, and mining operations were set up here because of the area's proximity to coal fields and to the Delaware River (and later to railroads), which provided efficient means to transport goods.

While residential and commercial areas have grown significantly along the "Main Line," the collective name for a series of communities that sprouted up along Route 30, the country's first toll road, the rural-agrarian nature of the southeast remains. Two-thirds of the land is still farmed—and although that's much less than even a decade ago, you can still drive for miles across wide open spaces and take in the sights, sounds, and smells of rural life.

BUCKS COUNTY   *map pages 101, E/F-1/3, and page 106*

Bucks County is perhaps best known for idyllic scenes of farm life, quaint towns that fill up on weekends with urbanites escaping city life for a few days. It's also filling fast with ex-urbanites who've traded in city life for green space and a long

Many have been drawn to
southeastern Pennsylvania
by the quality of light.

Edward Hicks's depiction of David Twining's farm in 1787 (painted circa 1845–47) idealized the farmers of Bucks County, where Hicks grew up. (Abby Aldrich Rockefeller Folk Art Center)

commute. The stretch of Route 32 (often signposted as River Road) that follows the Delaware River from Washington Crossing Historic Park north to Erwinna winds through one of the most history-laden sections of the state.

The two-lane road hugs the towpath of the old Delaware Canal, and a few hundred yards beyond that, often hidden in spring and summer by leafy birch, oak, and hickory trees, the shallow Delaware River rolls leisurely toward its outlet into Delaware Bay.

In late fall and winter, the river views are unobstructed. The soft afternoon light reflecting off the river is so unusual that painters have flocked to these Delaware banks hoping to capture it on canvas. An early-20th-century art movement known as Pennsylvania Impressionism was inspired here. The **James A. Michener Museum** in Doylestown has the most comprehensive collection of their work.

During the hour-long drive from Washington Crossing Historic Park to Easton, you can stop along the way at roadside produce stands, antique stores, and several wineries open for tastings and tours. Many of these attractions are located in tiny, picturesque villages—most of them former mill towns that have aged gracefully.

★ ANTIQUES ROW

Antique stores abound in village squares, along highways, and in giant warehouses. There are said to be more registered dealers in this area than in any other region of the country. The area's premier antiques row runs along a 15-mile stretch of Route 202, from Doylestown to Lahaska to New Hope, spilling onto a few side roads along the way. Some highlights are the dozen dealers in the **Lahaska Antique Courte** (Rte. 202, across from Peddlers Village); and **Best of France Antiques, Inc.** (3686 Rte. 202, Mechanicsville; 215/345–4523), whose spacious barn is packed with furniture from the owner's frequent trips across the pond and whose sprawling European-inspired gardens are populated with dramatic bronze and marble statuary. Buyers who haven't tapped out their energy or checkbooks by the time they get to New Hope can take a five-minute walk across the Delaware River Bridge (Rte. 202 East) and expect to kill more than a few hours in tiny Lambertville, New Jersey, which is dense with antique stores and furniture studios. For those who truly can't get enough, the **Golden Nugget Flea Market** (1850 River Rd.; 609/397–0811), one mile south of Lambertville, is a year-round favorite.

WASHINGTON CROSSING HISTORIC PARK   map page 101, F-2

A 45-minute drive northeast out of Philadelphia's Center City on I–95 brings you to Washington Crossing Historic Park, where Gen. George Washington and his demoralized, haggard troops rallied on the freezing Christmas night of 1776 to fight one of the decisive battles of the Revolutionary War. Climbing into cargo boats, 2,400 soldiers set out across the Delaware in a snowstorm, using poles to bash their way through a river choked with chunks of ice. After landing at Johnson's Ferry on the other side, the ragtag forces marched to Trenton, surprised the garrison of Hessian soldiers celebrating the holiday there, and captured the base in less than an hour.

The battle was Washington's first clear-cut victory, and it was a crucial one, giving the Revolutionary cause much-needed momentum—both physically and

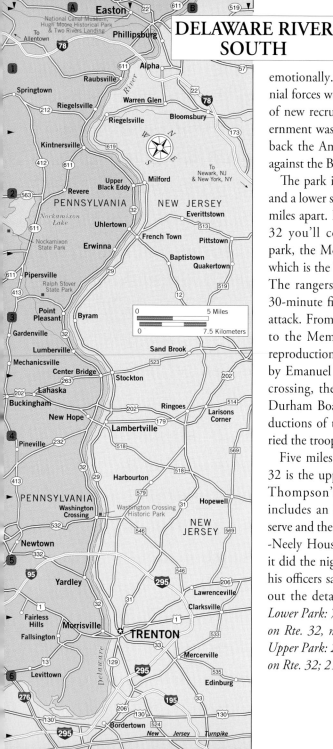

emotionally. Because of it, the colonial forces were bolstered by an influx of new recruits, and the French government was eventually influenced to back the American army in its fight against the British.

The park is split between an upper and a lower section, which are about 5 miles apart. Heading north on Route 32 you'll come first to the lower park, the McConkey's Ferry section, which is the best place to start a tour. The rangers are informative, and a 30-minute film recounts the surprise attack. From the visitors center, walk to the Memorial Building to see a reproduction of the famous painting by Emanuel Leutze of Washington's crossing, then proceed down to the Durham Boat House to view reproductions of the cargo boats that carried the troops to battle.

Five miles farther north on Route 32 is the upper part of the park, the Thompson's Mill section, which includes an 80-acre wildflower preserve and the 18th-century Thompson -Neely House, which looks much as it did the night that Washington and his officers sat in the kitchen hashing out the details of their attack plan. *Lower Park: 7 miles south of New Hope on Rte. 32, near junction of Rte. 532; Upper Park: 2 miles south of New Hope on Rte. 32; 215/493–4076.*

Seven miles north of Washington Crossing (and roughly 45 minutes north of Center City), on Route 32, you'll enter the town of New Hope, often referred to as the "jewel of Bucks County," where white clapboard and brick houses spread out along the banks of the slow-rolling Delaware River and its canal. Once known for its mills, which processed goods ranging from grain to metals, New Hope is now part artist colony, part historic site, and part shopping mall. Art galleries and boutiques line Main Street, interspersed with tacky T-shirt shops and hamburger joints. In summer, art lovers, souvenir hunters, history buffs, and city-weary wanderers clog town streets.

The village has been attracting offbeat characters for decades, and locals like to think of themselves as a people tolerant of unconventional lifestyles. Townspeople also figured prominently in several controversial events of the nation's past. In the summer of 1804, the town's most prominent citizens hid Aaron Burr from pursuing authorities after the fateful duel in which Burr mortally wounded Alexander Hamilton. In the Civil War years, many of the town's homes were used as safe houses along the Underground Railroad. The area has more recently become a popular destination for gay and lesbian tourists.

TOURING NEW HOPE

You can tour the New Hope area by rail, foot, and even barge. At one time New Hope was an important transportation center along the Delaware Canal—handling between 2,500 and 3,000 barges a month at its peak in 1862. The **Delaware River Canal Boat Company** (215/862–0758) brings this aspect of the town's past to life; old mule-drawn coal barges now ply the Delaware Canal to offer day rides, complete with tour guides singing folk songs.

The canal system met its demise with the advent of rail transport, but the town continued to prosper with the arrival of the **New Hope and Ivyland Railroad** (215/862–2332). Today you can take a 9-mile, 45-minute ride along the river in restored 1920s passenger cars pulled by a steam locomotive.

One of the best ways to see New Hope is to stroll down the three busiest blocks of Main Street, between Mechanic and Bridge. You'll encounter 18th-century stone houses with intriguing courtyards, alleys lined with cozy row houses, and cobblestone walkways that lead to the wooded trails that workers once followed out of town to various mills.

The entire town is listed on the National Register of Historic Places, and at the **New Hope Visitors Center** you can pick up a free guide or buy a "Walking

One of the great pleasures of visiting Bucks County is boarding a mule-drawn barge and riding down the Delaware Canal.

Tour of Historic New Hope" map with the important sights highlighted. *1 West Mechanic St., at Main St.; 215/862–5030.*

The stone **Parry Mansion** was built in 1784 for a wealthy lumber mill owner whose descendants occupied it until the New Hope Historical Society bought it in the 1960s. On the first and third weekends from May to October, you can tour eight rooms that reflect several generations of its occupants' decorating styles. *45 Main St., at Ferry St.; 215/862–5652.*

In the 1920s, an old gristmill was converted into the nationally recognized **Bucks County Playhouse,** which presents Broadway-caliber musicals and dramas to packed houses year-round. *70 South Main St.; 215/862–2041.*

Exotic is indeed the word at **Gerenser's Exotic Ice Cream,** a family-owned and -operated ice cream shop that has been selling out-of-the-ordinary flavors since the 1940s. Among the selections: Polish plum brandy, African violet, and Indian loganberry. *22 South Main St.; 215/862–2050.*

There are plenty of antiques and specialty stores. One favorite is **Hot Plates,** which carries '50s-style kitchenware, including Fiestaware in every shade and shape. *40 South Main St.; 215/862–3220.*

The crowded shelves at the family-owned **Farley's Bookshop** contain much fodder for browsing, including a section on books about the region. *44 South Main St.; 215/862–2452.*

LUMBERVILLE   *map page 101, F-2*

About a 10-minute drive north from the bustle of New Hope is quiet, tidy Lumberville, where you can leave the car and view the old homes crowded together on the main street. Lumberville has been a one-industry town since it was known as Wall's Saw Mills in the late 18th century, and its old buildings are on the National Register of Historic Places. Buy a picnic lunch at the **Lumberville Store** (3741 River Rd.; 215/297–5388), in operation since 1770, and enjoy it on the New Jersey side at Bull's Island, accessible by way of a sturdy footbridge over the river.

POINT PLEASANT   *map page 101, F-2*

Should you grow tired of driving along the river and prefer instead to get into the river, the mellow reach of water near Point Pleasant, just north of Lumberville, is perfect for the decidedly nonadventurous sport of "tubing." The folks at **Bucks County River Country** will outfit you with the right size inner tube for your weight—or with a canoe, raft, kayak, or Snuggle Tube built for two—and they also conduct guided raft trips. Call in advance to reserve your equipment. *2 Walters La.; Point Pleasant; 215/297–5000.*

ERWINNA   *map page 101, E-1*

A quaint town situated along the twists of River Road as it follows the river's sharp curves, Erwinna has several inns that serve lunch and dinner. There are also antique stores, the renowned **Tinicum Park** (River Rd.; 215/757–0571), which has well-marked hiking trails, and the **Sand Castle Winery** (755 River Rd.; 800/722–9463), which has a tasting room and offers tours.

EASTON   *map pages 101, E-1*

Just over the Bucks County line in Northampton County, Easton was, on July 8, 1776, the site of the second public reading of the Declaration of Independence. Those fateful words, "We hold these truths to be self-evident," were shouted from the steps of the Northampton County Courthouse on Centre Square.

Red crayon liquid is poured on a belt at the Crayola factory in Easton.

The land for the square had been presented to city founders in 1765 by William Penn's sons under a bill of sale that required the city to pay the Penn family an annual fee of one red rose. By the early 1800s, in large part because of its prime location at the confluence of the Lehigh and Delaware rivers, Easton had become an important link in the Pennsylvania canal system—Lehigh Navigation, known as the Lehigh Canal, and the Delaware Canal connected here. In the 1830s, railroad companies began constructing lines here, and by the mid-1860s, when the iron horse superseded canals as the favored mode of shipping transport, Easton was already securely established as an interchange point for five separate railroads.

Today, after a solid century of industrialism, Easton is in the midst of a major downtown revitalization initiative. The 1926 Hotel Easton has been converted into high-end condos, and several other historic buildings including the 1925 vaudeville State Theater are in different stages of restoration. Tourism is on the rise as the town fills up with places to shop and dine.

TWO RIVERS LANDING   *map pages 101, E-1*

An abandoned department store in downtown Easton has been reclaimed and put to new use as the Two Rivers Landing complex, whose three tenants are the

Delaware and Lehigh National Heritage Corridor Visitor Center; the Crayola Crayon Factory; and the National Canal Museum.

The **Delaware and Lehigh National Heritage Corridor Visitor Center,** on the first floor, has exhibits and a short film about the history of Easton and the Lehigh Valley, including displays on the area's ethnic groups, historic canals, and main industries.

On the second floor, at the ★**Crayola Factory,** you'll learn everything you want to know and then some about the history of crayons and Crayola. Perhaps more important, your kids can paint with melted crayons, draw all over the glass walls of the Creative Studio, and sink their hands into Model Magic (Crayola's answer to Silly Putty) to mold 3-D sculptures. On the third and fourth floors, the **National Canal Museum** charts the history of the country's extensive waterways transport system in the 19th century. The inland canal network is detailed in wall-size panels and in displays of equipment used to build the canals. Hands-on exhibits allow you to operate a model lock and pilot a scaled-down canal boat. *30 Centre Sq.; 610/515–8000.*

A short walk away is the **Easton Museum of Pez Dispensers** with 2,000 models of the Austrian candy dispenser first intended as a smoking-cessation tool. Cartoon heads were only added to the containers' tops when Pez was imported to America in 1952. The museum has a strong showing from the 1950s, '60s, and '70s, including Disney's *Jungle Book* characters (an original King Louie is worth $45) and *Winnie the Pooh. 15–19 South Bank St.; 610/253–9794.*

HUGH MOORE HISTORICAL PARK   *map page 101, E-1*

Named after the Easton businessman who made his fortune selling Dixie cups, and who also happened to have a fondness for canal history, this historic park runs along the banks of the Lehigh River for 6 miles on land bought by the city from the Lehigh Coal and Navigation Company. It includes a restored portion of the Lehigh Canal—on which you can take a ride aboard a mule-drawn canal boat, the *Josiah White II*—as well as the 1890s lock-tender's house, now a museum. Outside the house, canal boats enter Lock 47 and rise 8 feet in about five minutes as a hydrostatic valve is opened. Company founders Josiah White and Erskine Hazard invented the valve, which helped give the Lehigh Canal the largest carrying capacity of any canal in the country. Canal boat rides are offered May through September only. *2.5 miles north of I–78; 610/515–8000.*

CANALS

Pennsylvania's canal system was actively used between 1826 and 1900, and in its heyday had 900 miles of state-owned and 300 miles of privately owned canals. Charles Dickens was 30 years old when he traveled on the canal in 1842.

There was much in this mode of traveling which I heartily enjoyed at the time, and look back upon with great pleasure. Even the running up, bare-necked, at 5 o'clock in the morning from the tainted cabin to the dirty deck; scooping up the icy water, plunging one's head into it, and drawing it out, all fresh and glowing with the cold; was a good thing. The fast, brisk walk upon the towing-path, between that time and breakfast, when every vein and artery seemed to tingle with health; the exquisite beauty of the opening day, when light came gleaming off from everything; the lazy motion of the boat, when one lay idly on the deck, looking through, rather than at, the deep blue sky; the gliding on, at night, so noiselessly, past frowning hills, sullen with dark trees, and sometimes angry in one red burning spot high up, where unseen men lay crouching round a fire; the shining out of the bright stars, undisturbed by noise of wheels or steam, or any other sound than the liquid rippling of the water as the boat went on: all these were pure delights.

Canal Scene on the Juniata, by George Storm. (State Museum of Pennsylvania)

DELAWARE LOOP DRIVE *map page 106*

A popular day trip with New Yorkers, Philadelphians, and other travelers is the drive up the Pennsylvania side of the Delaware River through Bucks County, following Routes 32 and 611 to Easton, then crossing into New Jersey on I–78 and lazily following Route 29 back down the other side, stopping to scout antique stores and crafts shops en route. Before you get as far south as Trenton, New Jersey, you'll come to a bridge that will take you back over the Delaware to Washington Crossing. From there you can venture inland and absorb the rest that Bucks County has to offer.

BUCKS COUNTY WEST *map page 101, E-2*

Many people argue that the most bucolic region in Bucks County is along the Delaware, but some of the region's best sights and museums—among them the Moravian Pottery and Tile Works, the James A. Michener Art Museum, and the Pearl S. Buck House—lie well west of the river in Doylestown.

DOYLESTOWN AREA *map page 101, E-2*

Even though it's less than an hour's drive from Center City Philadelphia, the first thing you realize when you reach Doylestown's central business district is that the foot traffic on the tree-canopied streets eases along at a languid pace. First settled in the 1730s, and once a stop on the stagecoach line between Philadelphia and Easton, Doylestown is steeped in early American history, and much of the town is on the National Register of Historic Places. Take a stroll through downtown to see the hundreds of preserved and carefully restored buildings, many of which now house boutiques, cozy cafes, and restaurants.

MERCER MILE

Doylestown native Henry Chapman Mercer (1856–1930), a Harvard-educated millionaire, was a historian, archaeologist, and ceramist—"Renaissance man" is the term usually used to describe him—as well as a dedicated collector. Fascinated by the objects used in everyday life in pre-industrial America, he began to collect them in 1897, visiting junk dealers and selecting pieces that would tell the story of work and leisure in the American experience.

Today more than 50,000 objects reflecting Mercer's objective—the tools of more than 60 Early American trades and crafts, including bean hullers, log sleds, and cheese presses—are in the collection of the ★**Mercer Museum,** a large reinforced-concrete "castle," begun in 1913, completed in 1916, and constructed without the assistance of architects or blueprints. Some people find it bizarre, others unique. It is one of three buildings by Mercer, all now National Historic Landmarks and known collectively as the Mercer Mile. *84 South Pine St.; 215/345–0210.*

Artisanal crafts were Mercer's first love, and in 1898 he established the **Moravian Pottery and Tile Works**—named for his collection of Moravian stove plates—to produce ceramic tiles. In 1903, commissioned with creating tiles for the floor of the new state capitol building in Harrisburg, he turned out 377 tiles depicting Pennsylvania flora, fauna, and history. The reinforced-concrete building housing the factory, built in the style of a U-shaped California mission church, was completed in 1912. Today it is a combined museum and manufacturing plant specializing in the production of distinctive decorative tiles using traditional crafting and firing methods. A slide show and lecture introduce Mercer's world. Tours include a walk through the factory. *130 Swamp Rd.; 215/345–6722.*

The third concrete "castle," **Fonthill,** was Mercer's residence, built between 1908 and 1910 and inspired by whimsy rather than by any architect's plans. Mercer sketched it from the inside out and hired local laborers, none of whom had ever built a house before, to build it. The overall effect is of a haphazard, multitextured extravaganza. The basic structure is concrete, but other building materials include sand, grass, Mercer's precious tiles, and wooden posts. With 44 rooms, 18 fireplaces, 200 windows, and 32 stairwells, Fonthill is impressive in an odd sort of way, but exhausting to visit, and most people breathe a sigh of relief when they leave. The museum here includes Mercer's vast collection of decorative tiles, pottery, lighting devices, and prints. *East Court St. at Swamp Rd.; 215/348–9461. Guided tours only.*

The late James Michener, the Pulitzer-winning author of mammoth novels like *Hawaii, The Source, Centennial,* and *Chesapeake,* was raised in Doylestown, and the town's regional art museum is named after its famous native. The ★**James A. Michener Art Museum,** part of which was formerly the Bucks County Jail, built in 1884, contains five permanent and three rotating galleries of 19th- and 20th-century American art, including the most comprehensive collection of Pennsylvania Impressionists, whose prices at auction have surpassed the million-dollar mark. One serene room is devoted to the work of George Nakashima, a Japanese-American furniture maker who settled nearby and whose daughter, Mira, continues his legacy from the family's nearby compound. The museum also

Henry Chapman Mercer's Fonthill castle is an exuberant mix of sand, concrete, wood, and thousands upon thousands of decorative tiles.

BERKS COUNTY HEX BARN ART TOUR

map page 101, C-1/2

The following tour will take you through a wonderful region of the state, an area with more than a few memorable examples of Berks County hex signs. For a brochure on this drive, call the **Reading and Berks County Visitors Bureau** (352 Penn St., Reading; 610/375-4085 or 800/443–6610); or download it at www.readingberkspa.com—click on "Media Center: Brochures."

Continuing north from the western Bucks County area, take the Kutztown Road exit off U.S. 222, take a right, and drive through town, cutting through the leafy campus of Kutztown State University, then continuing to the junction of Kutztown Road and Crystal Cave Road. Set your odometer to zero and take a right toward Crystal Cave park. You'll roll through wooded countryside interspersed with open farms and fields, and at 5.0 miles **Barn One,** on the Stutzman farm, will be tucked behind a clump of trees on the right. The winding road crests out on a open hilltop, offering views to all sides, then descends rather

steeply, and at 5.5 miles you'll see **Barn Two,** the monstrous, weathered white barn of the Dreibelbis farm, with its fading but intricate hexes, sitting in the middle of a luxuriantly green pasture.

After 6 miles, take a left onto Route 143 south, and after another half-mile, **Barn Three** will be on the left; **Barn Four** is perched on a rise to the right at the 6.9-mile point. At 8.1 miles, keep your eyes peeled for easy-to-miss Route 662, and after turning right onto it proceed 0.3 miles, where just off the road on the right you'll find **Barn Five,** a beautiful red barn with four hexes painted on its broad side. There's a place to pull the car over and see it relatively close up, without being overly invasive.

The next 3.5 miles are barn-free, so take in the quiet, hilly countryside, stealing glances skyward for hawks riding on thermals, until you pass **Barn Six** on the left; then swing immediately right onto Windsor Castle Road and you'll pass **Barn Seven,** which is on the Christman farm, at the 12.2-mark on the right. When you hit the 13.7-mile marker, turn right onto Virginville Road. On the left side of the road, between here and mile 14.0, are **Barns Eight, Nine,** and **Ten.** They're all huge dairy barns painted with hexes of horse heads (the Amish Carriage Horse hex protects horses and livestock) and rows of hexes with birds (the Double

Distlefink hex, for double good luck), as well as the more standard star patterns. At the 14.9- and 15.0-mile points, **Barns Eleven** and **Twelve,** both on the Miller farm, will be on your left.

At 16.4 miles turn left onto Route 143 North. The Sunday farm barn is on the left at 16.7 miles and the Leiby farm is on the left at 17.2 miles. Off to the right at 18.4 miles is the **Dreibelbis Covered Bridge,** which bears a colorful, star-shaped hex over the entrance. At mile 20 you'll come to Old Route 22, also known as the Hex Highway, where you'll go left, continue one block to Deitsch Eck Restaurant, and turn right onto Route 143 North, which will take you to **Barn Fifteen. Barn Sixteen,** at 20.3 miles, is just ahead on the left, and, after passing under I-78, **Barn Seventeen** is also on the left, at 22.9 miles.

You'll wind past farms and scattered woods, then, after taking a left at mile 24.2 onto Hawk Mountain Road (just past Raberts Garage on the right), **Barn Eighteen** will be on the right at 24.5 miles followed closely on the right by **Barn Nineteen.** The land starts to be a bit more steep and wooded now as you follow along Kittatinny Ridge to your left. Coming through here in the late evening, the fading sunlight covers the countryside with subtle bursts of color, and in the distance the spire of a church and a small, rounded hill studded with tombstones are illuminated in the glow.

Climbing slowly up the ridge, you'll come to mile 28.1 and **Barn Twenty,** the shop of Robertsons Restoration, which is on the right and covered with a variety of hex designs. The final barn of the tour, **Barn Twenty-One,** sits 0.4 miles farther along on the right side of the road and is adorned with two starburst-design hexes.

has an outdoor sculpture garden. In 2002, a satellite gallery opened in New Hope. *138 South Pine St.; 215/340–9800.*

PEARL S. BUCK HOUSE   *map page 101, E-2*

Six miles north of Doylestown (take Route 313 to Dublin and turn left onto Dublin Road) is Green Hills Farm, former residence of the Nobel laureate and Pulitzer Prize–winning author of *The Good Earth* and *My Several Worlds.* Born in 1892 to parents who were missionaries, and raised in China from the age of four, Buck made her experiences with China and Chinese life the focus of much of her writing.

Buck and her second husband, Richard Walsh, purchased this 48-acre farm (dating from 1835) in 1934, as a home for themselves and their family, which included seven adopted children. The house, fancifully filled with American and Asian antiques, remains much the same as when Buck lived and wrote here.

In 1949, Buck founded Welcome House, to find homes for "unadoptable" mixed-race children, and in 1964, she formed the Pearl S. Buck Foundation to assist primarily Asian children not eligible for adoption. She died here in 1973 and is buried on the property, which is now the headquarters of Pearl S. Buck International, a humanitarian assistance organization that carries on her charity work. *520 Dublin Rd., Perkasie; 215/249–0100.*

BERKS COUNTY DUTCH HEX SIGNS

The Pennsylvania Germans who began settling in southeastern Pennsylvania in the late 1600s and early 1700s brought with them their language, their old-world customs, and their decorative arts—unique painted furniture, quilts, and other household articles with distinctive, geometric designs. In the mid-19th century (paint was too costly before then), these colorful designs began to appear on barns. For the Plain People of Lancaster County, such decoration would have signified vanity, so you will see more of this folk art in areas inhabited by the "fancy" Dutch, their less conservatively religious cousins. Berks and Lehigh counties have a lot of barn art.

Use of the term "hex" to describe these designs has been traced to a guidebook of the 1920s. Presumably, they were meant to ward off the influence of the devil. The symbolic meanings attached to them—stars for good fortune, hearts for love, tulips for faith, the stylized bird known as the distelfink for happiness—may well have roots in superstition. But it's more likely that when a Pennsylvania Dutch farmer sets out to touch up his barn stars today, he's doing it "chust for nice."

A farmer and his chickens in front of a barn in Berks County.

HAWK MOUNTAIN SANCTUARY   *map page 101, C-1*

The drive on Route 895 along Kittatinny Ridge passes through open farm country until you reach the 2,400-acre Hawk Mountain Sanctuary. Each year between mid-August and mid-December, more than 18,000 birds, including 16 species of raptors, pass by here on their annual migration to Central and South America. The preserve was founded by local conservationist Rosalie Edge in 1934 to save these magnificent creatures from hunters who slaughtered them wholesale for "sport" and under the guise of protecting their livestock. It was the first refuge for birds of prey in the world.

The best time to spot ospreys, American kestrels, and broad-winged hawks is in late August and September; peregrine falcons and merlins visit in October; and red-winged hawks and golden eagles in November and early December. The best viewing points are from the South and North Lookouts. From the visitors center, it's an easy five-minute stroll along a well-groomed path to the South Overlook, where a panoramic vista reveals the rolling farm country below. The trail to the North Overlook is rockier and a more strenuous 45-minute climb, but worth every step when you arrive at the top and gaze out over the sheer cliffs, rocky out-

Birders on the North Overlook at Hawk Mountain Sanctuary.

croppings, and dense forest in the valley below. *1700 Hawk Mountain Rd., off Rte. 895, Kempton; 610/756–6000.*

READING AREA   *map page 101, C-2*

Reading is a struggling post-industrial city reinventing itself to fit into a new economic niche—outlet shopping. Ten million consumption-crazed visitors flock here every year to grab bargains at the 300 outlet stores around the town. Mid-range brands like Jones New York, JC Penney, Bass, and Oneida dominate, though there are a few more upscale shops like Dooney & Bourke and Reebok. Reading was once a center for the manufacture of textiles, and its new incarnation is a fairly natural outgrowth of the sale of mill overruns and irregulars to employees. Just west of Reading in nearby Wyomissing, the VF Outlet Village, which has about 90 stores and offers some of the best selections and prices, occupies the old Berkshire Knitting Mill, once the largest hosiery mill in the world. The smaller Reading Outlet Center is also housed, in part, in an old factory that once produced silk stockings. The Reading Station Outlet Center, on the other hand, was the headquarters of the Reading Railroad.

Double your pleasure at the Kutztown German Festival.

THE PAGODA *map page 101, C-2*

The Pagoda is William Witman's seven-story apology to Reading for making an eyesore out of its highest point. After making his fortune as the owner of a rock quarry on that very visible mountain, Witman shut down the operation and in 1908 decided to cover the damage with a resort. Inspired by a postcard a friend brought back from the Phillippines, he modeled the resort after a cattle castle of the Shogun dynasty.

The resort failed, and the castle was neglected and abandoned by a series of owners until it was renovated by a local preservation group in 1969. It is now home to the Berks Arts Council. The second-floor gallery presents fine exhibits, but the real treats here are the peaceful Oriental garden and panoramic views of the Reading area. *98 Duryea Dr.; 610/655–6374.*

DANIEL BOONE HOMESTEAD *map page 101, C-2*

About 8 miles east of Reading, the Daniel Boone Homestead provides a unique view of what rural life was like for Pennsylvania families in the mid-1700s. Dense woodlands make up most of the 579-acre park, and you can see the foundation of the cabin where Boone lived until the age of 16. The remote feel of the area—it's a 3-mile drive from the entrance to the visitors center—makes it easier for the visitor to imagine how early settlers had to fend for themselves in remote sections of southeast Pennsylvania.

Boone gained the foundation of his legendary frontiersman skills while growing up here. Writes John Mack Faragher in his 1992 book, *Daniel Boone*, the young Daniel "found his forest teachers" among "backwoods hunters descended from European colonists ... [and] Indians of many ethnic varieties who also called friend this young hunter .... These men of the forest frontier instructed Daniel in a way of life that combined elements of both cultures and bridged many of the differences between Indian and European."

In 1750, Boone's parents had a falling out with the Quaker church, which disapproved when first one of their daughters and then a son married "worldlings." The family headed for North Carolina. The remains of the homestead they left behind include 14 miles of wooded trails, the ruins of the original cabin, and a two-story stone house built in the late 1700s after the Boones had moved on. *Daniel Boone Rd. off Rte. 422; 610/582–4900.*

HOPEWELL FURNACE NATIONAL HISTORIC SITE
map page 101, D-2/3

One of the earliest and now best-preserved iron manufacturing furnaces in the United States, the Hopewell Furnace, 17 miles southeast of Reading, churned out cannons and shot during the Revolutionary War and cooking stoves and farm tools during peaceful colonial times.

The furnace was built in 1771 by Mark Bird and operated until 1883, though its peak years were between 1820 and 1840. It is considered a fine example of a 19th-century iron "plantation," an entire community devoted to iron making. Such communities had to be built near good sources of iron ore (there were three mines nearby); wood, which was used to make the charcoal that fueled the furnace; and water. A waterwheel powered the bellows that blew air into the furnace, keeping it at nearly 3,000 degrees. The cast house, the big white building with the steeple containing the 32-foot stone furnace, is the centerpiece of Hopewell, but you can also visit the remaining three of 14 workers' houses, the ironmaster's mansion, the wheelhouse, and other buildings. The surrounding French Creek State Park was the source of Hopewell's raw materials; a century ago it was virtually denuded, but the forest has returned. *2 Mark Bird La., Elverson; 610/582–8773.*

PENNSYLVANIA DUTCH COUNTRY map page 101, B/C-3/4

Travelers from around the world flock to this region of southeast Pennsylvania to catch a glimpse of the quaint and simple life led by the Plain People, the members of several religious groups that have been quietly going about their business in this countryside for close to 300 years. Their plain dress, which makes them the most distinctive of the Pennsylvania Dutch, is the outward sign of their austere lifestyle, marked by separation from society and solidarity with their own community. They include the Old Order Amish (the large majority of the Amish), Old Order Mennonites (about a third of the Mennonites), and a few Old Order Brethren.

The Mennonites trace their origins to the Swiss Anabaptist movement of early 16th-century Europe. Their belief in adult baptism set them off from the mainstream Protestantism that emerged from the Reformation, and in 1693, the more rigorous Amish split off from the Mennonites. Fleeing religious persecution in the Rhineland-Palatinate and Alsace areas of present-day Germany and France, the first sizable groups of Amish and Mennonite settlers arrived in Lancaster County in the early 1700s. They were attracted by the promise of William Penn's "Holy Experiment" in religious tolerance and by the region's fertile soil.

About 22,000 Old Order Amish live in Lancaster County. They constitute 90 percent of Lancaster's Amish—more progressive groups make up the remainder. (About half the Amish in Pennsylvania live in Lancaster County.) They live in the countryside, especially southeast of Lancaster, around the towns of Ephrata, Bird-in-Hand, Intercourse, Paradise, and Strasburg, making this the second-largest Old Order community in the country, next to Holmes County, Ohio.

It's easy to spot the Amish: men and boys wear dark suits topped with broad-brimmed hats of straw or black felt; women and girls wear modest, solid-color, mid-calf-length dresses covered with an apron and a cape whose apex is fastened at the waistline in back and whose two sides are brought up over the shoulders, crisscrossed, and fastened. Black is the predominant clothing color; gray, green, blue, wine, and purple are also typical. No zippers hold things together, just safety and straight pins, buttons, snaps, and hooks and eyes. Men have untrimmed beards, but no mustaches, which these pacifists deem militaristic. Women never cut their hair, and wear it in a bun on the back of the head. If married, they wear a white prayer covering; if single, a black one. Over all goes a shawl, and a bonnet is worn. They do not wear jewelry, even wedding rings. The Amish feel their simple clothes encourage humility and signal their separation from worldly society.

An Amish family out for a spin in Lancaster County, home to an estimated 22,000 Old Order Amish.

Old Order groups drive horses and buggies and do not have electricity in their homes, although they may use electricity in their businesses, provided they generate it themselves and are not connected to the public utility lines. Their children attend school only through the eighth grade, in private, one-room schoolhouses— their fight for exemption from compulsory public school attendance resulted in jail time for many Amish people until the Supreme Court ruled in their favor in 1972. One of the subjects they study in school is English, because until they go to school, the Amish speak only Pennsylvania Dutch, the old dialect of German they use in everyday life—another sign of separation from the larger society. After school they work on the family farm or in the family business until they marry.

Traveling in this region, you'll notice a host of seeming contradictions: families in horse-drawn buggies clopping past the monstrous Wal-Mart store on Main Street in Ephrata; a young girl in a homemade dress, pigtails streaming behind her, schussing down a side road on a pair of Rollerblades. You'll witness the incongruity of a religious people seeking to distance themselves from the modern world, while the inhabitants of that very same world clamber for a closer look. There's a further paradox: As the Amish population grows, the four million tourists who head this way each year are helping more and more of them make a living.

A team of horses pulls a plow for this Amish farmer.

An Amish driver takes his buggy over the Jackson Mill covered bridge in Bart Township.

The Amish are anything but a dying community. Families with from five to seven children are common. At the same time, Lancaster County is one of the fastest-growing areas in the state, leading to a serious loss of farmland and raising land prices to record highs. The World Monuments Fund has placed Lancaster County on its list of endangered sites, and the National Trust for Historic Preservation has put the county on a similar list. During the 1990s the county developed a master plan to channel growth and safeguard its unique heritage. Preserving farmland by buying up development rights is part of the effort. Nevertheless, more and more Old Order groups are turning to nonfarm work. Fortunately, the crafts and baked goods that the tourists lap up are products suitable to their way of life. Another boon for Lancaster County farmers is the recent trend in the restaurant industry to source produce and other ingredients from local growers.

The Amish usually live under the radar of non-Amish people who don't live close enough to get stuck behind one of their buggies while driving to the store, but occasionally they're thrust into the spotlight. A 2002 documentary called *Devils' Playground,* by Lucy Walker, exposed an Amish custom called *rumspringa,* literally "running around" in Pennsylvania Dutch. Meaning "adolescence," the term refers to a period of time after age 16 and before an adult chooses to be baptized in the Amish faith or leave the community. During rumspringa, the Old Order rules are relaxed, allowing teens to experiment with normally taboo behaviors, such as wearing nontraditional clothes, using electronics and driving cars, using drugs and alcohol, and having sex. According to studies conducted by Ohio State University, 85 to 90 percent return to the fold.

The Amish capacity for tolerance and forgiveness was noticed around the world in 2006. After the tragedy at Nickel Mines, when five young girls were senselessly and brutally murdered in an Amish schoolhouse, dozens in the community, including some of the girls' parents, attended the murderer's funeral and offered condolences to his parents, widow, and children.

LANCASTER   *map page 101, B-3*

Lancaster, pronounced *Lank*-uh-stir, was founded in 1710 by lieutenants of William Penn and named by the town's chief magistrate, John Wright, for his home shire of Lancaster, England. Lancaster is known as the Red Rose City because the symbol of the English House of Lancaster was the red rose. By 1760 Lancaster had become the largest inland city in the colonies, with 4,200 people

Amish children attend school only through the eighth grade, in schoolhouses like the one above.

and 600 houses. With an abundance of craftsmen and nearby iron ore furnaces, it had become a gun-producing center: Swiss and German weapons makers developed the highly accurate Pennsylvania long rifle here.

During the Revolution, Lancaster supplied the Continental Army with high-quality arms and ammunition. The city was, for one day only—September 27, 1777—the capital of the colonies, after George Washington failed to stop the British advance at the Battle of Brandywine, which forced the members of the Continental Congress to flee Philadelphia. They paused to hold a session in the courthouse on Lancaster's Penn Square, thus making the city the temporary capital, and then went on to York, where they convened for nine months before heading back to Philadelphia. From 1799 to 1812, though, Lancaster served as the capital of Pennsylvania.

Lancaster's economy is based on agriculture, light manufacturing, retail trade, and tourism. The city of 56,000 people has a pleasant center with tree-shaded streets and rows of majestic colonial- and Victorian-era homes and historic churches. There is plenty to see, which makes Lancaster a good place to kick off a visit to Pennsylvania Dutch country.

The **Pennsylvania Dutch Visitors Center,** run by the Convention and Visitors' Bureau is just outside the city proper. Their short film, *Stories of the Land*, will give you an idea of what to expect during your visit. From May to November you can sign up for their one-hour Amish Farmlands Tour. Year-round, you can pick up a self-guided audio tour and select from a seemingly endless number of brochures and maps. *501 Greenfield Rd., just off of Rte. 30; 717/299–8901.*

You might want to start your walking tour of downtown by gathering your energy next to the life-size bronze statue of a newspaper reader sitting on the park bench at the entrance to **Steinman Park** (22 West King St.). The brick-paved and tree-shaded vest-pocket park is next door to the building occupied by Steinman Hardware from 1886 to 1965. The company is said to have been founded in 1744. Look above the door, and you'll see a Conestoga wagon in stained glass. The red wheels, white cover, and Prussian blue body were the standard colors of this early American freight hauler, which was invented in the nearby Conestoga Valley and for which Steinman Hardware used to supply parts.

LANCASTER SIGHTS

At the heart of downtown, in two old buildings dating from the 1790s—the old City Hall and Masonic Lodge Hall (where both the Marquis de Lafayette and President James Buchanan attended ceremonies)—the **Heritage Center Museum**

Martin's Pretzel Factory in Akron, outside Lancaster, is owned and run by Mennonites.

brings Pennsylvania Dutch history to life with fine examples of regional furniture, grandfather clocks, redware pottery, *Scherenschnitte* (scissor art), metalwork, needlework, and birth and baptismal certificates and other documents in the decorative Fraktur style. The museum shop sells the works of local artisans, including Ned Foltz, a well-known creator of Pennsylvania redware pottery. The museum is closed during the winter. *13 West King St., at Penn Sq.; 717/299–6440.*

The **Lancaster Quilt and Textile Museum**'s core collection is the Esprit Collection of Amish quilts acquired in 2002. An Esprit founder began collecting the quilts in the 1970s. Before returning to their place of origin, the 82 quilts hung in the company's San Francisco headquarters. Now they're the foundation of this museum in the Beaux Arts Lancaster Trust Building. Rotating exhibits highlight other local crafts. *37 Market St.; 717/299–6440.*

Not far from the quilt museum, ★**Central Market,** in a redbrick Romanesque Revival building erected in 1889, is the country's oldest publicly owned farmers market. Open on Tuesdays, Fridays, and Saturdays, the market is a worthy attraction for tourists, though it is much more than that, as the procession of locals entering it with shopping baskets tucked under their arms will tell you. Inside is booth after booth of locally produced meats, sausages, and cheeses, fresh fruits and vegetables, prepared foods, baked goods, flowers, and craft items. Many of the vendors are Amish or Mennonite, and although you can buy a bagel, a southern sweet-potato pie, or gourmet coffee, this is really the place to stock up on local items like scrapple, corn on the cob "pulled this morning," and shoofly pie. Scrapple, consisting of slices of pork mush (made of the leftovers of the pig after butchering) that are usually fried, is a breakfast staple for many in these parts. Shoofly pie is a gooey concoction, heavy on the molasses. *Penn Sq.; 717/291–4723.*

The history of the **Fulton Opera House** is the history of the American theater, they'll tell you, and as you read the names of those who have appeared here, you realize that's no idle claim: Tom Thumb, Mark Twain, Buffalo Bill and Wild Bill Hickok, Sarah Bernhardt, and Al Jolson. The theater was built in 1852, and early audiences had to put up with smoke and gunpowder drifting down from a shooting gallery on the top floor and the smell of fertilizer and tobacco, which were stored in the basement. A drastic remodeling in 1873 transformed the structure into a European-style opera house, although operas were not performed here immediately. Another renovation in 1904 added a second balcony with pew seating to accommodate the growing audiences attracted by vaudeville and, later, talkies.

By the 1960s the theater was slated for the wrecking ball. Saved by community spirit and designation as a National Historic Landmark, the building underwent

Amish and Mennonite bakers sell their edibles at the Romanesque Revival Central Market.

a lavish restoration and is once again a gem of plaster rosettes, scrolls, and cherubs decked out in gilt and Victorian-correct colors, with red velvet seating and chandeliers imitating the original gaslight. You can tour the building daily year-round or see it during one of the shows put on by one of its home companies. *12 North Prince St.; 717/397–7425.*

The paintings of Lancaster native Charles Demuth, a pioneer of modernism, are in museums all over the world. Most of them were created in his studio on the second floor of the 18th-century **Demuth House.** Demuth gained early recognition for his watercolors of flowers, fruits, and vegetables—subjects he could see in the flower garden his mother, Augusta, tended in the courtyard beneath his window and in the farmers markets not far away. Later, influenced by exposure to cubism during travels to Europe, he turned to architectural themes and became known for his precisionist style. His famous *My Egypt,* in New York City's Whitney Museum of American Art, depicts the Eshelman grain elevators that once stood nearby; *Chimney and Water Tower* depicts the Armstrong plant; and *Welcome to Our City* the Lancaster Courthouse.

Next door is the **Demuth Tobacco Shop,** opened in 1770 by Christopher Demuth and now the oldest continuously operated tobacco shop in the country.

It was the prosperity of this enterprise that spared Charles Demuth, who was sickly and suffered from diabetes, the worries of earning a living, allowing him to paint. The shop displays some ancient smoking bric-a-brac (plus some antique firemen's hats) and sells mainly pipe tobacco and cigars, including the locally made Amish Fancy Tails and Amish Palmas. The shop keeps regular business hours; the house is closed in January. *114–120 East King St.; 717/299–9940.*

Modern-day Lancaster artists are found along **Gallery Row** on Prince Street, the hub of the city's unofficial, fast-growing arts district. LancasterARTS, a cooperative born in 2005, is doing a great job of both wooing the creative class and turning the area into an arts destination. Some of the fruits of their labor are **City Folk** (146 North Prince St.), exhibiting exquisite contemporary and traditional folk art; **Gallery Two** (140 North Prince St.), the home of two local artists, Freiman Stolzfus and Liz Hess, with very different styles; and the **Living Light Gallery** (150 North Prince St.), a two-story gallery in a pre–Civil War building that shows the work of emerging and well-known local painters. These galleries as well as the highly browseable shops on the 300 block of North Queen Street are open late on the first Friday of every month.

James Buchanan, the only president from Pennsylvania (1857–61) and the only bachelor president—he often said publicly that he entered politics in his 30s as a diversion from grief after the death of his fiancée, a Lancaster woman—bought ★**Wheatland,** a Federal-style mansion, in 1848. He lived in it, except for his term as the 15th president, until his death. On his diplomatic missions he was accompanied by his orphan niece, Harriet Lane, who also served as his First Lady in the White House. She lived at Wheatland until her marriage in 1866, inherited it, and used it as a summer house until she sold it in 1884. The two-story house, built in 1828, reflects her sophisticated style—it was she, for instance, who bought her uncle the desk at which he wrote his memoirs, *Mr. Buchanan's Administration on the Eve of the Rebellion.* Everything but the floor coverings and draperies is of the period, and many of the larger pieces of furniture are original to the house. The Wilsons, who occupied it from 1884 to 1934, upgraded the bathroom: note the wood-encased tin tub

This late-19th-century weathervane reveals the craftsmanship of Pennsylvania Dutch metalworkers. (Heritage Center Museum)

This Lancaster County birth record is an example of the Pennsylvania Dutch art of decorative illumination known as Fraktur. (Heritage Center Museum)

and the bidet. Then go out back to the original privy, with three adult seats on one side—for servants, perhaps?—and two adult and three smaller seats of graduated heights on the other. Well-marked herb and flower gardens are behind the estate. The house is closed from January through March. *1120 Marietta Ave.; 717/392–8721.*

The outdoor ★**Landis Valley Museum,** 2.5 miles north of Lancaster, depicts the rural life of the Pennsylvania Dutch from the 1740s through 1940. It consists of about two dozen buildings, some original to the area and some relocated, laid out to form a crossroads village and its adjoining farms. You can wander from barn to blacksmith shop, from tavern to tin shop to print shop, and listen to costumed docents explaining the work of artisans and farmers. The museum also has several Conestoga wagons; these massive covered vehicles, developed in Lancaster County in the mid-18th century, were the tractor-trailers of their day, hauling freight between Lancaster and Philadelphia and points west. The museum is home to the Heirloom Seed Project, which seeks to preserve vegetables, herbs, and flowers lost to the effects of hybridization and mechanized agriculture.

Save time to browse through the museum's shop, whose inventory includes handmade dolls, beeswax candles, shirts and bonnets, handwoven linens, paintings, and some of the crafts—wood carvings, paper cuttings, paintings on tin,

Lancaster County is working to preserve its endangered farmland.

and others—demonstrated by artisans at the museum. *2451 Kissel Hill Rd. (Rte. 272/Oregon Pike); 717/569–0401.*

INTO THE COUNTRYSIDE

Anyone interested in getting a taste of the authentic Amish experience must venture out to the smaller towns and gently rolling farm country where the Amish live and work. There's really no "best way" to tour the region, but the relative proximity of the towns, and the small area that contains them, tends to encourage you to follow your own impulses. Good places to start are the corridors heading east out from Lancaster: toward Bird-in-Hand and Intercourse along Route 340; toward Paradise along Route 30; and toward Strasburg, at the junction of Routes 896 and 741.

In Lancaster County, handmade Amish quilts and Mennonite furniture—more like works of art than household goods—are sold from the makers' own homes and at retail outlets that come recommended by visitors bureaus. Other valued Pennsylvania Dutch crafts include needlework, such as tablecloths and napkins; gardening tools; leather goods; pottery; and toys. Primary locations include

Lancaster, Intercourse—where the Amish conduct much of their regular business—and Bird-in-Hand.

Visitors centers throughout the region carry standard warnings that while there are reputable dealers who offer the best Pennsylvania Dutch craftwork, imitations are common, so the buyer must beware. Be sure to ask shopkeepers where quilts and other crafts are from. Another reality check: much of the best work here passes by the local market and is handled through galleries in large cities such as Philadelphia and New York.

The sights below are organized roughly in a counterclockwise spiral that begins southeast of Lancaster.

Five miles south of Lancaster, the stone ★**Hans Herr House** was completed in 1719. The oldest building in Lancaster County, it is one of the best examples of medieval German architecture in North America. Hans Herr was the patriarch of a group of Swiss Mennonites who arrived in the area in 1711, and the house, built by his son, Christian, was probably lived in by both men and their families. Because they were both Mennonite bishops, the house was used for services, making it the oldest Mennonite meeting house in the Western Hemisphere. Artist Andrew Wyeth, a descendent of Herr, included the house, which is open from April through November and by appointment the rest of the year, in several of his paintings. *1849 Hans Herr Dr., in the town of Willow St.; 717/464-4438.*

This hope chest, crafted about 1792 in Lehigh or Berks County, exemplifies the furniture built by German craftsmen from the late 18th to the early 19th century. (Philadelphia Museum of Art)

About 3 miles east of Lancaster via Route 462, the **Mennonite Information Center** is a good place to get background information on the lives and history of the Mennonites. There are audiovisual displays and a 20-minute film plays regularly. Contact the center if you wish to stay in a Mennonite guest home or find a Mennonite tour guide. *2209 Millstream Rd., Lancaster; 717/299–0954.*

STRASBURG AND INTERCOURSE   map page 101, B/C-3

At the **Amish Village** you can take guided tours through a farmhouse from the 1840s that has been authentically furnished as an Old Order Amish home. A barn with animals, a blacksmith shop, a one-room schoolhouse, and a smokehouse are also on the site. To get to the village, head east from Lancaster along U.S. 30. *Rte. 896, about 2 miles north of Strasburg.*

The state-maintained ★**Railroad Museum of Pennsylvania and Railway Education Center** chart railroad history from its beginnings in the early 1800s to the present and does a great job of showing how the railroads transformed the state's economy and the face of the nation. You can climb into a caboose at the museum, or walk beneath a 62-ton steam locomotive. More than 100 preserved locomotives and rail cars are on display in the cavernous original Rolling Stock Hall. Another 40 or so are outside in the Restoration Yard, where there's a working Reading Railroad turntable from 1928. *300 Paradise La., off Rte. 741, Strasburg; 717/687–8628.*

Just down the road from the museum is the antique **Strasburg Rail Road,** whose trains wind for 9 miles round trip between Strasburg and Paradise, passing through beautiful farm country. On view through the windows are horse-drawn buggies paying no mind to cars swooshing by on backcountry roads and Amish men in their wide-brimmed straw hats directing horse-drawn plows along ever-so-neat rows. Before or after you board the train, inspect the opulent private coach that catered to the president of the Reading Railroad. The car, which is on static display, cost more than $100,000 to build back in 1913 and contains separate sleeping, dining, and meeting compartments. The lavish decor includes cut-glass chandeliers and floor-to-ceiling mahogany paneling. *Rte. 741, Strasburg; 717/687–7522.*

You can dine while you ride on the Strasburg Rail Road in the **Lee E. Brenner dining car** (717/687–6486 for reservations) or pack a lunch: the train stops at a picnic area just before Paradise. Or you can stick to the railroading theme and eat on the outskirts of Strasburg in the Victorian dining car that serves as the res-

A Strasburg Rail Road train passes a corn maze near Paradise.

taurant of the **Red Caboose Motel** (316 Paradise La.; 717/687–5000), so-called because its rooms are in recycled cabooses, mail cars, and baggage cars.

★**Kitchen Kettle Village** got its start in 1954 as a mom-and-pop business making jams and jellies out of a two-car garage. Over the years, other shops grew around the original preserves-making operation and today the place is a veritable shopping and eating mecca with 39 shops, two restaurants, and a handful of hotels. The original "mom," Pat Burnley, is still involved as are her kids and grand-kids. Go to sample some of her 70 types of relishes, jams, and jellies, including her award-winning sweet-and-sour Chow Chow, packed full of end-of-the-season garden vegetables. The Rhubarb Festival in late May is a huge and tasty celebra-tion. *Rte. 340, Intercourse; 717/768–8261.*

The **Old Country Store** is an outlet for locally made crafts, including quilts of exceptional value. The **People's Place Quilt Museum** on the second floor is a wonderfully serene place to go and contemplate some stunning quilts before head-ing downstairs to consider buying one of your own—or possibly buying the fabric to make one. You can also purchase quilts in the museum shop, although these tend to be art pieces, not in traditional style and not necessarily locally made. The

Quilting is one of the most renowned Pennsylvania Dutch crafts.

The Ephrata Cloister is now open to the public.

adjacent **Village Pottery** sells the works of various American potters. *3510 Old Philadelphia Pike (Rte. 340), Intercourse; 717/768–7171.*

BACK ROADS TO EPHRATA   *map page 101, C-3*

Some of the most appealing, authentically Amish farm country lies between Intercourse and the town of Ephrata to the north.

The ★**Ephrata Cloister,** a community of religious celibates, was founded by Conrad Beissel in 1732 and practiced a no-frills existence with an emphasis on self-denial. Unlike other strict religious societies of the times, however, the group believed they honored God best when they were singing or engaging in artistic pursuits. Ephratans were admired for their skill in a form of calligraphy known as Fraktur—broken lettering. The cloister has a library filled with hand-lettered books, and many others that were produced here are held in rare book collections and research libraries.

A perfect time to tour the cloister is on a cold, gray winter's day, when you'll get a heightened sense of how drafty and austere the medieval-style buildings can be. Be sure to walk the grounds around the complex—still set off from modern society by a wooded park—and visualize how much more remote the community was 250 years ago. The last celibate member died in 1813, but the cloister continued to be occupied until 1934 by married members of the German Seventh-Day Baptist Church. *At Rtes. 322 and 272, Ephrata; 717/733–6600.*

ADAMSTOWN   *map page 101, C-2/3*

Just a few miles north of Ephrata is Adamstown, known as "Antiques Capital USA," where people still talk about the time in 1989 when one lucky Philadelphian bought a painting for $4 at a local flea market because he liked the frame. He found a folded up Declaration of Independence tucked between the canvas and its backing and had it appraised. It was real, and it sold for $8 million at auction. That kind of find only happens once in a century—but hey, we *are* in the next century.

The license plates in the lot at ★**Renninger's Antiques and Collector's Market** read Illinois, Massachusetts, and Virginia, revealing just how far people will come to this legendary flea market that's on plenty of national top-10 lists. The crowd browsing the stalls is a mix of locals, experienced pickers, young couples look-ing to furnish their starter homes, recreational flea marketers, and looky-loos who're just here to soak up the atmosphere. During three annual "extravaganza weekends," approximately 900 vendors set up shop in the surrounding fields and under two covered pavilions, adding to the 200 vendors selling inside every Saturday. *Rte. 272, Exit 21; 717/336–2177.*

The guy who added collectibles to Renninger's in the mid-'60s got the idea from nearby **Shupp's Grove,** founded in 1962. Now around 200 vendors (closer to 500 on extravaganza weekends) set up on creaky wooden tables under the trees. Each weekend highlights a theme, such as vintage kitchen utensils, cast-iron goods, or textiles, but you'll find everything else, too. Among them are a china dealer with a large supply of vintage Hall; several vendors showing five-point Mennonite stars made from reclaimed tin in all sizes and colors; and some impressive displays of glassware and vintage magazines. It's open weekends April through October. *Off Rte. 897, south of Adamstown; 717/484–4115.*

LITITZ   *map page 101, B-3*

Along quiet Route 772, at the intersection with Route 501, is peaceful Lititz, founded by a religious group, the Moravians, that originated in Moravia and Bohemia in what is the present-day Czech Republic. The Moravians may be the oldest of the Protestant denominations. Followers of John Hus, a Protestant reformer who predated Martin Luther and was burned at the stake for heresy in 1415, the Moravians came to America by way of Germany, where they had

The Wilbur Chocolate Company has been a Lititz institution for nearly a century.

sought refuge from persecution in the early 18th century. Moravian missionaries arrived in the Lititz area in 1746 and, among others, converted a local farmer who deeded his property to the congregation 10 years later. A church was built and a town laid out, and until 1856 only church members were permitted to own land and live in Lititz.

The town really deserves to be described as "charming." The clean, tree-shaded streets are lined with beautiful 18th-century buildings of fieldstone and aged red brick, many housing antique stores and craft shops.

You can pick up a walking-tour map of the Main Street at the Lititz **Welcome Center** (Lititz Springs Park), housed in a replica of the 1884 Lititz train station. Before you even start your stroll, however, you may find yourself following the sweet smell of chocolate that wafts from the Wilbur Chocolate Company's **Candy Americana Museum & Factory Candy Store.** Here, next door to the train station, you can see the confections being made, sample some Wilbur Buds—which the company has been making since 1894—and stock up on enough chocolate to last you until you get to Hershey. *48 North Broad St.; 717/626–1131.*

The walking tour wraps up at the spiritual heart of town, the wonderfully preserved **Moravian Church Square.** Bordering the square are the Moravian

Church, built in 1787 but not the first on the spot, and Linden Hall, which was founded by the church in 1746 and is the oldest girls' boarding school in the United States.

Across the street are two old gray stone buildings owned by the Lititz Historical Foundation. One, built in 1793, houses the **Lititz Museum** (145 East Main St.; 717/627–4636), with historical artifacts. The other building, the **Johannes Mueller House** (137–139 East Main St.), was built in 1792 and is furnished as it would have been when its original occupant, a Moravian cloth dyer, lived there. The house was inhabited until 1962, and so little had been done to it over the years that it hardly needed restoration. The museum and house are both open from Memorial Day through October; the museum stays open on weekends to mid-December.

The ★**Julius Sturgis Pretzel Bakery** is the first commercial pretzel bakery in the country. The nominal tour fee gets you not only a pretzel as a ticket but also the chance to make your own pretzel. As the story goes, Julius Sturgis was baking bread in this 18th-century stone house in 1850 when, in thanks for a kindness, a passing hobo gave him a pretzel recipe. They proved so popular that by 1861 the bakery was twisting pretzels full time. Nowadays the hard pretzels are made by machine, but the soft pretzels are still done by hand and baked in the old brick oven. *219 East Main St.; 717/626–4354.*

MARIETTA   *map page 101, B-3*

After a 10-minute drive southwest of Mount Joy, at the junction of Route 772 and Route 441, you'll find the sleepy riverfront town of Marietta, where at least half of the buildings have earned designation on the National Registry of Historic Places. Stroll along Norman Rockwell–esque streets lined with elegant colonial, Federal-style, and Victorian homes, complete with manicured lawns, towering shade trees, and huge American flags flying from front porches. That this newly polished former mill town is nurturing a growing artist's community is evident in many galleries, studios, and antique shops in the village center.

CHICKIES ROCK COUNTY PARK   *map page 101, B-3*

Give the Amish a break and pull off at this riverfront park to gawk at the swans and green herons gracefully plying the slow-rolling waters of the Susquehanna and at the ospreys and bald eagles skimming the surface to snatch fish in their talons. You may see rock climbers (humans, not birds) scaling the walls at Chickies Rock itself, because this is considered the best place for the sport in the area. The

If you have time on your hands, visit the National Watch and Clock Museum in Columbia.

444-mile-long Susquehanna River is shallow and rocky here, its flow contained by hydroelectric dams. The park has two spectacular overlooks from which you can observe the wildlife along the steep banks of the river. *Rte. 441 between Marietta and Columbia; 717/295–2055 or 717/299–8215.*

COLUMBIA   *map page 101, B-3*

Two easy miles south of Marietta on Route 441 is the placid town of Columbia, stretching languidly the riverfront and peppered with B&Bs, good restaurants, and antique shops. The town is best known for the more-interesting-than-it-sounds **★National Watch and Clock Museum,** with 12,000 items in the collection. Hanging over the reception desk is the Latin motto *Tempus vitam regit*—"Time rules life." But time gets lost here amid the various timepieces, which include an Egyptian pot that measures time with dripping water, American railroad watches, an entire room of cuckooing cuckoo clocks, and, perhaps the museum's greatest treasure, the Engle Clock, the first American-made monumental clock, an 11-by-8-by-3-foot timepiece in an exquisitely carved case. Made by Stephen Engle, a clock-maker from Hazleton, it has 48 moving figures, including Jesus, the 12 Apostles, and Engle himself as one of the three Ages of Man. Engle worked on the clock for 20 years before completing it in 1877; he then turned it over to a pair of Philadelphia entrepreneurs, who took it on tour around the eastern United States, advertising it as the Eighth Wonder of the World. *514 Poplar St., Columbia; 717/684–8261.*

HERSHEY   *map page 101, A-2*

The smell of chocolate permeates part of Lititz, but here's a town where, no matter the direction of the wind or time of day, the aroma of chocolate wafts through the air. It has a main street named Chocolate Avenue, and street lights in the shape of foil-wrapped Hershey's Kisses. Chocolate addicts can follow their noses directly to Hershey's Chocolate World, but to fully appreciate the significance of the place, it's best to know a little about the man who built the world's largest chocolate factory.

Native son Milton Snavely Hershey produced a lot more than just chocolate. After early failed attempts to manufacture and sell candy in Philadelphia and New York City, Hershey returned to Lancaster County, where his innovative use of fresh milk in making caramels proved highly successful. In 1900 he sold his Lancaster Caramel Company for $1 million, and in 1903 he bought a cornfield in his Derry Township birthplace, constructed a manufacturing plant, and set out to perfect the chocolate bar. The rest is history, but only part of the story.

A Pennsylvania Dutchman of Mennonite stock, Milton was not only hard-working but also endowed with a strong sense of moral responsibility. For his employees, he built a model company town, full of comfortable, worker-owned one- and two-family homes, tree-lined streets, and landscaped grounds. He built a bank, an inn, churches, schools, a trolley system, and a community center. He opened a park with a swimming pool, a ballroom, and a zoo. He kept on building through the Depression, to keep everyone working. He and his wife, Catherine, were childless, but he founded a vocational boarding school for orphaned boys in 1909 and endowed it, nine years later, with all of his Hershey Chocolate Company stock. Today, the Milton Hershey School is one of the wealthiest schools in the world. It serves 1,700 disadvantaged boys and girls from pre-kindergarten through grade 12 and has plans to expand the enrollment to 2,100 students by 2013.

At Hersheypark, Reese's Peanut Butter Cups dance, chocolate bars hop, and Hershey's Kisses dispense hugs.

THE HERSHEY COMPLEX

Hershey is basically a factory town, sweetened with a tourist destination that draws 1.5 million visitors a year. To get to the Hershey attractions, take Hersheypark Drive exit off Route 322. *Call 800/437–7439 for more information, directions, and lodging reservations.*

HERSHEY'S CHOCOLATE WORLD

The official visitors center of the Hershey Foods Corporation serves as an introduction to the chocolate-making process. An automated Disney-esque ride along a conveyor belt begins in a rainforest where cacao beans grow, glides along to a barnyard scene featuring animatronic cows, and ends with the Hershey kitchens where you can see chocolate-bar, -kiss, and -patty–making machines. At the end you get a little reward and the chance to buy your very own five-pound, personalized Hershey bar. *800 Park Blvd.; 717/534–4900.*

★HERSHEYPARK

Candy man Milton S. Hershey opened the park in 1907 as a recreational area for his workers. Dancing six-foot Reese's Peanut Butter Cups and Hershey Bars bop around this amusement park's 60 or so rides and attractions—including 11 roller coasters, from a vintage wooden coaster circa 1946 to the Fahrenheit, a vertical-lift inverted coaster added in 2008. An 11-acre wildlife park has more than 200 animals, and the Boardwalk area, built in 2007 for the park's centennial, pays homage to the boardwalks of Coney Island and the Jersey Shore. Among the thrilling water rides is the 70-foot-tall East Coast Waterworks. The park is open from Memorial Day to Labor Day, weekends only in May and September. *Hersheypark Dr., off U.S. 422; 717/534–3090.*

HERSHEY GARDENS

Purge the aroma of chocolate from your nose with a stroll through these 23 acres of stunning and fragrant botanical gardens. They've come a long way since the site's establishment as a single rose garden in 1936. *170 Hotel Rd.; 717/534–3492.*

HERSHEY MUSEUM

A memorial to Milton Hershey's life, the museum exhibits wonderful black-and-white photographs of the town's progression from a one-horse way station to a world-famous city. The collection of folk art, furniture, and other artifacts of early Pennsylvania Dutch life is another highlight, and there are exhibits of 19th-century firefighting equipment and Native American objects. *170 West Hersheypark Dr.; 717/534–3439.*

GETTING AROUND

Since the real allure of the region lies on the back roads, and since Pennsylvania Dutch Country and Bucks County are hardly touched by mass transit, a car is a necessity. A good, detailed map will help you navigate the well-marked back roads that snake throughout the countryside. The Pennsylvania Turnpike (I–76) travels east–west across the northern part of Lancaster County, with Exit 20 (Rte. 72, Lancaster-Lebanon), Exit 21 (U.S. 222, Lancaster-Reading), and Exit 22 (Rte. 23, Morgantown) the most convenient to the area.

Amtrak's *Keystone* train service, from New York through Philadelphia, stops in Lancaster, Mount Joy, and Harrisburg. The *Pennsylvanian,* coming to Philadelphia from Chicago and Pittsburgh, also stops in Harrisburg and Lancaster, as does the *Three Rivers,* also from Chicago and Pittsburgh. Capitol Trailways buses connect New York and Philadelphia with Lancaster, Reading, Hershey, and Harrisburg. Bieber Tourways buses connect New York and Philadelphia with Kutztown and Reading. Doylestown is reachable via SEPTA trains from Philadelphia.

FAVORITE PLACES TO EAT

Bube's Brewery. 102 North Market St., Mount Joy (Lancaster area); 717/653–2056. $–$$$

There are three restaurants in this 19th-century working brewery. Bottling Works has nachos, burgers, and salads; Alois, in the highly decorated "Victorian Hotel" portion of the complex, serves a six-course, $36 prix-fixe that begins with cocktails in the parlor; and Catacombs, in the cellar, offers fine dining a la carte.

John J. Jeffries. Lancaster Arts Hotel, 300 Harrisburg Ave., Lancaster; 717/431–3307. $$–$$$$

Choose from inspiring small and large plates off a daily seasonal menu . Typical dishes are warm goat-cheese custard, duck breast confit with roasted root veggies, and Darjeeling-tea crème brûlée.

Jules Thin Crust. 78 South Main St., Doylestown; 215/345–8565. 300 Sycamore St., Newtown; 215/579–0111. $–$$

Twenty-eight (and counting) toppings, using the freshest, locally produced organic ingredients, are baked on top of a crispy, wafer-thin crust. This is practically diet pizza.

Marsha Brown. 15 South Main St., New Hope; 215/862–7044. $$$

Southern hospitality and Cajun food—like eggplant Ophelia (mashed eggplant with shrimp and crab)—are dished up in a converted stone church on the town's main drag. Stop by the bar if you want to check out the dramatic interior but don't feel like having dinner.

The Meritage at Groff's Farm Golf Club. 650 Pinkerton Rd., Mount Joy (Lancaster area); 717/653–2048. $$–$$$$

The restaurant in this 18th-century farmhouse serves contemporary cooking like hazelnut sea scallops and pan-seared duck breast with white-bean ragout.

Millers Smorgasbord. 2811 Lincoln Hwy. E (Rte. 30), Ronks.; 717/687–6621. $–$$

For $21, return as many times as you'd like to the lunch or dinner buffet—the spread stretches on forever. Hearty offerings from the carving stations are supplemented by chicken potpie and baked cabbage in cream sauce. Save room for the homemade shoofly pie and bread pudding.

FAVORITE PLACES TO STAY

Ash Mill Farm. 5358 York Rd., Holicong (Lahaska area); 215/794–5373. $$–$$$

A cheerful white 1790 farmhouse is now a B&B on a working farm. Children love the sheep and pygmy goats, while adults will appreciate the wireless Internet and flat-screen TVs.

Bridgeton House. 1525 River Rd., Upper Black Eddy; 610/982–5856. $$–$$$$

This charming B&B in an 1836 building stands right on the banks of the Delaware. Its 12 rooms are each decorated differently, with clever trompe l'oeil paintings, Victorian wood furniture, and fluffy floral comforters. It feels secluded, with benches and a little dock on the river, but it's actually a short walk from the Delaware Canal Park and a 20-minute drive from New Hope.

Doylestown Inn. 18 West State St., Doylestown; 215/345–6610. $$

Continuously operating since 1902, this inn was created when the original owners combined a turreted 1871 building with its neighbor. The 11 rooms are light-filled with dark woods and traditional furnishings, including four-poster and sleigh beds. The inn's central location means attractions like the Mercer and Michener museums are within walking distance.

Hotel Hershey. 100 Hotel Rd., Hershey; 717/533–2171. $$$–$$$$

Milton Hershey began construction on this lavish resort in 1932, conscious of the need for work among local townspeople. The hotel is set high on a hilltop above town and its grand interiors are inspired by Hershey's European travels. The on-site spa is famous for its chocolate fondue wrap and other sweet treatments.

Lancaster Arts Hotel. 300 Harrisburg Ave., Lancaster; 717/299–3000. $$–$$$

This hip boutique hotel in a former tobacco warehouse exhibits local artists' work in its art gallery, public spaces, and 67 rooms and suites. Exposed brick walls, wood floors, and chestnut beams feel both rustic and contemporary.

The Woolverton Inn. 6 Woolverton Rd., Stockton, NJ (New Hope area); 609/397–0802. $$–$$$$

A grand stone manor (built in 1792) on a 300-acre country estate, the luxurious Woolverton Inn is the perfect place to celebrate a special occasion. Tastefully decorated country-style rooms come with every amenity: fireplaces, spa tubs, and Egyptian cotton towels, plus quaint window seats overlooking sweeping woodlands and grazing sheep.

NORTHEAST
AND THE POCONOS

In northeastern Pennsylvania, forested mountains with spectacular views rise up from all directions. In the eastern section are the steep ridges of the Poconos; in the west, the hills of the Appalachian Plateau. Exit the Interstate anywhere in the Poconos and you'll be rewarded with a back-road drive through mountain forests.

The Delaware Water Gap is where the Delaware River slices through a ridge a thousand feet high that runs across the borders of Pennsylvania and New Jersey. Views of the mountains and river are spectacular.

Roads west of the Delaware River will take you past former coal towns, such as Scranton and Jim Thorpe, and the heavily forested nature areas of Lehigh Gorge State Park and the "Endless Mountains" of the western Appalachian Plateau.

LANDSCAPE

The dominant landform in northeastern Pennsylvania is the heavily forested Appalachian Plateau. A narrow section of the Allegheny Mountains reaches in from the southwest to touch the region around Scranton. The Poconos stretch from the Allegheny Mountains in the south to the Moosic Mountains in the west, near Lehigh Gorge State Park, gradually subsiding into lower Wayne County in the north. They are bounded by the Susquehanna River to the west and the Delaware River to the east. The Pocono Escarpment plunges from 2,300 feet above sea level down to the Delaware River, creating dramatic vistas along the way.

In the north, the Poconos are covered by second-growth forests of pine, beech, birch, oak, and maple; in the south and east with hickory-mixed oak; in Monroe and Pike counties with hemlock and white pine. These are still young woodlands, as the virgin forests were cut down during the 19th and early 20th centuries.

The Delaware River forms the border between Pennsylvania and New Jersey, cutting through the mountains at a spot known today as the Delaware Water Gap, but originally called Pohoqualine, or "river passing between two mountains," by the indigenous Lenni Lenape Indians. English trappers and settlers shortened the name to the Poconos, a term that later came to refer to the entire area.

The northeast's forested Poconos and the shores of the Delaware and Susquehanna rivers have remained beautiful and, for that reason, a place of retreat. In spring, creeks and streams swell from melting snow and carry icy water

A bucolic scene along the Susquehanna in Bradford County.

on a sharp, winding descent to the rivers. Marking the steeper drops along that journey are 30 waterfalls, nearly half of all the significant falls in Pennsylvania. Mountain meadows and fields here are dominated by the pinkish-white mountain laurel, Pennsylvania's state flower, which blooms from May through July.

HISTORY

Before the first European settlers arrived, hunting trails used by the Lenni Lenapes crisscrossed northeastern Pennsylvania. Indigenous tribes must have heard rumors of the growing European presence in North America, but it was not until 1725 that a French Huguenot fleeing religious persecution became the first settler in the northeast. He was Nicholas DePui, who purchased 3,000 acres at the southern end of the Delaware Water Gap from the Wolf Clan of the Lenni Lenapes and established good relations with the native tribes. DePui and his wife raised nine children here and supported their family by hunting, farming, and growing apples.

If the settlers who followed had been as honorable and peaceful as DePui, Pennsylvania might have been a very different place. Instead, the English settlers who followed him drove out the region's Indians in order to claim the homesteads they had been promised by the Penn family and its agents in London. Angered, the Lenni Lenapes, Shawnees, and Nanticokes joined the French in fighting the English during the French and Indian War. Raiding parties descended upon small farms, terrorizing settlers. Entire families were butchered, farms burned, and children kidnapped.

CONNECTICUT VERSUS PENNSYLVANIA

In the mid-1700s, Connecticut challenged Pennsylvania for control of the Wyoming Valley. To establish his state's claim, Connecticut's governor sent hundreds of families to settle in the region that would later be called Wilkes-Barre. The arrival of these Connecticut settlers in the middle of the Wyoming Valley infuriated the Lenni Lenapes, who were already dispossessed of their original territory. In 1763, a Lenni Lenape war party went on the rampage, destroying hundreds of settlements.

Pennsylvania's new colonial governor, John Penn, grandson of William, exhorted settlers streaming into the region to respect American-Indian treaties, but to no avail. The Indian raids continued, and Penn descended to offering bounties for the scalps of Indian warriors. The conflict escalated into the Yankee-Pennamite Wars. The fighting was interrupted by the Revolutionary War, but it began again after the British surrendered. The dispute was ultimately resolved by the Decree of Trenton in 1782, ceding the valley to Pennsylvania.

REVOLUTIONARY WAR

In 1778, in the midst of the Revolutionary War, Native American tribes from the Northeast joined British loyalists in defending the area's grain stores from confiscation by the Continental Army.

On July 3, 1778, the British and their Indian allies attacked the colonists in the Wyoming Valley. Outnumbered three to one, the farmer-soldiers were overwhelmed and more than 220 of them were killed. The Indians proceeded to ravage the unprotected homesteads—events later referred to as the Wyoming Massacre.

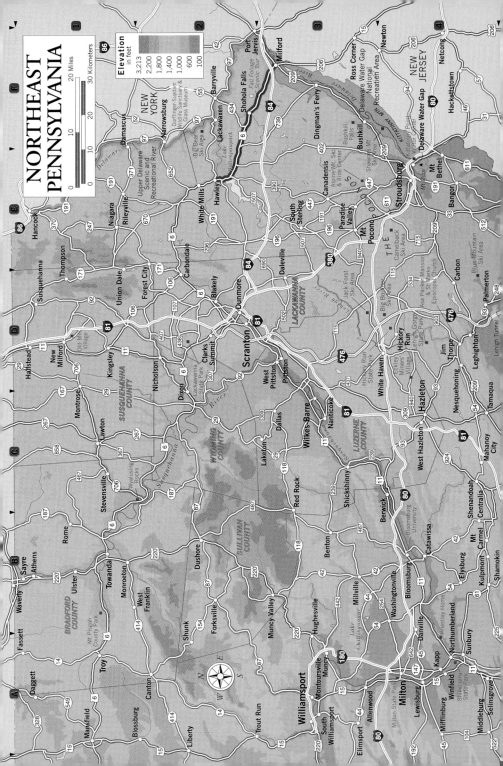

This train belonged to the Jersey Central Lines, which were built in the 19th century to transport coal to and from cities throughout northeastern Pennsylvania.

After the Revolutionary War, the new American military forces retaliated by destroying scores of Indian villages. By 1795, Indian resistance had been overcome and peace finally came to the region. With borders secure and immigrants free to settle, farms prospered and towns expanded.

LOGGING, MINING, AND IRON

In the decade after the War of Independence, prospectors discovered huge anthracite coal deposits—"black diamonds" as this hot-burning and almost smokeless coal became known. In the decades before the Civil War, anthracite, along with timber, fueled Pennsylvania's economic expansion. Coal from Pennsylvania's new mines was hauled along makeshift roadways, and as access improved, logging operations flourished. Bark was stripped from oak trees to supply tannin for tanneries in Stroudsburg and Tannersville, and hardwood trees—lashed together as rafts and floated down the Delaware—were milled into lumber for homes in the rapidly developing western settlements. By the 1840s, virtually all usable timber had been logged from the Poconos.

As the demand for railroads expanded, so did the need for coal to fuel locomotives. The last barrier to widespread mining operations in the region—lack of a cost-effective transportation system—ended when railroad tracks were laid to the Pocono Plateau. With its plentiful coal, iron foundries, and rail system, Pennsylvania emerged from the Civil War with its economy roaring full steam ahead.

UNION MOVEMENT

The burgeoning mining industry was centered in Carbon County and in Jim Thorpe, known then as Mauch Chunk. Industrialists in this region amassed fortunes while miners toiled underground, going into debt buying their food in company stores. Many of the toughest mining jobs went to the Irish, who resented their treatment in the mines and saw it as a continuation of what they had endured under the British in Ireland. In the 1840s, laborers who dug coal were making 50 cents a day. There was no federal regulation of pay or working conditions, and the courts were vigorously anti-union.

A secret terrorist group, the Molly Maguires, formed in the coal-mining region, its roots in a similar violent gang that targeted land barons in Ireland for assassination. The name derived from a legendary Irish woman who brought murderous vengeance on those who had wronged her. Before long the Maguires had graduated from sending greedy mine owners to their graves to targeting people at all levels of mine management and community members seen as industry sympathizers. The gang's hold on the region was so strong that killings often took place in public, in front of dozens of witnesses, none of whom would cooperate with police.

Eventually, the public became fed up with the violence and began to testify at trials. Ironically, it was an Irish contingent of the Pinkerton Detective Agency—a private police force employed with bloody results decades later in Pittsburgh steelworker union strikes—that infiltrated the Maguires and brought them down. (The 1970 movie *The Molly Maguires,* starring Sean Connery, explored the conflict and was filmed in Jim Thorpe.)

In 1902, an emerging labor crusade against unsafe conditions in the coal mines and an increasing reliance on oil as an industrial fuel source brought coal production nearly to a halt. By the 1930s, underground coal mining had been followed by strip mining, which left large scars on the land. And by the 1970s, the iron foundries were idle and once-prosperous Scranton lay fallow in the heart of the "Rust Belt."

TODAY

The Lehigh and Wyoming valleys and the forested Poconos bear little evidence today of the heavy industry of the past. In most valley communities, the rusty skeletons of old steel mills, iron foundries, and mining operations stand as depressing monuments to yesterday. But in Scranton and Jim Thorpe, those same facilities have been turned into museums. Other vacant industrial sites have been reborn as office parks for high-tech businesses.

In mountainous areas, forests cover most peaks and spectacular waterfalls drop precipitously through two major plateaus. Eight state parks crisscrossed with hiking trails and studded with glimmering lakes preserve this natural beauty. Although development continues to encroach on animal habitats—the state gaming-control board decided in 2006 to allow the development of casinos in the region—officials in this area are more protective of the environment than in the past. Community groups and state environmental workers have improved habitats for bald and golden eagles and ospreys, and for the white-tailed deer, the state animal, which was hunted almost to extinction in the 1800s.

ABOUT THE POCONOS

Emerging from the Lehigh Tunnel on the northeastern extension of the Pennsylvania Turnpike (I–476), you will notice a dramatic change in the mountains. In this part of the Appalachian Plateau, the Poconos rise up steeply, in contrast to the long ridges of the Allegheny Plateau. These are hardly the Rockies, however; the loftiest elevations are at best a few thousand feet. Drive through the back roads of these woodlands, and you'll come upon dairy farms, ski resorts, and, in the fall, a gorgeous display of foliage.

The reputation of the Poconos as a honeymoon destination began during World War II, when servicemen rushed here with their brides before leaving for war. In 1963, Morris Wilkins introduced the first heart-shaped bathtub at his Cove Haven Resort. A photo feature about the tub in *Life* magazine earned the area a reputation as the "Honeymoon Capital of the World." The razing in 2001 of Mt. Airy Lodge, a resort that catered to newlyweds for more than 50 years, marked the end of that era, and today the Poconos are caught between their kitschy past and a future marked by casinos, destination spas, and mountain retreats aimed at hikers and skiers.

SKIING

Thanks to an average of 60 inches of snow per year, the Poconos have seven major winter recreation resorts. Whether your tastes lean toward fast downhill runs, groomed cross-country trails, snowboarding, or powdery snowshoe hikes, most resorts can accommodate you, whatever your skill level. For general skiing information, you can call the **Pocono Mountains Snow Hotline** at 570/421–5565 or go to www.poconoski.com.

With 15 lifts and 33 trails, **Camelback** is the biggest of the resorts and is only going to keep growing. It has options for all levels of skiers and snowboarders, including night skiing, plus a separate tubing park. *1-80, Exit 299, Tannersville; 570/629–1661.*

Blue Mountain, with 9 lifts and 30 trails, offers less variety than Camelback but towers above all the resorts at 1,082 feet, allowing for mile-long runs. Each of the seven resorts caters to families, but Blue Mountain's Explorer Hill for beginning skiers and boarders provides a nice, protected environment for those who're still on wobbly legs. *1660 Blue Mountain Dr., Palmerton; 610/826–7700.*

In between these two superlatives—the biggest and the highest—are Shawnee, Jack Frost, Big Boulder, Alpine, and Big Bear. **Jack Frost** (570/443–8425) and **Big Boulder** (570/722–0100), sister properties a few miles apart, are the granddaddies of Poconos skiing. One ticket covers both hills: Big Boulder has the giant terrain park, Jack Frost has more options for skiers. **Shawnee** (570/421–7231) is closest to New Jersey and New York, and has a good terrain park and beginners' learning area. **Alpine** (800/233–8240) and **Big Bear** (570/685–1400) are the smallest resorts, with only five lifts each. Alpine is know for its 400-foot-long half-pipe. Big Bear is a good bet for young kids and beginners who prefer slow and gentle runs.

★ DELAWARE WATER GAP NATIONAL RECREATION AREA
map page 153, F-3, and page 160

Unsuspecting travelers heading west on I–80 from New Jersey might not be pre-pared for the dramatic entry point into the state of Pennsylvania, a breach in the long ridge of Kittatinny Mountain made by the waters of the Delaware River and known as the Delaware Water Gap. How did the gap come to be? In a previous eon of geologic history, an uplift (a rise in the earth's surface in relation to adja-cent areas) began beneath the river. The uplift was slow enough that the river's course eroded the rock underneath while the mountains rose on either side of it. As the mountains grew, so did the stone wall, creating a stunning cross-section. The twisted bands of metamorphic quartzite visible today cause geologists to pull off the highway for a closer look. Even those with little interest in geology stop to take in the views.

A thrill ride at Knoebels Amusement Park in Elysburg. The Poconos have long been a family destination as well as a honeymoon retreat.

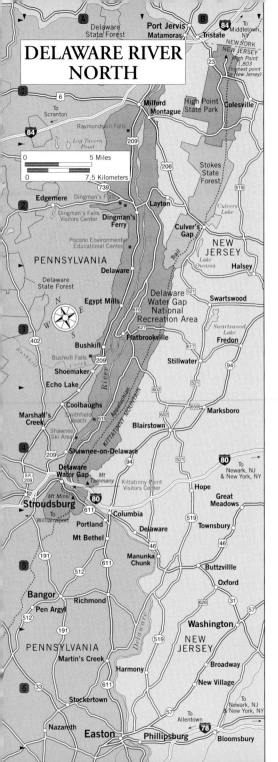

DELAWARE RIVER NORTH

The 70,000-acre Delaware Water Gap National Recreation Area protects both sides of the Delaware River, which for 40 miles forms the border between Pennsylvania and New Jersey. The protected area is, at its widest point, about 6 miles across. You'll want to follow Route 209 South, which winds along the river and turns into River Road once you enter the park. Stop in the small villages, at the swimming beaches, or canoe launches. There's not much development along this road, so gas up before you go. You can also hike in this area, starting at one of the many marked trailheads.

The upper Delaware River is slow-moving, shallow, and clear, lined with trees and filled with fishing birds, beaver, and, in season, Canada geese. Following a serpentine course, the river makes an S-curve on its mile-long journey through Kittatinny Ridge

The Delaware is the only major waterway on the East Coast that has not been dammed. It narrowly escaped that fate 35 years ago when the federal government announced plans to flood the valley and create a giant reservoir. Opposition was fierce, and in the 1970s Congress added two sections of the Upper Delaware to the National Wild and

A WALK NOT RECOMMENDED

The Appalachian Trail runs for 230 miles in a northeasterly arc across the state, like the broad end of a slice of pie. I never met a hiker with a good word to say about the trail in Pennsylvania. It is, as someone told a *National Geographic* reporter in 1987, the place "where boots go to die." During the last ice age it experienced what geologists call a periglacial climate—a zone at the edge of an ice sheet characterized by frequent freeze-thaw cycles that fractured the rock. The result is mile upon mile of jagged, oddly angled slabs of stone strewn about in wobbly piles known to science as *felsenmeer* (literally, "sea of rocks"). … Lots of people leave Pennsylvania limping and bruised. The state also has what are reputed to be the meanest rattlesnakes anywhere along the trail, and the most unreliable water sources, particularly in high summer. The really beautiful Appalachian ranges in Pennsylvania—Nitanny and Jacks and Tussey—stand to the north and west. For various practical and historical reasons, the AT goes nowhere near them. It traverses no notable eminences at all in Pennsylvania, offers no particularly memorable vistas, visits no national parks or forests, and overlooks the state's considerable history. In consequence, the AT is essentially just the central part of a very long, taxing haul connecting the South and New England. It is little wonder that most people dislike it.

—**Bill Bryson,** *A Walk in the Woods,* **1998**

Scenic River System, protecting 73.4 miles of natural resources along the New York–Pennsylvania border.

If you come west from New York City on I–80, or north from Philadelphia on Highway 33, you'll arrive at the southern end of the park, near Stroudsburg. Near the entrance is the **Kittatinny Park Visitors Center** (908/496–4458), where you can pick up maps and ask the rangers any questions. **Park Headquarters** (570/426–2452) is at the Fernwood Resort in Bushkill, on River Road a mile east of U.S. 209.

Interstate 80 follows the
course of the river through
the Delaware Water Gap
near Stroudsburg.

SWIMMING, CANOEING, AND TUBING

In summer, you can swim, canoe, and ride inner tubes or rafts down the slow-moving Delaware. Access points to the river are located every 8 to 10 miles. Two beaches are recommended for swimming: Smithfield, at the south end of the park, near Shawnee-on-Delaware; and Milford, at the north end. These are family-friendly, with lifeguards, and get fairly crowded. Water temperatures rise from the mid-50s in late spring to the mid-70s in July.

For information on camping and canoe and raft trips, call the park's visitor line at 570/426–2452 or visit www.nps.gov/dewa.

FISHING

The Delaware River contains shad, trout, walleye, and bass. You can pick up the required license at tackle and hardware stores and even local Wal-Marts.

TRAILS

Sixty miles of hiking trails traverse the forest. Interesting day hikes include the trail up Mount Tammany (1,527 feet) and Mount Minsi (1,463 feet). A 42-mile segment of the Appalachian Trail, which in its entirety covers the East Coast from Maine to Georgia, winds through the park, most of it on the New Jersey side of the river. Get maps and hiking recommendations at one of the visitors' centers in the Delaware Water Gap Recreation Area.

CAMPING AND LODGING

Overnight accommodations here include cabins and campgrounds. In nearby towns, youth hostels and hotels abound.

★ *BUSHKILL FALLS*   *map page 153, F-3*

Much of what is beautiful about northeastern Pennsylvania can be sampled at Bushkill Falls, a large park in the Poconos (part of the Delaware Water Gap National Recreation Area) with eight roaring waterfalls. Known to many as the "Niagara of Pennsylvania," the waterfalls are easily reached by trails and bridges that take hikers through some of the state's most densely forested areas. It's an easy 20-minute walk to Main Falls, the highest of these cascades, where water plunges from a 100-foot-high cliff into a creek and then courses through a gorge strewn with gigantic boulders. Several trails (some challenging, some not) lead to

Bushkill Falls encompasses eight waterfalls; trails lead to them through densely wooded forests.

Deer abound in northeastern Pennsylvania.

the less vertigo-inducing Bridal Veil Falls and Bridesmaid's Falls. The most efficient way to get to Bushkill Falls is via I–80 to Stroudsburg, then heading north to U.S. 209. *Bushkill Falls Rd., 2 miles northwest of U.S. 209; 888/287–4545.*

POCONO ENVIRONMENTAL EDUCATION CENTER
map page 160, A-2

This 38-acre compound in the middle of the Delaware Water Gap National Recreation Area was once a well-known honeymoon getaway. In 1972 it was taken over by bird-watchers and environmentalists and is now the largest center for environmental education in the Western Hemisphere. More than 2,500 people come annually to study nature-related topics ranging from bird-watching to wildlife photography to the flora and fauna of the Poconos.

Trails within the complex cut across forests, open fields, and boggy wetlands. Otters, common in the Water Gap area, can be spotted here, as well as beavers, coyotes, foxes, porcupines, and snakes (timber rattlesnakes and copperheads). If lucky, you'll catch a glimpse of a bald eagle soaring in the late afternoon updrafts, searching for fish in the Delaware River.

The golf course of the Shawnee Resort, one of the premier hotels along the Delaware River, can be seen on the island below.

A three-day, two-night Family Nature Getaway at the center will cost a family of four about $700. Included is basic bed and board plus educational and recreational activities. Check www.peec.org for dates of family-getaway weekends. Day passes are available. *Off U.S. 209, north of Bushkill Falls; 570/828–2319.*

DINGMAN'S FALLS   *map page 160, A-2*

Close to the Delaware River and used as a canoe-launching site is the small town of Dingman's Ferry, where a privately owned toll bridge spans the river. Less than a mile west of U.S. 209 is Dingman's Falls, a tranquil place where a half-mile trail (keep the stream in sight) threads among rhododendrons and hemlocks to two waterfalls, the cascading Dingman's Falls and the more delicate Silver Thread Falls. There is a visitors center and a small picnic area. *Johnny Bee Rd., off Rte. 209; 507/828–2253.*

Autumn leaves form a carpet of gold, obscuring the green of a grassy meadow.

★ MILFORD   map page 160, A/B-1

This waterfront town on the Delaware Water Gap has been working to restore its buildings to better reflect its Victorian-era past as a summer retreat for wealthy Manhattanites. The circa-1852 Hotel Fauchère once hosted such esteemed guests as Mae West and Charlie Chaplin. Its current owners bought the clapboard building in 2001 and spent five years restoring it with the Inn at Little Washington as their model. Since the Fauchère's reopening in 2006, regard for the area has risen a notch.

Look for the $1 brochure that outlines a self-guided architectural tour around town; it's available at most of the shops and B&Bs. True to its name, Milford is also filled with mills. The first one was built in 1740, and by the 1800s, Milford had at least seven water-powered mills, in which flour and seeds were ground and wood was sawed and planed. The **Upper Mill** (150 Sawkill Ave.; 717/296–3134), powered by a still-working waterwheel, is open for tours. Other must-see attractions are the **Columns Museum** (608 Broad St.; 570/296–8126), home of the bloody flag upon which President Lincoln laid his head after being shot by John Wilkes Booth; and **Grey Towers** (151 Grey Towers Dr.; 570/296–9630), an imposing mansion on 100 acres that was home to Gifford Pinchot, the first chief of the U.S. Forest Service and the father of the Conservation Movement. He and President (Teddy) Roosevelt resolved in the early 1900s to save the nation's vanishing forests from lumber barons and development, a mission that's still relevant today.

ALONG SCENIC U.S. 6   *map page 153, A/F-1/2*

U.S. 6 provides a scenic northern route across Pennsylvania. Its most beautiful stretch is from Milford west to the outskirts of Scranton. Don't be in a hurry if you take this route. The going may be slow but the views are splendid.

MILFORD TO WHITE MILLS   *map page 153, E/F-2*

From Milford, U.S. 6 meanders west through forests of thick evergreens and hardwoods, country villages, and the occasional resort. South of Hawley is **Lake Wallenpaupack,** a 5,700-acre man-made lake formed by the Pennsylvania Power and Light Company in 1926. Fishing is a big pastime here, with typical catches yielding walleye, panfish, pickerel, largemouth bass, muskellunge, brown trout, and rainbow trout. The lake is surrounded by woodlands with walking trails and campsites.

Five miles north of Lake Wallenpaupack on U.S. 6 is White Mills, a homey burg with upscale antique stores and cozy restaurants. Getting here is a real treat because U.S. 6 travels though some of Pennsylvania's most drop-dead gorgeous countryside. It's a nice trip at any time of the year, but especially so in autumn, when leaves explode with color.

For information about fall foliage driving tours of the region, call the **Pocono Mountains Visitors Bureau** (800/762–2667).

In 1862, the world-celebrated glassmaker Christian Dorflinger bought 600 acres in White Mills to build a home and workshop for his glassmaking enterprise. When Dorothy Grant Suydam, the widow of Dorflinger's grandson, Frederick, died in 1979, she stipulated in her will that the property should become a wildlife sanctuary, and the land was donated to the community. Trails at the **Dorflinger-Suydam Wildlife Sanctuary** wind through generous forests and over fields bursting in spring and summer with flowers. There is a small lake, and deer, raccoons, foxes, and Canada geese live in peace. The grounds are open year-round, and in summer, music festivals and art shows take place. *Long Ridge Rd. and Elizabeth St., White Mills; 570/253–1185.*

The **Dorflinger Glass Museum,** near the entrance to the wildlife sanctuary, displays more than 700 pieces of cut glass and crystal, including etched vases, jewelry boxes, paperweights, and ornaments. The Dorflinger studio took commissions from U.S. presidents and other notables, and many of the pieces crafted for chiefs of state are exhibited here. The museum is open from mid-May through October.

ENDLESS MOUNTAINS   map page 153

The Endless Mountains region was named for its rolling forested hills, which appear to go on forever. A branch of the Allegheny Mountains, this 3,000-square-mile area cuts a wide swath through Bradford, Sullivan, Susquehanna, and Wyoming counties.

Much of this territory was settled by Native Americans, but it later became the stomping ground of fur traders, French expatriates, European immigrants, farmers of all sorts, lumberjacks, industrialists, and coal miners. Sports enthusiasts and nature lovers are mostly what you will see today, as the mountains provide great opportunities for bird-watching, fishing, hiking, bicycling, and cross-country skiing. Game hunting is permitted on thousands of acres of state forest or game lands. *570/265–1528.*

COAL COUNTRY

West of the Poconos is the coal country of Lackawanna and Luzerne counties. If you come from the Poconos, you'll pass low rolling hills and manicured farmland.

SCRANTON   map page 153, D-2

Those interested in Pennsylvania's railway and mining heritage—or in the setting for NBC's hit sitcom, *The Office*—should visit Scranton, a city of 75,000 on the Lackawanna River. Lackawanna County is the youngest in the state, and Scranton's history as an industrial town began in the 1840s, when it became a manufacturing center for iron rails. The success of the mills brought several railroads to Scranton. The city flourished in the 1850s and became known as the "Anthracite Capital of the World" when the town began mining and transporting anthracite coal.

The **Lackawanna Railroad Depot** is one of Scranton's architectural gems. The 1906 French Renaissance–style building was converted into a hotel in 1983 and is now a Radisson, but most of the structure's original features remain intact, includ-

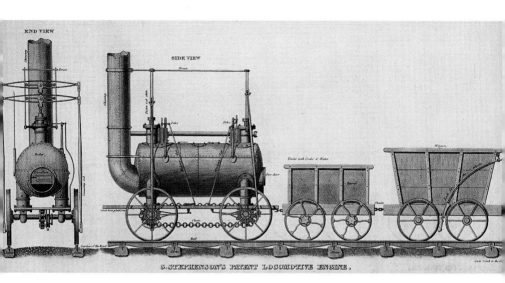

(above) Engineer and architect William Strickland's 1826 design for a locomotive steam engine. (Library of Congress) (below) Raymond Loewy, instrumental in defining the streamlined aesthetic of 20th-century industrial design, stands atop his prototype for the S-1 engine, created for the Pennsylvania Railroad. (Laurence Loewy)

FOREIGNERS

Theodore Dreiser was an Indiana native who often wrote about Pennsylvania. In 1915, he and a friend took a motor trip that covered most of the northeastern part of the state. Here are some of his reflections on the many foreigners he saw and met.

What becomes of all the Poles, Czechs, Croatians, Serbians, etc., who are going to destroy us? I'll tell you. They gather on the street corners when their parents will permit them, arrayed in yellow or red ties, yellow shoes, dinky fedoras or beribboned straw hats and 'style-plus' clothes, and talk about 'when I was out to Dreamland the other night,' or make some such observation as 'Say, you should have seen the beaut that cut across here just now. Oh, mamma, some baby!' That's all the menace there is to the foreign invasion. Whatever their original intention may be, they can't resist the American yellow shoes, the American moving picture … the popular song, the automobile, the jitney. They are completely undone by our perfections. Instead of throwing bombs or lowering our social level, all bogies of the sociologists, they would rather stand on our street corners, go to the nearest moving pictures, smoke cigarettes, wear high white collars and braided yellow vests and yearn over the girls who know exactly how to handle them, or work to someday own an automobile and break the speed laws. They are really not so bad as we seem to want them to be. They are simple, gauche, de jeune, 'the limit'. In other words, they are fast becoming Americans.

—Theodore Dreiser,
A Hoosier Holiday, **1916**

ing the facade and the Grand Lobby, which has a mosaic-tile floor, marble walls, and a vaulted Tiffany stained-glass ceiling. *700 Lackawanna Ave.; 570/342–8300.*

A few blocks north of the hotel is **Steamtown National Historic Site** and **Electric City Trolley Museum,** the only museum devoted to trains that's operated by the National Park Service. The 52-acre yard has a fleet of vintage steam locomotives and passenger and freight cars, most of which can be boarded for close-up inspection. The history museum reveals railroad history with vivid displays of archival photographs, documents, and videos, and there's a 1930s-era

Abundant snowfall in the Poconos makes the region a prime destination for cross-country skiers.

roundhouse with locomotives. Sixty-minute steam train excursions to nearby Moscow are offered a few times a day, Wednesday through Sunday, from April to December. *150 South Washington Ave.; 570/340–5200, www.nps.gov/stea.*

A pedestrian bridge connects the historic site to a two-story shopping mall. On the other side of that mall is Scranton's downtown, a basic (and hilly) grid with a growing number of restaurants and shops. Local government has focused on revitalization since the 1980s. Some successes include the establishment of a AAA team that plays at the PNC Field, and, of course, *The Office.* Not since coal has anything drawn so much attention to Scranton.

There are other attractions here besides *The Office* convention held in late October. The **Everhart Museum,** a gift to the city from Dr. Isaiah Everhart, is about fifteen blocks from the city center in Nay Aug Park. The museum was founded in 1908 as a natural history collection with an ornithological bent, and is now a full-blown museum with 20th-century American art, decorative art, and folk art collections. Highlights of the collection include portraits by Alex Katz, Violet Oakley, and Ivan Olinsky. *1901 Mulberry St.; 570/346–7186.*

Vestiges of Scranton's gilded past can be seen in old neighborhoods like Greenridge and the Hills, where the mansions of onetime coal barons still stand. Most are private homes, but you can tour two fine ones, the **Tripp House** (1011 North Main St.; 570/961–3317) and the **Catlin House** (232 Monroe Ave.; 570/344–3841), a 16-room, English Tudor–style mansion.

The master magician Harry Houdini pulled off some of his most memorable contortionist tricks and speedy escapes in Scranton, which explains the presence of the ★**Houdini Museum** here. Created by adoring fans, the museum presents magazine articles, photographs, and film clips chronicling his exploits—which were often underwritten by Scranton businesses as a way to advertise their products. Workers at hardware manufacturer J. B. Woolsey & Co., for instance, shut him in a packing crate secured with seven pounds of nails. It took him six minutes to pop out. The museum is open on a regular basis during the summer and intermittently the rest of the year. *1433 North Main Ave.; 570/342–5555.*

McDade Park has 200 acres of beautiful woodlands and wetlands, picnic groves, an Olympic-size swimming pool, ball fields, and a fishing pond. Several nearby institutions relate the sometimes-harrowing story of coal mining in this region. *Off North Keyser Ave.; 570/963–6764.*

Photographs and archival documents at the **Anthracite Heritage Museum** reveal the difficult lives of the men and women who came to this region in the 19th and early 20th centuries to work in coal mines, mills, and factories. Particularly poignant are the stories museum guides tell about the hardships and obstacles overcome by immigrants on the bottom rung of the employment ladder. *McDade Park, off North Keyser Ave.; 570/963–4804.*

At the **Lackawanna Coal Mine,** visitors descend 300 feet below ground in railcars to reach a former "working city" of underground stables, offices, storage rooms, and living quarters for hundreds of workers. Former miners lead the tour and give sobering lectures about the risks early miners faced, from poison gas eruptions to roof and wall cave-ins. *51 McDade Park, off North Keyser Ave.; 570/963–6463.*

WILKES-BARRE *map page 153, C-3*

Scranton and Wilkes-Barre are so close geographically it's easy to think of them as one city. The smaller of the two, Wilkes-Barre, was named in the late 18th century for John Wilkes and Isaac Barre, fellows of the British Parliament who lent sympathetic ears to the American colonies. A monument in the town square honors both men. Wilkes-Barre was considered tiny until thousands of immigrants

Eckley Miners' Village, a restoration of a 19th-century company town.

came to the region in the early 1900s to work in the anthracite mines. By 1917, more than 100 million tons of coal had been mined in the Wilkes-Barre/Scranton area. Exhibits at the **Luzerne County Historical Society** (49 South Franklin St.; 570/823–6244) trace the history of the mining industry in Wilkes-Barre.

ECKLEY MINERS' VILLAGE   *map page 153, D-4*

This 19th-century anthracite mining village, about 25 miles south of Wilkes-Barre in the little town of Eckley, is a fine example of the company towns of the industrial era, in which everything from the store to houses and schools was built and run by a single company. A walking tour of the town takes in about two dozen sites, including two churches, a miner's dwelling, and a general store. *Take Rte. 309 south from I–81, then Rte. 940 east; 570/636–2070.*

LEHIGH GORGE   *map page 153, D-4*

Lehigh Gorge State Park follows the course of the Lehigh River for 26 miles, encompassing some of the most dramatic scenery in the Poconos. White-water rafting is popular here, and a typical raft trip organized by one of the compa-

Jim Thorpe was one of the best all-around athletes in American history. (Cumberland County Historical Society)

nies operating in the park goes from White Haven to Jim Thorpe and takes 10 to 12 hours. (Inexperienced boaters should not attempt this trip without qualified guides. All boaters must enter and leave the Lehigh River at designated access areas.)

The northern terminus of the **Lehigh Gorge Trail** is at White Haven. An abandoned railroad bed follows the river through the park, making it an ideal trail for hiking and mountain biking. Here, the landscape is a series of steep cliffs and jagged rocks. In the spring, rhododendrons bloom along parts of the trail. *Take I–80 to Exit 40, White Haven; 570/427–5000.*

JIM THORPE   *map page 153, D-4*

The town of Jim Thorpe bills itself as Little Switzerland, which is a bit of a stretch, but the setting is pretty and the town's Victorian homes, Italianate and Romanesque public buildings, and quaint streets lined with 19th-century row houses merit a walking tour. The town is so quiet, it's hard to believe that the brutality of the Molly Maguires saga played out here. The seven Irish miners hanged in front of the former Carbon County Jail are said to haunt the structure that's now the Old Jail Museum and Heritage Center (128 West Broadway; 570/325–5259).

The town's name was changed from Mauch Chunk ("sleeping bear" in the Lenni Lenape language) in 1954, when it merged with two nearby towns into one self-governing district and assumed the moniker of the country's most famous athlete. Born in Oklahoma of Fox and Sauk Indian lineage, Thorpe played football for coach Glenn Scobey "Pop" Warner at Pennsylvania's Carlisle Indian Industrial School, becoming an All-American in 1911 and 1912. He won the

The citizens of Mauch Chunk, a gritty coal town, renamed their city after athlete Jim Thorpe.

pentathlon and decathlon at the 1912 Olympic Games in Stockholm but was stripped of his two gold medals when Olympic Committee members discovered he had played a season of professional baseball. In 1982, nearly 30 years after his death, the Olympic Committee reinstated the medals. **Thorpe's mausoleum**—20 tons of granite—is in a park a half mile east of town.

From the 1888 Railroad Station you can take a leisurely 40-minute **train ride** over tracks that became part of the former Nesquehoning Valley Railroad in 1872. *Contact Rail Tours Inc.; 570/325–4606.*

St. Mark's Episcopal Church is a fine example of late Gothic Revival architecture, and one of the most intriguing structures in the area. The windows are Tiffany stained glass and the altar is white Italian marble. *21 Race St.; 570/325–2241.*

The **Asa Packer Mansion** is visible from just about anywhere in Jim Thorpe. Packer, an industrialist and philanthropist who founded the Lehigh Valley Railroad and Lehigh University, was worth $54 million in 1879. His mansion, built in 1850 and remodeled in 1877 for the then-staggering sum of $85,000, is worth a visit for its many beguiling and eccentric touches. The exterior is a playful cadenza of Gothic arches, gingerbread detailing, and embellishments like those seen on Italian villas. Inside, elegant wood carvings adorn the main hallway, and

THE LONG, SLOW BURN

A subterranean fire has been burning in Centralia since 1962.

Centralia has been called a modern-day ghost town. *In the early '60s this very typical small town about 15 minutes south of Bloomsburg on Route 42 had a population of 1,435. Today it's all but abandoned, and the cause is far from typical. In 1962, a fire in a trash dump on the edge of Centralia found its way into a deep pit underground where it spread through a labyrinth of coal mines, and continues to burn to this day.*

In the '60s and '70s, various plans were advanced to fight the fire. Huge volumes of water were poured onto the coal seams but simply evaporated due to the extreme underground temperatures. The only method proven effective against this sort of fire—digging out the blaze, extinguishing it, then refilling the dig area —was the most expensive, and funding in Centralia ran out.

The area had become a frightening place to live, with ground temperatures recorded at close to 1,000 degrees Fahrenheit and glowing hot spots visible across the landscape at night. Sudden cave-ins claimed backyards and basements, and increasing levels of carbon monoxide seeped into homes made people sick.

In 1983, Congress allocated $42 million to purchase the town's homes, relocate its population, and bulldoze the buildings. The residents voted to accept the offer, and today only a stubborn few remain. All routes into Centralia are closed but remain passable. Its streets are deserted, driveways lead to empty lots, and only a few houses remain scattered around. An overall view of what's left of this once-typical American town can be had from the mountain north of town. Experts say the fire could burn for another thousand years.

A sleigh rally in Forksville, Sullivan County.

there are stained-glass windows in the dining room. The house is closed from mid-December through March. *30 Elk St.; 570/325–3229.*

GETTING AROUND

Many scenic routes wind through the region. Interstate 84 begins in Pennsylvania at Point Jervis and skirts the Poconos to I–380, which leads to Scranton. Scenic Route 6 (U.S. 6) begins in Milford and wends its way slowly across the northern half of the state, hitting some of the region's most wondrous natural settings, including the areas around White Mills, Carbondale, and Dixon. U.S. 6 also offers connections to the region's many lesser-traveled back roads, which lead through mile after mile of unspoiled wilderness and past small towns filled with friendly locals. Route 209, running the length of the New Jersey and Pennsylvania border, is the easiest route to the Delaware Water Gap, Dingman's Falls, Delaware State Forest, and Bushkill Falls. Martz Lines (800/233–8604) has regular bus service running through the Poconos from Stroudsburg to Wilkes-Barre and Scranton.

FAVORITE PLACES TO EAT

Bar Louis and the Delmonico Room.
Hotel Fauchère, 410 Broad St., Milford;
570/409–1212. $–$$ and $$$$

The Hotel Fauchère's two restaurants
are day and night. Casual dining,
including sushi and pizza, is in the
basement at cozy, hip Bar Louis. Fine
dining and a swanky menu (lobster
Newburg, prime Angus ribeye) are
upstairs in the Delmonico's elegant,
candlelit room. Both are excellent.

Coney Island Lunch. 515 Lackawanna
Ave., Scranton; 570/961–9004. $

This downtown institution has been
in the same family for three generations
and specializes in the Texas Weiner,
a grilled all-beef dog topped with
mustard, onions, and chili sauce.

Deer Head Inn. 5 Main St., Delaware
Water Gap; 570/424–2000. $$$

The oldest continuously running jazz club in
the country is really known for its live music,
but the food is good, unfussy, seasonal fare.
Light dishes and sandwiches are served late.

Moya. 24 Race St., Jim Thorpe;
570/325–8534. $$

Locals come here for good, straightforward
crowd-pleasers like pan-roasted chicken,
seared scallops, and potato gnocchi. The
dining room vibe is warm and relaxed.

Barley Creek Brewing Company.
Sullivan Trail and Camelback Rd.,
Tannersville; 570/629–9399. $–$$

This family-friendly pub near
Crossings Outlet and Camelback
has an extensive menu of bar grub
to go along with its home brews.

FAVORITE PLACES TO STAY

Hotel Fauchère. 401 Broad St., Milford; 570/409–1212. $$$$

A Victorian-era inn rescued from total disrepair by two design-savvy entrepreneurs, the serene and chic Fauchère offers crisp beige-and-white rooms with original wide-plank floors and Kiehl's bath products.

The Lodge at Woodloch. 109 River Birch La., Hawley; 866/953–8500. $$$$

Two former consultants for Canyon Ranch are the masterminds behind this worthy splurge. Everything is top-notch—the healthy food, the forest views from scores of floor-to-ceiling windows, the spa treatments—and the price includes meals and activities. Treat yourself to a hydromassage from the indoor pool's heated waterfall.

Mt. Airy Casino and Resort. 44 Woodland Rd., Mount Pocono; 877/682–4791. $$–$$$$

Mt. Airy Lodge, a symbol of honeymoons past, was razed in 2001. In 2007 this slots casino and hotel sprung up in its place. It's the Poconos on steroids imported from Vegas, with oversize fieldstone pillars and a massive waterfall in the lobby. Rooms are standard-issue.

Skytop Lodge. Rte. 390, Skytop (near Canadensis); 800/345–7759. $$$$

A grand historic hotel with something for everyone, this sprawling stone lodge has traditional rooms plus freestanding cottages. There are 5,500 acres with hiking trails, pools, a lake, clay-shooting, and nature walks. Kids make a beeline for the lodge's basement game room. Price includes meals and activities.

CENTRAL PENNSYLVANIA
THE HEARTLAND

The author Robert Louis Stevenson, traveling through central Pennsylvania on a railroad journey in 1868, wrote in his diary:

> I saw one after another, pleasant villages, carts upon the highway and fishers by the stream, and heard cock-crows and cheery voices in the distance. And then when I asked the name of the river from the brakesman, and heard that it was called the Susquehanna, the beauty of the name seemed to be part and parcel of the beauty of the land.

Except for rolling farmland near Gettysburg, central Pennsylvania is a region of wooded ridges and narrow valleys. To the west, rising above all, is the Allegheny Ridge. Fed by dozens of creeks and streams, the wide Susquehanna River is the third-largest river in the state, flowing from Pennsylvania's northern border with New York south through Harrisburg to the Chesapeake Bay. Indigenous Americans called it "Long Reach River."

Because many parts of the Susquehanna are not navigable and its forests were once impenetrable, the Seneca and Iroquois tribes lived here largely undisturbed until the late 1700s, when William Penn annexed the land for settlement. Soon roads were built along the Iroquois trails, tying the region to the state's major towns. White pine was the chief export, but there were also mining and refining operations on coal, iron ore, and limestone deposits. When these resources were exhausted—mainly in the 1950s and '60s—the area was abandoned, its ridges stripped bare and its streams polluted from mine drainage. In 1977, state lawmakers passed legislation to reclaim abandoned mine sites. Now the land has begun to heal, and much of its natural beauty has been restored.

Today, visitors to Central Pennsylvania can enjoy the region's seemingly infinite ribbon of lush valleys, forested mountains, and gurgling streams. In addition to plenty of hiking opportunities, the region is rich with reminders of the past. The smoke has long since cleared from the Gettysburg Battlefield, yet you can practically hear the footsteps of General Lee's Confederate troops during a visit to the site. Architectural treasures are as diverse as the frescoed capitol rotunda in Harrisburg and the perfectly preserved covered bridges that dot Bedford County.

BEAUTIFUL SUSQUEHANNA

The Susquehanna, though more than two hundred miles longer than the Hudson, is born among men. A few yards from the lake it is not quite four feet deep, and there children swim, shadowed sometimes by the high bank across from Riverbrink. Canoes drift here and fishermen, hardly expecting a catch, idle with short lines dangling in water so clear that the fish can see them. In spring and summer, lawn and stream and high bank across meld varying shades of green, making a lush and subtly arranged background for the fading hues of the house, like a landscape by the French painter, Courbet. And, somehow, ever consistent, through other backyards and through coal towns, through deep chasms and wide flat bottoms, the Susquehanna always keeps a relationship to the men on its banks. Sometimes dangerous, sometimes friendly, it ever maintains its unique unchanging quality, minding its own business, a "character" among streams.

—Carl Carmer, "The Susquehanna,"
1955, in *The Way It Was*

And, of course, Pennsylvania's industrial past continues to characterize towns like Altoona, where a railroad museum transports you back to the days when steam engines passed through with loads of coal, lead, and lumber.

Sports fanatics can get their game on with Penn State during football season, while kids—and those simply young at heart—may want to catch the action at the Little League World Series if traveling through Williamsport in the fall.

HARRISBURG

Harrisburg has come a long way from its roots as a sleepy ferry town on the Susquehanna's eastern bank. During the early 1700s, it had a single trading post and one tavern. But the city underwent several transformations during the 19th century, finally becoming a key transportation hub, first as a link on the Main Line Canal from Pittsburgh to Philadelphia and later as a railroad interchange. State leaders chose Harrisburg as the capital in 1812, citing its location in the middle of Pennsylvania. Although government remains the primary industry, these days Harrisburg is characterized by recreational and cultural events. The sixth-largest city in Pennsylvania, with 47,000 residents, Harrisburg has a thriving commercial district with unique boutiques, art galleries, trendy restaurants, and nightlife. More in the mood for a hot dog and peanuts? City Island is an energetic park, hosting

A choral group performs in the state capitol's rotunda.

SOUTH-CENTRAL PENNSYLVANIA

Harrisburg's own minor-league baseball team and plenty of kid-friendly attractions, such as a carousel, an 18-hole water golf course, and trolley rides.

STATE CAPITOL   *map page 186*

When Theodore Roosevelt came to the dedication of the Pennsylvania State Capitol in October 1906, he gazed up at the great dome, which was modeled after St. Peter's Basilica in Rome, and declared it "the handsomest building I ever saw." The six-story building, designed by Joseph Huston, cost more than $13 million to construct, a princely sum for its time. The ornate interior includes a grand staircase and murals by Edwin Austin Abbey. The artist's crowning work is *The Apotheosis of Pennsylvania,* which depicts 35 of the state's historic figures, including William Penn, Benjamin Franklin, Daniel Boone, Gen. George Meade, and Chief Justice Thomas McKean (founder of the Democratic party). Thirty-minute guided tours of the Senate chambers, the House of Representatives, the Supreme Court, and the Rotunda leave every half hour. *Third and State Sts.; 717/787–6810.*

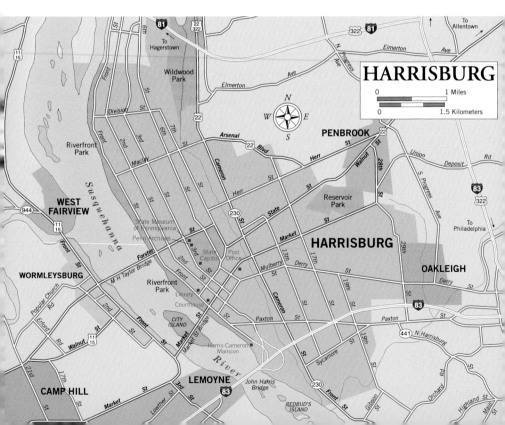

The State Capitol's dome was based on that of St. Peter's Basilica in Rome.

★ STATE MUSEUM OF PENNSYLVANIA   *map page 186*

The state's official museum has exhibits that encompass Pennsylvania's history from prehistoric times to the 21st century. The first floor contains a detailed re-creation of a colonial street, with storefronts and furnished rooms from a typical family home. The Civil War gallery includes paintings, uniforms, and munitions from the war, as well as a collection of artifacts and weaponry used by the state's native peoples. But the highlight is one of the largest paintings of the Battle of Gettysburg ever created, by artist Peter Rothermel. In the Hall of Industry and Technology are models and photos of steamboats, trains, gristmills, and auto-mobiles. Kids age 2 through 7 can build trucks and pretend to be farmers in the Curiosity Connection. The museum's planetarium presents shows each weekend. *300 North St., at Third St.; 717/787–4980.*

JOHN HARRIS–SIMON CAMERON MANSION   *map page 186*

Among the first settlers to arrive in this area was John Harris, sent by the Penn family to mitigate conflicts between settlers and native peoples. His son, John Harris Jr., who went on to found Harrisburg in 1784, built this splendid mansion overlooking the river in 1766. Simon Cameron, President Lincoln's first Secretary of War, bought the house in 1863 for $8,000. He spent a considerable sum to

The Millersburg Ferry crosses the Susquehanna about 20 miles upriver from Harrisburg.

redecorate it with furnishings acquired during his travels in Europe, and the mansion appears today much as it did during Cameron's residency. Two 14-foot-tall pier mirrors in the parlor hail from France, while the fireplace mantles are made of hand-carved Italian marble, and the alcove window glass is from Bavaria. The master bedroom has a magnificent Victorian bed and a fully appointed bathroom. The house is now the home of the Historical Society of Dauphin County, where photographs, manuscripts, and paintings trace 200 years of local history. *219 South Front St.; 717/233-3462.*

MILLERSBURG *map page 185, D-3*

About 20 miles upriver from Harrisburg is the historic town of Millersburg, on the banks of the Susquehanna. Deeded to one Daniel Miller in 1790, the town is the site of the Millersburg Ferry, which has been crossing the river to a landing about 2 miles south of Liverpool, in Perry County, since the early 18th century. Today, it's the last remaining ferry on the Susquehanna River and possibly the last wooden paddlewheel ferry in the United States. The tranquil one-mile ride is a journey back in time. As the ferry meanders amid the mountain peaks it is often accompanied by raptors from a nearby wildlife preserve. The ferry operates, water conditions permitting, from May through October. *From Harrisburg, take Rtes.*

22/322 West to Rte. 147 North. Follow into Millersburg and turn left onto North St. toward the river. 717/692–2442.

THREE MILE ISLAND   *map page 101, A-3*

Ten miles south of Harrisburg lies the Three Mile Island nuclear power plant. Today, its looming towers betray no hint of the drama that unfolded March 28, 1979. At 4 A.M. that day, a minor malfunction in the system that feeds water to the steam generators at the Unit 2 reactor set off a chain of events that led to the worst nuclear accident in U.S. history. Temperatures within the reactor rose precipitously, and the unthinkable, a nuclear meltdown, suddenly seemed possible. Radioactive gases escaped into the containment vessel and some also seeped into the atmosphere. Meanwhile a hydrogen bubble in the reactor threatened to explode.

Confronted with contradictory information about the potential for radiation exposure from the plant's operator and officials at the Nuclear Regulatory Commission, Gov. Richard Thornburgh struggled over whether to evacuate a quarter-million area residents. Initially, people living nearby were ordered to remain indoors with their windows closed. But on March 30, officials evacuated

President Jimmy Carter leaving Three Mile Island nuclear power plant, April 1, 1979. (National Archives)

children and pregnant women living within a 5-mile radius. Although President Jimmy Carter attempted to calm fears by touring the plant two days later, thousands had fled by the time Thornburgh declared the crisis over April 9.

The partial core meltdown required a dozen years and $1 billion to clean up. TMI's damaged reactor is permanently off-line, but the undamaged reactor restarted in 1985 and remains in operation. Officially, the incident caused no long-term adverse health or environmental effects. Regardless, no new nuclear power plants have been ordered in the United States since the accident.

CIVIL WAR TRAIL

The Cumberland Valley in Franklin County saw more military activity during the Civil War than any other region in the North. Four important historical sites can be visited in this area, about an hour's drive from Lancaster. The most important is the site of the Battle of Gettysburg, where the Confederate Army was dealt a devastating blow in July 1863. Live dramatizations of the battle take place for three days over the July 4 holiday, drawing 10,000 to 15,000 reenactors, and twice that many spectators. If you drive to Gettysburg, take back roads, where quiet farms and small towns are the norm.

Route 34 is among the most scenic routes into Gettysburg. If you're coming from Maryland, drive through **Waynesboro,** known for its high-quality antiques shops.

GETTYSBURG
map pages 185, D-6, and page 191

In downtown Gettysburg, the streets radiating from Lincoln Square are lined with souvenir shops, art galleries, and bistros. The 800-seat Majestic Theater, renovated in 2005, hosts Broadway-style shows,

Official army drawings of Union and Confederate cavalry officers.

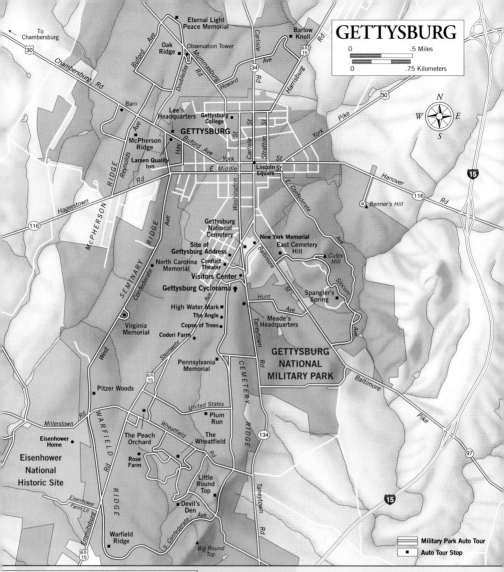

To Chambersburg

30

Chambersburg Rd

Eternal Light
Peace Memorial

Oak
Ridge

Observation Tower

Carlisle St

Barlow
Knoll

BR
15

34

Howard

Harrisburg

Buford Ave

Mummasburg Rd

Doubleday Ave

Pike

York

Lee's
Headquarters

Gettysburg
College

GETTYSBURG

McPherson
Ridge

Larsen Quality
Inn

Hay

Buford Ave

York

Carlisle St

Stratton St

Lincoln
Square

E Middle

St

Hanover

116

Rd

15

Benner's Hill

Hagerstown Rd

116

Reynolds Ave

SEMINARY

RIDGE

MCPHERSON RIDGE

Confederate Ave

Gettysburg
National
Cemetery

Site of
Gettysburg Address

North Carolina
Memorial

Conflict
Theater

Visitors Center

Gettysburg Cyclorama

Baltimore St

E Confederate Ave

New York Memorial
East Cemetery
Hill

Culp's
Hill

Ave

Slocum

Spangler's
Spring

Virginia
Memorial

West

High Water Mark
The Angle
Copse of Trees
Codori Farm

Steinwehr

Hunt

Ave

Meade's
Headquarters

Taneytown

GETTYSBURG
NATIONAL
MILITARY
PARK

Ave

Baltimore

Pike

BR
15

Pennsylvania
Memorial

Pitzer Woods

WARFIELD

PY

RIDGE

Eisenhower
Home

Eisenhower
National
Historic Site

Millerstown

Eisenhower
Farm Ln

Fairfield Rd

BR
15

The Peach
Orchard

Rose
Farm

Warfield
Ridge

S Confederate Ave

United States Ave

Wheatfield

Plum
Run

The
Wheatfield

Rd

Little
Round
Top

Devil's
Den

Ave

Big Round
Top

CEMETERY RIDGE

Taneytown Rd

134

Baltimore Pike

97

15

Military Park Auto Tour

Auto Tour Stop

GETTYSBURG

0 .5 Miles

0 .75 Kilometers

N
W E
S

GETTYSBURG CAMPAIGN 1863

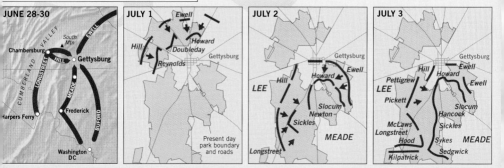

JUNE 28-30

CUMBERLAND VALLEY

South Mtn

Chambersburg

Gettysburg

EWELL

HILL

LONGSTREET

MEADE

BUFORD

Harpers Ferry

Frederick

Washington
DC

JULY 1

Ewell

Hill

Howard
Doubleday

Reynolds

Gettysburg

Present day
park boundary
and roads

JULY 2

Gettysburg

Hill

Ewell

LEE

Howard

Slocum
Newton

Sickles

MEADE

Longstreet

JULY 3

Hill

Gettysburg

Ewell

Howard

Pettigrew

LEE

Pickett

Ewell

McLaws
Longstreet
Hood

Hancock

Slocum

Sickles

Sykes

Sedgwick

MEADE

Kilpatrick

concerts, and films. The Historic Gettysburg Railroad Station, built in 1859, served as a field hospital during the Battle of Gettysburg—and then converted back to its original purpose in time to receive President Abraham Lincoln in November 1863.

Nearly 7,500 permanent residents and 2,000 students attending Gettysburg College live here, while nearly 2 million people visit each year. The 6,000-acre Gettysburg National Military Park surrounds the town on all but its west side. Trees and Civil War–era wood-frame homes line the streets, and closer to the town center are older Federal-style brick row houses with white trim.

In the town itself, centrally located Lincoln Square contains memorials to the battle and is surrounded by historic buildings with bronze plaques explaining their significance. Many of the town's houses and buildings still bear the scars of bullets and cannon shells fired during the three-day campaign. The Farnsworth House, a bed-and-breakfast on Baltimore Street, is dotted with some 100 bullet holes from the fighting.

GETTYSBURG NATIONAL MILITARY PARK   *map page 191*

The park that commemorates the Battle of Gettysburg consists mostly of rolling hills and groves of oaks and hickory. The 17-acre cemetery is inside the park, just south of town. More than 1,300 markers, memorials, and monuments lining 26 miles of paved roads throughout the park identify battle points and pay homage to soldiers and regiments from the Confederate and Union armies.

THE GETTYSBURG MUSEUM & VISITORS CENTER

The Gettysburg Museum & Visitors Center opened in 2008. Its gallery features the **Gettysburg Cyclorama,** a 26-foot-high, 360-foot-long, circular oil-on-canvas painting that depicts Pickett's Charge, the final and fateful confrontation of the Battle of Gettysburg. The French artist Paul Philippoteaux labored over the work between 1882 and 1884. Unveiled in Boston, the work, weighing three tons, wasn't brought to Gettysburg until 1913. Exhibits describe the history of this masterpiece and its conservation. *1195 Baltimore Pike; 717/334–1124.*

★GETTYSBURG NATIONAL CEMETERY

Two days after the Battle of Gettysburg, Gov. Andrew Curtin of Pennsylvania toured the battlefield, where he viewed the bodies of hundreds of young men—Union and Confederate—buried in shallow graves or decaying in the hot summer sun. By nightfall, the shaken governor had ordered the immediate purchase of

BATTLE OF GETTYSBURG

In the third year of the Civil War, after an important but costly Confederate victory at Chancellorsville, Virginia, Gen. Robert E. Lee urged the Confederate president, Jefferson Davis, to move the war north and strike at Pennsylvania. A victory there, he reasoned, could weaken the North's will to fight, raise Southern morale, and at the same time improve chances for European recognition of the Confederacy. Furthermore, Pennsylvania's farms were supporting the Union army, its factories were supplying weapons, shoes, and clothing, and its railroads were moving troops and supplies with great efficiency. Cutting the flow of supplies from Pennsylvania to Union soldiers could turn the course of the war. In June 1863, nearly 75,000 Southern troops crossed the Mason-Dixon Line, the border between Maryland and Pennsylvania.

DAYS PRECEDING THE BATTLE

The Union army had received reports of the movement but was unsure of Confederate intentions. Lee kept enough troops in Virginia to deceive the Union generals into thinking that Washington, D.C., was his objective. When the newly appointed commander of the Union Army of the Potomac, Gen. George Meade, heard reports that Confederate troops had occupied Chambers-burg, Greenwood, and York in southern Pennsylvania, he ordered 90,000 Union troops north.

Meade moved quickly. The Confederate army was spread out over the rural area around Harrisburg and was planning an assault on it. A unit of Confederate Gen. A. P. Hill's cavalry was just north of Gettysburg when they met with a division of Meade's advance cavalry, commanded by Gen. George Buford. The Confederates drove the Union forces south of Gettysburg, where they entrenched themselves along Cemetery Ridge, determined to fight until Meade's reinforcements arrived.

DAY ONE

On July 1, the Battle of Gettysburg began with Confederate troops attacking Union troops on McPherson Ridge, west of town. Though outnumbered, the Union forces managed to hold until afternoon, when they were overpowered and driven back through town. In the confusion, thousands of Union soldiers were captured before they could rally on Cemetery Hill, south of town. Long into the night, Union troops labored over their defenses while the bulk of Meade's army arrived and took positions.

DAY TWO

On July 2, battle lines were drawn up in two sweeping arcs. The main portions of

Photographs in this essay were taken during the
filming of the Civil War movie *Glory*.

both armies were nearly a mile apart on two parallel ridges: Union forces on Cemetery Ridge facing Confederate forces on Seminary Ridge to the west. Lee ordered an attack against both Union flanks. James Longstreet's thrust on the Union left broke through D. E. Sickles's advance lines at the Peach Orchard, left the wheat field strewn with dead and wounded, and destroyed the base of Little Round Top. R. S. Ewell's attack proved futile against the entrenched Union forces on East Cemetery Hill and Culp's Hill.

DAY THREE

On July 3, Lee's artillery opened a bombardment, but did little to weaken the Union center on Cemetery Ridge. The climax of the Battle of Gettysburg came when Maj. Gen. George E. Pickett led an infantry assault of 12,000 Confederate troops across the open field toward the Union center on Cemetery Ridge. Raked by artillery and rifle fire, Pickett's men reached but failed to break the Union line. In 50 minutes, 7,500 men and 5,000 horses were killed, and the attack —known as Pickett's Charge—became history.

AFTERMATH

The failure of Pickett's Charge saved the Union. More than 51,000 total casualties make Gettysburg the bloodiest battle in American history. On July 4, Lee prepared for an attack that never came. That night, in a downpour, Lee began his withdrawal to Virginia with an army that was physically and spiritually exhausted. Lee would never again attempt an offensive operation of such proportions.

Meade, though he was criticized for not immediately pursuing Lee's army, had carried the day in the battle now known as the "high-water mark" of the Confederacy. The war was to rage for two more years but would never again be fought north of the Mason-Dixon Line.

On November 19, 1863, President Abraham Lincoln delivered his Gettysburg Address as part of the dedication ceremony for the National Cemetery.

A monument in Gettysburg National Military Park.

burial ground that would be turned over to the federal government to honor those who had given their lives. Four months after the battle, an emotional President Abraham Lincoln came here to dedicate the cemetery.

Today, the Gettysburg National Cemetery is the final resting place for American veterans who served in wars from 1846 to the present day. The site is dotted with significant monuments, such as the Soldiers National Monument, placed in 1869 as a national memorial of sorrow. The figure of Liberty, holding a sword in one hand and the wreath of peace in the other, crowns the monument. Cemetery designer William Saunders arranged burial plots, each distinguished by the state from which the men served, in a semicircular pattern around the central point where this monument stands. The headstones are curved granite markers inscribed with the names and regiments of the dead, ignoring distinction between officers and enlisted men. In another part of the cemetery, near where Lincoln gave his famous address, are headstones for veterans from subsequent wars. *97 Taneytown Rd.; 717/334–1124.*

A grave marker in Gettysburg National Cemetery.

GENERAL ROBERT E. LEE HEADQUARTERS

The 18th-century stone farmhouse commandeered by Lee as his battlefield head-quarters contains exhibits of Civil War military equipment, such as uniforms belonging to officers who fought in the Battle of Gettysburg and the saddle Major General John Reynolds was sitting in when enemy gunfire threw him off his horse to his death. Also exhibited are artifacts from the Lee family, including a piano cover, eating utensils, and a family photograph. The collection includes a book signed by Confederate President Jefferson Davis. The headquarters are open from March to November. *Larsen Quality Inn, 401 Buford Ave. (Rte. 30 West); 717/334–3141.*

EISENHOWER NATIONAL HISTORIC SITE

President Eisenhower and his wife, Mamie, purchased this farm in Gettysburg in 1950. He used it as a weekend retreat during his presidency, often hosting national and world leaders. After leaving the White House in 1961, "Ike" and Mamie made the farm their primary residence. Ike died in 1969, and Mamie lived here until her death in 1979. The following year the property was opened to the public and has since expanded to include 690 acres. Exhibits trace Eisenhower's

GETTYSBURG ADDRESS

President Abraham Lincoln arrived by train from Washington, D.C., for the cemetery's dedication in 1863. There, 15,000 people gathered on Cemetery Hill for the ceremonies. After listening to a two-hour speech by former Massachusetts Senator Edward Everett, Lincoln rose to deliver his address. Although it lasted just two minutes, this dedication reaffirming the principles of democracy and assuring that no soldier had died in vain is considered as significant as the battle itself.

Four score and seven years ago our fathers brought forth on this continent a new nation, conceived in liberty and dedicated to the proposition that all men are created equal.

Now we are engaged in a great civil war, testing whether that nation or any nation so conceived and so dedicated can long endure. We are met on a great battlefield of that war. We have come to dedicate a portion of that field as final resting place for those who here gave their lives that that nation might live. It is altogether fitting and proper that we should do this.

But, in a larger sense, we cannot dedicate—we cannot consecrate—we cannot hallow—this ground. The brave men, living and dead, who struggled here have consecrated it far above our poor power to add or detract. The world will little note nor long remember what we say here, but it can never forget what they did here. It is for us, the living, rather, to be dedicated here to the unfinished work which they who fought here have thus far so nobly advanced.

It is rather for us to be here dedicated to the great task remaining before us —that from these honored dead we take increased devotion to that cause for which they gave the last full measure of devotion; that we here highly resolve that these dead shall not have died in vain; that this nation, under God, shall have a new birth of freedom; and that government of the people, by the people, for the people shall not perish from the earth.

—Abraham Lincoln, 1863

The following day, Senator Everett wrote to Lincoln: "I should be glad if I could flatter myself that I came as near to the central idea of the occasion in two hours as you did in two minutes."

life from his childhood in Abilene through his military and political careers. The house is furnished with antiques, family heirlooms, and gifts from heads of state. A self-guided tour of the grounds takes you past a putting green, rose gardens, and the guest house. A farm tour explores the Eisenhowers' cattle operation and farm machinery. Shuttle-bus service, the only way to reach the site, departs from the Gettysburg Museum & Visitors Center. *1195 Baltimore Pike; 717/338–9114.*

CHAMBERSBURG   *map page 185, B/C-5*

After the crucial victory in September 1862 at the Battle of Antietam, where General Lee's advance on Maryland was stopped, Chambersburg became an important hospital and supply center for the Union army. When 400 wounded soldiers were evacuated from battlefields to the town, residents opened up their homes to them.

The Confederate army occupied Chambersburg several times from 1861 to 1863. A month before the Battle of Gettysburg, General Lee and 65,000 troops camped in the area, and Lee and his generals held strategy sessions in the town center. This is where Lee made the fateful decision to lead his troops east, toward Gettysburg, after scouts reported that the Union army was headed in their direction. In 1864, a Confederate force under the command of General John McCausland held Chambersburg ransom and threatened to burn the city unless officials paid $100,000 in gold or $500,000 in U.S. currency. To dramatize the point, Confederate soldiers fired a cannon into the west wall of the Franklin County courthouse. No gold was offered, the general's deadline passed, and the town's buildings were set ablaze. Residents ran for refuge to the Cedar Grove Cemetery at the edge of town.

McCausland and his forces spared only a few buildings, including the **Masonic Temple** (74 South Second St.)—supposedly as a gesture of respect from Confederate brother Masons. The building, completed in 1824, is among the oldest Masonic institutions in the country. **The Old Jail** (175 East King St.), built in 1818, also survived the Great Fire and exists today as a stellar example of Georgian architecture. It claims the longest continuous use of any jail in the state, operating until 1971. Runaway slaves hid in the basement dungeons of the jail as they journeyed along the Underground Railroad. Today the Old Jail is a museum and houses the **Franklin County Historical Society–Kittochtinny** (717/264–1667), open from May to October.

Chambersburg looks very much as it did when founder Colonel Benjamin Chambers laid it out in 1788. Chambers, a Scots-Irish immigrant, chose to settle

These columns were all that remained of the Bank of Chambersburg after it was burned by Confederate soldiers. (Kittochitinny Historical Society)

in the area knowing the Conococheague Creek could provide power for his gristmill and sawmill. Route 30 West, off Exit 6 of I–81, takes you through the town square, past budget hotels and fast-food chains, and finally through tree-lined residential neighborhoods made up of tidy 20th-century homes fronted by manicured lawns. The business district begins several blocks beyond a large hospital complex and continues to the town square, beyond the intersection of routes 30 and 11.

In the square is a four-tier, cast-iron fountain created in 1878 as a monument to local Union soldiers who died in the Civil War. In front of the fountain, a full-size sculpture of a Union soldier guards against the return of southern invaders. The town's loveliest residential architecture—restored Civil War–era homes built of local gray limestone and wood—can be seen along Philadelphia Avenue off Route 11 North.

MERCERSBURG *map page 185, B-6*

The seeds of the Battle of Gettysburg were sown in 1862 with a series of Confederate cavalry raids in the Cumberland Valley. The citizens of Mercersburg supported the Union cause, and the Confederate soldiers made it a regular target. During the first Chambersburg raid, General J.E.B. Stuart and his staff took over the side porch of the **Steiger family house** (120 North Main St.) as temporary headquarters. They avoided actually entering the house because the Steiger children had German measles. When the tide turned against the Confederacy in 1863, wounded rebel soldiers were captured and placed in makeshift hospitals throughout Mercersburg. Many of the soldiers are interred in the local cemetery. Much less conspicuous than the soldiers' cemetery at Gettysburg is the **Zion Union Cemetery,** often referred to as the Black Cemetery, at the end of Bennet Avenue. Hundreds of United States Colored Troops are buried here, including members of the 54 Massachusetts, made famous in the 1990 film *Glory.*

Acres of lush farmland and dairy pastures extend in every direction from Mercersburg. Route 16 runs east–west directly through the small downtown, a four-block area with a small green square bordered by large-limbed oaks.

Most people make the trip here to tour the **Mercersburg Academy,** an exclusive prep school for 440 boarding and day students. The stately buildings stand on 300 acres of grassy knolls. Ralph Adams Cram, a leading proponent of neo-gothic ecclesiastical architecture, designed the school's distinctive chapel, dedicated in 1927. President James Buchanan was born in a log cabin that sits on the campus, and the late actor Jimmy Stewart is among the school's illustrious alumni. *300 East Seminary St.; 717/328–6173.*

BEDFORD COUNTY BRIDGES AND TRAILS *map page 185, A-5*

Forty miles northwest of Mercersburg is a region of forested hills and valleys known especially for its covered bridges. Craftsmen working almost entirely by hand built these 14 bridges about 100 years ago. They strived to create structures capable of withstanding the rain, snow, and hard use of travelers. The **Bedford County Visitors Bureau** (141 South Juliana St., Bedford; 814/623–1771) provides maps of the bridge region. You can cross them by car, but bicycling is far more fun. **Grouseland Tours** (467 Robinsonville Rd., Clearville; 814/784–5000) arranges tours and rents bikes.

More than 40 log homes and shops from all over Pennsylvania were transported to Old Bedford Village, a simulation of a pioneer-era settlement.

Old Bedford Village is a living-history village with log cabins that replicates a colonial-era settlement. A gun shop, a farmhouse, a one-room schoolhouse, and a broom shop are among the several dozen buildings that simulate life in 18th- and 19th-century Pennsylvania. The village also hosts military reenactments, colonial craft demonstrations, and holiday festivals. It's open Memorial Day through Labor Day. *220 Sawblade Rd., Bedford; 814/623–1156.*

ALTOONA AND SURROUNDINGS *map page 185, A-3*

Altoona, the largest town in Blair County and an old-time railroad center, lies at the base of the Allegheny Ridge. In 1850, it was a farm community next to an iron plant, but then the Pennsylvania Railroad made Altoona the site of its maintenance facility. At its peak, the workforce reached 17,000, and railroad life so dominated the city that train schedules governed even tasks as mundane as laundering clothes. Monday was the citywide day for hanging garments on backyard lines because trains were inside maintenance buildings instead of spewing thick clouds of coal dust.

As diesel fuel replaced the less-efficient coal-powered steam systems, the maintenance operation became obsolete and Altoona's economy slumped. Then, during the 1990s, the Consolidated Rail Corporation (Conrail), a descendant of the Pennsylvania Railroad, retrofitted the old steam-engine repair complex to accommodate diesel locomotives. Today, more tons of freight travel the Main Line rails through Altoona than at any time in the city's history. With the increased traffic, Altoona has experienced a renaissance. New residential and retail developments are helping create a vibrant downtown once again, with pedestrian-friendly storefronts, live theater, and upscale dining options.

Altoona's railroad boom years are captured in the **Altoona Railroaders Memorial Museum.** This is a memorial not to corporate tycoons but to the laborers who laid the track, repaired the cars, and worked on the lines. The museum tells the social and cultural story of these people through audio and video narratives. Exhibits recreate Altoona neighborhoods like Dutch Hill and Little Italy. Among the many residents you meet is a newsboy (a holograph of one, anyway) who recalls old Altoona. The building is across from the Amtrak station. Each October, the museum organizes excursions on historic trains to local towns in the region as part of its Railfest celebration. *1300 Ninth Ave.; 814/946–0834.*

Fishermen try their luck next to a covered bridge.

Seventeen miles northeast of Altoona is the village of **Tyrone,** whose lovely Victorian homes belonged to yesteryear's railway executives. The adjacent town of **Sinking Valley** is home to **Fort Roberdeau** (From Rte. 220/I–99S, take the Bellwood Exit; 814/946–0048), built in 1778 to protect lead mines in the region from attacks by various Native American tribes. Today, visitors can see how soldiers lived in the barracks set up inside the fort. Fort Roberdeau is on 45 acres of fields and woods, with nature trails and picnic facilities. It's open May through October.

HORSESHOE CURVE   map page 185, A-3

The Allegheny Ridge, which rises steeply 1,200 feet above Altoona and Hollidaysburg, long presented a major barrier to east–west traffic. Pennsylvania Railroad chief J. Edgar Thompson and engineer Herman Haupt devised a dramatic railroad curve to skirt this obstacle. The plan called for a ravine to be filled between one of the main mountain ridges and a bed to be carved out of the mountainside. About 450 Irish immigrants worked for three years digging and sculpting the new grade. After Horseshoe Curve was completed in 1854, travel time between Philadelphia and Pittsburgh shrank from four days to just 15 hours. You can view this marvelous expanse of track just outside Altoona in the foothills of the Alleghany Mountain Range. The curve was designated as a National Historic Landmark in 1966 and is now listed on the National Register of Historic Places. Ride the funicular from the visitors center up to the train tracks, or if you prefer a physical challenge, climb the 194 landscaped steps to the top.

During World War II, Horseshoe Curve was considered so strategically important that the Nazis targeted it for attack. The saboteurs landed by U-boat on the East Coast, but were almost immediately apprehended in a bar. *Horseshoe Curve Rd., about 5 miles northwest of Altoona; 814/946–0834.*

ALLEGHENY PORTAGE RAILROAD HISTORIC SITE
map page 185, A-4

From 1834 to 1854 the Portage Railroad operated as a 36.5-mile link in the Main Line canal system running between the Delaware and Ohio rivers. Here, passengers, cargo, and canal boats were transported over the summit of Allegheny Mountain between Hollidaysburg and Johnstown—enabling continuous barge traffic between the Ohio and the Susquehanna rivers. A series of stair-step locks connected by track hauled barges from one platform to another up the mountain and then down the other side. This system of inclined planes and a 900-foot tunnel carved through solid rock by Welsh coalminers was so treacherous it injured

A train winds around the famous Horseshoe Curve.

A canal boat is pulled up an incline on the Allegheny Portage Railroad.
(Pennsylvania Historical and Museum Commission)

travelers on a weekly basis. The trip took five days Still, for 20 years it was the fastest way to venture through this jagged terrain. By 1854, with the more practical Horseshoe Curve and Gallitzin Tunnels in operation, the Portage Railroad became obsolete. On view at the site are models of the horses and vehicles used to operate the system. *U.S. 22, 12 miles west of Altoona; 814/886–6150.*

BLACK MOSHANNON STATE PARK   *map page 185, B-2*

Once the site of a stagecoach way station, this park lies on the Allegheny Plateau in Centre County, in the middle of Moshannon State Forest and about 30 miles northeast of Altoona. Among the park's features is a bog that serves as habitat for rare wildlife, as well as for cranberries and blueberries. Sedges, leatherleaf shrubs, and viburnum are among the species that thrive in this acidic body of water. During the 1800s, lumberjacks harvested most of the area's white pine and hemlock trees. During the Great Depression, the Civilian Conservation Corps built the park. Today, Black Moshannon is vibrant with a well-planned network of trails. Lodgings include 13 cabins that can be charitably described as "rustic." *Moshannon State Forest, Rte. 504 and Julian Pike; 814/342–5960.*

STATE COLLEGE   *map page 185, B-2*

In 1855, James Irwin, a Union general and cofounder of Centre Furnace Works, donated 200 acres of woodland as the site for an agricultural technology school for central Pennsylvania farmers. Today, his modest land grant is known as Penn State University. State College performs double-duty as university town and flagship municipality of the region commonly referred to as Happy Valley.

Amid a sea of cornfields and rolling hills, State College is a hub for arts and culture. Like most college towns, the streets running through campus are lined with cafés, bookshops, pubs, and record stores. On fall weekends, when the nationally ranked Nittany Lions football team plays at home, returning alumni and fans from across Pennsylvania overwhelm the downtown area. *Rolling Stone Magazine* recently bestowed an "honorable mention" on State College's music scene, ranking it among the best in the country.

Each July the five-day **Central Pennsylvania Festival of the Arts** (University Park Campus; 814/237–3682) takes over State College streets. Artists from across the country set up booths displaying their original paintings, jewelry, blown glass, and other handmade artwork. Live performances and ethnic food booths keep the 125,000 or so visitors entertained and well fed.

Lemon Inn on the Portage Railroad (ca. 1850), by George Storm. (State Museum of Pennsylvania)

PENN STATE UNIVERSITY   *map page 185, B-2*

Stroll from the point where town meets gown—the corner of East College Avenue and South Allen Street—along the main walkway across campus to the university libraries, the highest point on campus. On the way, near Schwab Auditorium, you'll pass **Old Main** (Pollock Rd.; 814/231–1400), the 1862 building where top administrators have their offices. Noted muralist Henry Varnum Poor painted the frescoes in the grand entrance foyer between 1939 and 1949. They depict the champions of the federal Land Grant Act that created Penn State, and salute the university's contributions to engineering, mining, and agriculture. *207 Mitchell Blvd.; 814/865–5403.*

The extensive collection of the **Palmer Museum of Art** includes 8th-century pottery from Greece, 17th-century decorative arts from Europe, 19th-century portraiture, and contemporary works on paper by Donald Judd, Louise Nevelson, Henry Moore, Sol LeWitt, and Willem de Kooning. *Curtin Rd., Penn State University campus; 814/865–7672.*

Penn State football games draw massive crowds of die-hard fans.

STATE COLLEGE SNACKS

It's easy to gain the freshman 15 at State College. Decades after graduation, alums continue to reminisce about the "grilled stickies," decadent cinnamon buns served hot off the griddle since 1929 at **Ye Old College Diner** (126 W. College Ave.; 814/238–5590). **The Penn State University Creamery** (Corner of Bigler and Curtain Rds.) sells ice cream, sherbet, and cheese—all churned out by students enrolled in the College of Agricultural Sciences. Ben Cohen and Jerry Greenfield, notorious for Ben & Jerry's brand ice cream, are 1978 alumni of the creamery's correspondence course in ice cream–making. Finally, late night partiers are willing to stand in line for **Canyon Pizza** (260 E. Beaver Ave.), which serves massive slices for just a buck fifty.

BOALSBURG   *map page 185, C-2*

Boalsburg, a 10-minute drive east from State College, was settled by Scots-Irish immigrants in the early 1800s. Strolling down Main Street here is like stepping from a time machine into 1830s America. Nineteenth-century homes and shops selling antiques line the clean, tree-shaded streets.

Memorial Day is said to have begun at **Boalsburg Cemetery** in October 1864, when Emma Hunter, Sophie Keller, and Elizabeth Meyers decorated the graves of all the war dead in the cemetery. The tradition was quickly adopted by the townspeople. A life-size bronze statue at the cemetery honors the three women. Gen. John Logan officially established Memorial Day in 1868, and today 25,000 people or more attend ceremonies here. *U.S. Business Rte. 322, across from Pennsylvania Military Museum.*

The **Boal Mansion Museum and Columbus Chapel** are the town's most important sights. Captain David Boal, the Irishman who founded Boalsburg and encouraged further Scots-Irish settlement before leaving to fight in the Revolutionary War, began building the mansion in 1789. Nine generations of Boals made it their home. The furniture and keepsakes on display reflect their colorful personalities. A family descendant and owner of the museum currently resides in the house.

One of the Boal wives was the niece of a direct descendant of Christopher Columbus. Because her aunt and uncle died childless, she inherited significant relics from the chapel at Columbus Castle in Asturias, Spain. They include a desk studded with gilt cockleshells, 16th-century Renaissance paintings, and a silver reliquary containing pieces of what is purported to be the True Cross. *163 Boal Estate Dr., parallel to U.S. Business Rte. 322; 814/466–6210.*

Army officers from Pennsylvania who served in the south of France at the end of World War I created the **Pennsylvania Military Museum.** One of the soldiers was Col. Theodore Boal, a great-great-grandson of Boalsburg's founder. Each year he organized a group to place memorial plaques on a stone wall bordering Spring Creek to honor those who "gave their lives in defense of freedom." The state purchased this shrine of the 28th Division in 1931 and transformed it into the museum.

While the museum explores the role Pennsylvanians have played throughout military history, a highlight of a visit here is a tour through a replica of a World War I battlefield trench, with the re-created sounds and light flashes of rifles and artillery. The museum also displays uniforms, weapons, and medals from the Revolutionary and Civil wars. *U.S. Business Rte. 322; 814/466–6263.*

BELLEFONTE   *map page 185, C-2*

Bellefonte, "Central Pennsylvania's Victorian Secret," is about 10 miles northeast of State College. While many towns bulldozed their original architecture under the guise of urban renewal, Bellefonte's Victorian homes, and municipal, commercial, and industrial buildings, dodged the wrecking ball. The borough's historic district has some 400 buildings and houses in architectural styles including Italianate, Second Empire, Romanesque, and Queen Anne. Naturally, it's on the National Register of Historic Places.

Bellefonte was founded in the late 18th century. Surveyors poking around the area in the 1770s found an enormous natural spring that generates, according to current estimates, 11.5 million gallons of water a day. In 1785, William Lamb saw the value of such a resource and purchased 750 acres around the spring. Settlers flocked to the area, which became known as Spring Creek.

The name didn't stick. When the French statesman Charles-Maurice de Talleyrand visited the area in 1795 and sampled the water, he reputedly exclaimed *"Oh, belle fontaine!"* Impressed by the Frenchman's elocution, Bellefonte's citizens built a creekside park in his honor. In a nod to French taste, Talleyrand Park has a sculpture park and a gazebo.

The **Bellefonte Historical Railroad Society** has on display a two-car diesel train that once snaked through central Pennsylvania. The famous Edwin G. Budd Company of Philadelphia built these stainless steel cars in 1953 and 1962 for the New Haven and Reading railroads, respectively. The society also operates special train excursions when fall foliage is at its most brilliant. During the Christmas season, join the Santa Run in a meticulously restored historic train decorated for the holidays. Bundled under blankets, passengers enjoy a one-hour round-trip ride to Milesburg entertained by Christmas music and holiday stories. *320 West High St.; 814/355–2917.*

BALD EAGLE STATE FOREST   *map page 185, C-1*

In Bald Eagle State Forest (not to be confused with Bald Eagle State Park, north of Bellefonte), the leaves of tall oaks form dramatic canopies that allow only slivers of light to reach the ground.

One section of the Mid-State Trail descends along the north flank of Thick Mountain, crosses Woodward Gap Road, and leads to a natural spring. Part of the hike follows an abandoned Penn Central Railroad grade and trestle that goes under Paddy Mountain by way of a 280-foot-long tunnel. Maps are available at the R. B. Winter State Park Visitors Center, where trails begin and end. *Off Rte. 150, Howard; 814/625–2775.*

POE VALLEY STATE PARK   *map page 185, C-2*

A 9.6-mile leg of the Mid-State Trail begins in Poe Valley State Park and leads you to spectacular views of a hollow flanked by tall oaks. From the park's concession stand, look for the blue-blaze path. *Poe Valley, off Rte. 322; 814/349–2460.*

CAVES   *map page 185, C-2*

Caves in Pennsylvania formed as far back as 20 million years ago, typically as a result of various chemical reactions, erosion caused by water, tectonic forces, microorganisms, pressure, and atmospheric influences. Spelunking, or caving, is a fascinating journey back to prehistoric times. Most caves are closed to the public,

Autumn colors brighten a Boalsburg street.

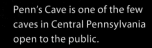

Penn's Cave is one of the few caves in Central Pennsylvania open to the public.

SUGAR VALLEY LOOP DRIVE
map page 185, C-2

North of Woodward is a stretch of low-lying land named for its sugar maple trees. This beautiful canoe-shaped valley, about 20 miles long and two miles wide, is surrounded by sandstone mountains. In rural Sugar Valley, Amish are frequently spotted in their horse-drawn buggies. Drivers or fit bicyclists can take a 25-mile-long ride that leads past a 19th-century gristmill, a covered bridge, a schoolhouse, old churches, and graveyards.

Take I–80 Exit 27, and head south on State Road 477 toward Loganton. After Loganton, turn right on Rte. 880 to Carroll-Tylersville Rd.

but two of the biggest can be toured. Wear comfortable shoes and a jacket, as the temperature in these caverns hovers at about 50 degrees year-round.

Immense springs flow into ★**Penn's Cave,** making it possible to coast through the one-mile tour entirely by boat. The cave was formed by a shallow sea that existed millions of years ago. In 1773 a relative of Edgar Allan Poe bought the cave, and the dark interior would seem a likely setting for one of his horror stories. Owners Jesse and Samuel Long opened the cave to the public in 1885, and its narrow limestone passages still lead visitors through the underground world of slowly elongating stalactites (ceiling limestone formations) and stalagmites (those anchored to the floor). *222 Penns Cave Rd., Centre Hall; 814/364–1664.*

Woodward Cave, 22 miles west of Penn's Cave, was also filled with water until 1923. That's when engineers turned the creek flow away from the cave and removed tons of clay and river sediment, revealing hundreds of Native American drawings on cave walls and artifacts secreted away in unexplored spaces. Passageways lead to chambers such as the Ballroom, once actually used for square dances and banquets. Another space contains a 50-ton stalagmite, estimated to be two million years old. Tours are given April through October. *Rte. 45, 22 miles east of State College; 814/349–9800.*

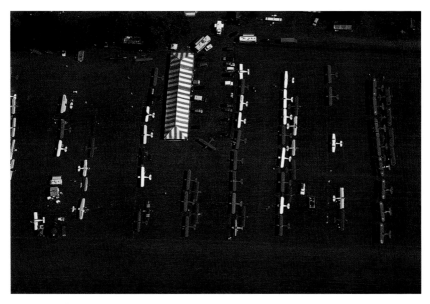

A reunion of Piper Cub pilots, seen from the air.

LOCK HAVEN   *map page 185, C-1*

On the banks of the western branch of the Susquehanna River, 20 miles west of Williamsport, sits the small city of Lock Haven. Logging operations during the late 1830s made millionaires out of many native sons in small communities like this one. Stroll down the Water Street block known as Mansion Row to see how the swell folks lived. While some homes have fallen into disrepair, others have been restored and are open for tours.

Aviation aficionados will enjoy Lock Haven's **Piper Aviation Museum.** An oil prospector and businessman, William T. Piper teamed up with aeronautics engineer Walter Jamouneau in 1937 to build the first assembly-line-produced private airplane. For 47 years the company produced the J3, or "Piper Cub," a small aircraft for leisure flying. Mr. Piper died in 1970 at the age of 89, while still living in Lock Haven. The sole plant operating today, in Vero Beach, Florida, is called the New Piper Aircraft Corporation. This museum, established in 1985, has prototype aircraft, photographs, films, artifacts, and memorabilia relating to the development of the Piper Cub and aircraft it inspired. *William T. Piper Memorial Airport, Hangar One, 1 Piper Way; 570/748–2586 or 570/748–8283.*

WILLIAMSPORT *map page 185, D-1*

Northeast of Lock Haven on U.S. 220 is Williamsport, the seat of Lycoming County. The town's location along the Susquehanna River's scenic western

Millionaires' Row mansion.

A game in progress at the Howard J. Lamade Little League Baseball Stadium.

branch, in the shadow of the Allegheny Mountains, makes it worth a visit. In the 1880s, when it was the center of the timber industry, Williamsport had the most millionaires per capita of any place in the world. The local high school marching band is The Millionaires, and an opulent stretch of mansions along West Fourth Street remains as evidence of Williamsport's flush days. The **Lycoming County Historical Society** (570/326–3326) offers tours of some of these historic homes, including the fanciful **E. A. Rowley House** (707 West Fourth St.), the first mansion on the street to have electric lights and a dumbwaiter. Other noteworthy residences include the **Eutermarks-Harrar House** (915 West Fourth St.), an Italianate design, and the **Emery House** (835 West Fourth St.), an impressive example of the Richardson Romanesque style.

Exhibits at the **Thomas T. Taber Museum** trace local history from its Native American roots to the present. Highlights include pottery and stone tools of the Woodland Indians, period rooms filled with Victorian furniture, paintings by 19th-century still-life painter (and 10-year Williamsport resident) Severin Roesen, and a 300-piece toy train collection. *Fourth and Maynard Sts.; 570/326–3326.*

Williamsport is also famous for the Little League Baseball World Series, played here each year at Howard J. Lamade Stadium in late August. (Little League was born here in 1939.) Adjacent to the stadium is the **Little League Baseball Museum,** which displays photographs of players and teams, as well as other memorabilia. *Howard J. Lamade Stadium, Rte. 15, South Williamsport; 570/326–3607.*

GETTING AROUND

Interstate 76, the Pennsylvania Turnpike, runs through Harrisburg and then moves south through Bedford County, Shanksville, and Laurel Hill. Route 81, south from Harrisburg, is the most direct route to Chambersburg and provides easy access to Shippensburg, Mercersburg, and Waynesboro. Route 15 south from Harrisburg is the most direct route to Gettysburg. Central Pennsylvania's interior is crisscrossed by back roads that wind through hilly woodlands and small towns, and past family farms with barns made of fieldstone and logs. U.S. Route 322 cuts through the central part of the state, skirting Boalsburg, State College, and Bald Eagle Mountain, before connecting with U.S. 220, which heads south to Altoona.

FAVORITE PLACES TO EAT

Dobbin House. 89 Steinwehr Ave., Gettysburg; 717/334–2100. $$$

Homemade candles cast a romantic glow on the tables, setting the scene for a meal à la Valentines Day. After you've made your selection, servers dressed in Colonial garb bring in plates of duck, prime rib, and pork loin. The Dobbin House has gained a reputation for its authentic historic atmosphere and traditional menu.

Duffy's Tavern. 113 E. Main St., Boalsburg; 814/466–6241. $–$$

Just five minutes from the Penn State campus, the formal dining room in this historic stone tavern promises a delicious twist on classic dishes. The seafood crepe is stuffed with fresh shellfish and a creamy Mornay sauce. At the pub, try the Boalsburger—a feast for carnivores— with ham, cheese, and mushrooms stacked on top of chopped sirloin.

Mamie's. 25 Carlisle St., Gettysburg; 717/337–8200. $

This café inside the Majestic Theater is an ideal lunch spot, with an emphasis on sal ads, soup, and sandwiches. Named for First Lady Mamie Eisenhower, the artful interior design—done in monochromatic shades of turquoise—is an homage to the 1950s.

Slick Ivy's Stone Restaurant. 8785 William Penn Rd., Osterburg; 814/276–3131. $

Anyone who believes McDonald's idea to stack bacon on a pancake is an original recipe has clearly never eaten at Slick Ivy's. Since 1978, the joint has been serving roast turkey and chicken over waffles, accompanied by stuffing and gravy. Wash it all down with a slice of flakey bumbleberry (mixed-berry) pie. Slick Ivy's is open only April through December.

Sophia. 403 Walnut St., Harrisburg; 717/236–3980. $$$

The walls of this intimate restaurant are covered in murals depicting the tranquil waters of the Mediterranean. And the simple southern Italian entrées, influenced by the chef's childhood in Naples, are equally pleasing. During warm weather months, dine on the patio. BYOB.

FAVORITE PLACES TO STAY

Aikens Cabins at Bear Meadows.
400 Bear Meadows Rd., Boalsburg;
814/466–9299. $$

*Nestled in a quiet wooded setting, adjacent
to the Rothrock State Forest and minutes
from State College, these cabins are a
unique alternative to a chain hotel. Each
cabin has a kitchen and living room.*

Best Western-Gettysburg Hotel.
1 Lincoln Sq.; 717/337–2000. $$–$$$

*Built in 1797, this beautifully restored
hotel in the heart of Gettysburg's historic
district strikes the perfect balance between
historic vibe and modern comforts. Suites
have gas fireplaces and Jacuzzi tubs.*

The Farnsworth House.
401 Baltimore St., Gettybsurg;
717/334–8838. $

*This bed-and-breakfast dedicated to
soldiers who fought on both sides of
the Civil War is far more comfortable
than their trenches. Curl up in a four-
poster bed in one of the supposedly
haunted rooms and awake to the
smells of a full country breakfast.*

**The Peter Herdic House & Peter
Herdic Inn.** 411 W. Fourth St.,
Williamsport; 570/326–0411. $$

*These two lovingly restored Victorian
mansions sit on Williamsport's historic
Millionaires' Row. Two sisters and their
mother run this bed-and-breakfast,
where the Victorian rooms have
authentic touches like marble-topped
dressers and original gold wallpaper.*

Ramada Inn-Altoona.
Rte. 220, Plank Rd. Exit, Altoona;
814/946–1631. $

*This affordable, pet-friendly hotel offers
comfortable and tastefully decorated
rooms. Take advantage of the free
Internet access and complimentary
breakfast buffet on weekday mornings.
After a long day of sightseeing,
splash around in the indoor pool.*

PITTSBURGH
S T E E L   C I T Y

Pittsburgh was founded at the point where the Allegheny and Monongahela rivers converge to form the mammoth Ohio River. The two rivers unite at Point State Park, a spacious green at the tip of a bustling area known as the Golden Triangle. Synonymous with downtown Pittsburgh, the area is filled with fine restaurants, shops, and historic landmarks. Beyond the buildings, a ring of forested hills encircles the city.

Off Pittsburgh's North Side, a weathered steel bridge reaches across the Alleghany River to a strip of land formerly called Herr's Island, renamed Washington's Landing. Well-manicured running and biking trails line both shores, but few of the joggers and cyclists on the paths know that before the island was a park it was the site of a meatpacking plant whose odors, according to a Pittsburgh resident "were foul enough to make a fellow just about swear off breathing." In the late 1980s, Washington's Landing underwent a dramatic transformation, during which contaminants leftover from the old plant were cleaned up and the land developed to include residential and commercial real estate, in addition to the park. Now Washington's Landing and its old pedestrian bridge stand as symbols of a city that has scraped off the rust of its industrial past, cleansed its three rivers, and built up its skyline, in the process becoming one of the country's most livable cities.

HISTORY

BRITISH AND FRENCH FIGHT FOR CONTROL

By 1750, the French recognized that control of the land at the confluence of the Monongahela and Allegheny rivers was the key to the defense of an important inland trade route linking France's colonies in Canada with New Orleans on the Gulf of Mexico. The Ohio River, created by that confluence, led to the Mississippi River and directly to New Orleans.

The British also recognized the area's strategic importance and sent George Washington, then a 21-year-old major in Virginia's colonial militia, north with some soldiers. He carried with him a letter from Virginia's Ohio Company, a group of businessmen granted a British charter for 500,000 acres of land in the Ohio Valley, protesting French plans to build forts in the area. "I spent some time

Pittsburgh's skyline reveals a patchwork of architectural styles, a reflection of a city on the move.

George Washington raises his hat as the British flag is hoisted over Fort Duquesne in 1758. (The Granger Collection, New York)

in viewing the rivers and the land at the Fork, which I think extremely well situated for a Fort," he wrote in his journal in 1753.

The French officer who commanded Fort Le Boeuf, on French Creek to the north, wined and dined Washington but replied that the French were in western Pennsylvania to stay. The exchange was a polite preview of the bloody confrontation to come—the French and Indian War.

On this first trip through western Pennsylvania, Washington nearly drowned in the Allegheny River. His version of the story, told to dinner companions in his years as president, was that he saved himself from the river and also fought off an Indian attack. The version offered by a companion on the trip, missionary Christopher Gist, was that Washington fell in and Gist was forced to dive in, save him from drowning, and haul him to the island now known as Washington's Landing.

Heeding Washington's advice, British forces were dispatched to the area to build a fort and establish a presence. The French, better manned and supplied, surrounded the fort and forced the British out. They then set about building Fort Duquesne, a larger defense post that gave them command of all points of entry. In 1758, with their naval blockades proving highly effective against the French, the British attacked Fort Duquesne. The French burned it to the ground rather than see it overrun.

The British rebuilt the fort and named it for their prime minister, William Pitt, who had taken over management of the French and Indian War in 1757 and is largely credited with Britain's ultimate success.

PITTSBURGH AND THE REVOLUTION

During the American Revolution, colonial governor of Virginia John Murray, the fourth earl of Dunmore, took over the fort and rebuilt it. Virginia and Pennsylvania, working together in support of the Revolution, used the fort to host conferences with Native Americans, ultimately achieving a tenuous neutrality between the Continental government and local Native American nations. In 1777, the Continental Congress appointed Gen. Edward Hand to take control of Fort Pitt. Hand made it the Western District headquarters of the Continental Army. The first peace treaty the United States signed with Native Americans was negotiated at Fort Pitt on September 17, 1778.

In the fall of 1776, the first of many Ohio Valley volunteers joined George Washington's army to fight in the Revolutionary War. As a reward to veterans, one of the first official acts by Pennsylvania lawmakers was to offer discounted land about a mile north of the fort and the confluence of the Allegheny and Monongahela rivers. By 1786, the area had a fledgling settlement and its own newspaper, the ancestor of the largest newspaper in the city today, the *Pittsburgh Post-Gazette.*

If cheap land lured settlers to the area, rivers provided Pittsburgh with the means to grow and prosper. The nation's first steamboat, the *New Orleans,* was built in 1811 on a riverbank near what is now Try Street. The popularity of steamboat travel, combined with the efficiency of barge transportation, made Pittsburgh a premier inland port. During the War of 1812, the city's location facilitated timely transport of military supplies

The *New Orleans* was launched in Pittsburgh in 1811. (Historical Society of Western Pennsylvania)

Emma Gibson's *View of the City of Pittsburgh in 1817.*
(Historical Society of Western Pennsylvania)

and was key to America's victory in that conflict. After the war, the city's economic life and the quality of the environment would change forever as Pittsburgh became a major manufacturing center.

INDUSTRY AND IMMIGRANTS

By 1816, Pittsburgh and its 10,000 citizens were thriving. Word of job opportunities spread literally around the world, and soon immigrants were arriving in droves to work in glass and other manufacturing industries, and to build the city's bridges and roads. Housing for workers sprang up in the shadow of most factories and mills, usually in ethnic enclaves. In 1852, when the first rail line in the region was completed, cutting in half the four-day journey between Pittsburgh and Philadelphia, many immigrants moved to neighborhoods along the tracks.

In the years following the Civil War, Pittsburgh became a magnet for the industrial revolution's most successful magnates. Andrew Carnegie created a steel empire; Henry Clay Frick produced the coke (processed coal) that fired the blast furnaces in the steel foundries; Alfred E. Hunt and five partners started what later became the Alcoa aluminum company; Henry J. Heinz took processed foods to a new level; and George Westinghouse invented that watershed gadget, the air brake.

Pittsburgh, with its abundant low-cost labor, water for processing and transportation, and nearby coal mines, became a stronghold of the steel refining and manufacturing industries. Unfortunately, however, as blast furnaces along the rivers multiplied, a thick haze that would last more than a century settled over the city. When mills were chugging along at full capacity, from the late 1910s through the 1940s, it was common practice for business executives to go home on their lunch hours to change their white shirts, which had turned gray during the morning from the coke ash in the air.

Pittsburgh industrialists controlled their labor forces as they saw fit and working conditions, according to historical accounts, were horrific. Employers paid

The Bessemer converter revolutionized steel production so dramatically that a factory whose output had measured in tens of tons began producing in the thousands of tons. (Library of Congress)

A pall of smoke from steel factories hangs over Pittsburgh in this 1903 stereograph. (Library of Congress)

workers barely enough to live on and made no provisions for time off, health care, disability payments, or compensation for work-related accidents. In Pittsburgh, the gap between rich and poor was a yawning chasm with few opportunities for mill workers to move up.

Pioneering unions organized to help workers, but their leaders underestimated the ruthlessness and determination of businessmen who fought unions using every tactic available. In 1877, a strike by conductors and porters protesting a wage reduction turned violent and 25 people were killed. The most famous union-versus-management battle came 15 years later when 3,000 workers at Andrew Carnegie's Homestead Steel Mill walked off their jobs to fight management's attempt to lower wages by 22 percent and to break the union. Carnegie's chief executive at the mill, Henry Clay Frick, pitted a force of armed guards from the private Pinkerton security agency against the strikers. By the time the battled ended, nine strikers and three Pinkertons had died in the confrontation.

The intervention of the National Guard in the conflict played right into Frick's strategy of depicting the strikers as lawless thugs, and shut down the largest union

PITTSBURGH NOTABLES

Whether by birth or circumstance, those who have called Pittsburgh home recognize its nurturing character, especially in close-knit neighborhoods like Polish Hill and the Serbian South Side. Although many high-tech industries have moved into the city, working-class blood still pulses in Pittsburgh's veins, and its ethnic enclaves provide daily reminders of the immigrant backs and brawn that made this city work. Although Pittsburgh is home to prestigious educational and arts institutions and counts philanthropists, research scientists, lawyers, and other professionals among its population, the town's blue-collar image lingers. Despite media portrayals and preconceived notions about Pittsburgh, just 23 percent of the city's job base is comprised of blue-collar occupations, according to government statistics. These famous people are associated with Pittsburgh:

ACTORS
Jeff Goldblum, F. Murray Abraham, Sharon Stone, Shirley Jones, Michael Keaton

ARTISTS
Mary Cassatt, Andy Warhol, Philip Pearlstein

AUTHORS
George S. Kaufman, Annie Dillard, Rachel Carson, August Wilson

BASEBALL PLAYERS
Bill Mazeroski, Roberto Clemente

COMPOSERS
Stephen Foster, Henry Mancini, Samuel Barber

CHILDREN'S-SHOW HOST
Fred "Mister" Rogers

DANCERS
Martha Graham, Gene Kelly, Paul Taylor

ENTREPRENEURS
Andrew Carnegie, Henry Clay Frick, Henry J. Heinz

INVENTOR
George Westinghouse

MUSICIANS
Erroll Garner, Billy Strayhorn, Earl "Fatha" Hines, George Benson

QUARTERBACKS
Johnny Unitas, Joe Montana, Dan Marino

SINGERS
Lena Horne, Patty LuPone, Christina Aguilera

In the 1950s, J&L Steel, concerned about the increased use of aluminum and plastic, ran advertising campaigns showing happy consumers glowing with pride over their steel products. (National Museum of American History)

in the nation at the time—the Amalgamated Association. Twenty years would pass before organized labor would reemerge as a strong voice for workers.

RUST BELT REALITIES AND MODERN RENEWAL

For nearly 150 years, Pittsburgh's scenic splendor was buried under the haze of mill smoke, and its rivers ran with industrial waste. But Mayor David Lawrence began an organized effort to clean up the city when he took office in 1945. His administration severely restricted the use of coal. Railroad engines were switched to diesel; coal-burning furnaces, the standard heating method for most Pittsburgh homes, were outlawed. As the post–World War II era progressed, declining steel production led to population loss in southwestern Pennsylvania. Between 1975 and 1990, nearly 800,000 residents moved out of the area. The mills and their supporting industries withered in the face of competition from factories in countries like China, Japan, Russia, and Eastern European nations, which had lower labor costs and often more efficient production techniques.

Many riverside mill towns near Pittsburgh still haven't recovered from the loss of steel-related jobs. Pittsburgh's economy has survived, however, with the growth of the high-tech, health care, and medical research industries, financial management, banking, and some light manufacturing. Under the leadership of Mayor Richard Caliguiri in the late 1970s and '80s, the city began transforming itself economically and aesthetically. Caliguiri is credited with bringing a spirit of coop-

A BEAUTIFUL THREE DECADES

From 1968 to 2001, the late Fred Rogers hosted the PBS kids' show *Mister Rogers' Neighborhood,* produced in Pittsburgh. Rogers, famous for his cardigan sweaters and mild manner, was such a legend here that his picture appeared on billboards and posters, his opinions were sought out by local newspapers, and area baseball teams asked him to throw out the first ball of the season.

Rogers would have been revered in any town, but he was especially loved in Pittsburgh, a city whose close-knit and friendly neighborhoods served as inspiration for the nurturing society at the heart of the show. Recurring characters like friendly Lady Aberlin, Handyman Negri, Mr. McFeely, and Police Officer Clemmons reflect a sense of community and small-town know-how that are as much a reality of everyday Pittsburgh as the show's "neighborhood trolley," corner bakery, and local library. "Pittsburgh has distinct and unique neighborhoods, and so does the show," said Rogers, who was born in 1928 in Latrobe, 30 miles east of Pittsburgh.

Mister Rogers' Neighborhood is among the longest-running programs in PBS history. And though the show stopped production in 2001, Rogers didn't hang up his cardigan. In 2002, he received the Medal of Freedom from President Bush and a star on the Hollywood Walk of Fame. Rogers died in February 2003.

Children's TV is all about love for Fred Rogers. (Family Communications, Inc.)

eration and civility to the mayor's office, which fostered public–private partnerships and encouraged corporations to build new skyscrapers, including the Mellon Center and PPG Place. He also convinced the Pirates to remain in Pittsburgh when the baseball team threatened to leave town. A commitment to wise use of the riverfronts may be the greatest legacy of Mayor Tom Murphy, who served three terms ending in 2005. His administration emphasized providing public parks and walkways along the rivers and downtown. Former City Council member Luke Ravenstahl became mayor of Pittsburgh in 2006, at the age of 27. He took over when newly elected Mayor Bob O'Connor lost his battle with lymphoma.

Signs of transformation from Pittsburgh's sooty past to its cosmopolitan present are everywhere in this compact downtown, just two miles in diameter. The former Penn Station, with its ornate oak and glass doors and skylight-lit concourse, has been reborn as a luxury apartment building. The former Mellon Bank headquarters on Smithfield Street, a perfect example of Industrial Age design, with marble columns lining the corridors, is now retail space. The original terminus for the Pittsburgh & Lake Erie Railroad, on the banks of the Monongahela River, is now

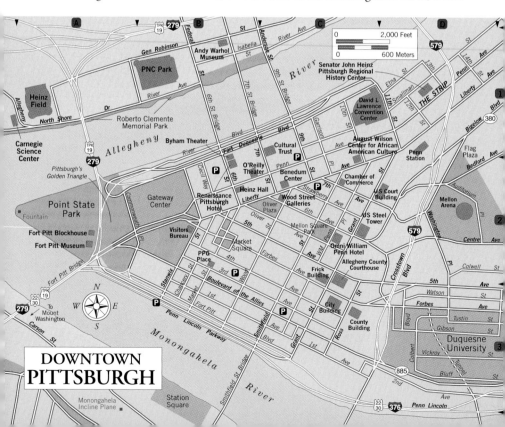

A view of Pittsburgh's growing skyline.

part of a popular retail and entertainment complex. Mount Washington, the 367-foot-high peak that overlooks Pittsburgh, was previously known as Coal Hill because miners excavated surface seams of coal here. Today, incline cars operated by the Port Authority of Allegheny County carry riders to a row of upscale restaurants on the mountain.

Among the more high-profile projects in Pittsburgh's renaissance is the $370 million expansion and redesign of the eco-friendly David L. Lawrence Convention Center (by Rafael Viñoly, also architect of Philadelphia's Kimmel Center). The revamped structure, named after one of Pittsburgh's most beloved mayors (1946–58), is the largest "green" building in the world. Its design maximizes daylight and natural ventilation, while a water reclamation system reduces potable water use.

This progressive design is typical of the city's ongoing rejuvenation. Factor in the low cost of living here and the super-sized cultural scene—from art galleries to theater companies and a professional orchestra—and it should be no surprise that since 1985 Pittsburgh has landed on the Rand McNally Top 20 Most Livable Cities list. Today, the population is 312,800 within city limits and 2.6 million in the metropolitan area.

DOWNTOWN

Downtown Pittsburgh is an 11-square-block area bounded by the Monongahela and Allegheny rivers. Rife with contrasts, its lush waterfront parks and glimmering skyscrapers stand in opposition to the railcars chugging over the rusty trestles and the shadows cast by Victorian-era gothic church spires. Pirates and Steelers fans soak in the skyline view from swank downtown sports stadiums, while articles about high school games still grace the front page of the daily newspaper. It's this distinct medley of architecture, activity, and history that lends downtown Pittsburgh its unique character. No wonder several condo buildings have gone up since 2000 and more are underway.

THE POINT AND FORT PITT   *map page 232, A-2/3*

Nearly every adventure in downtown Pittsburgh begins or ends in ★**Point State Park,** where an impressive fountain forms the apex of a geographical triangle whose base is a series of crosstown ramps and expressways known as I–579. By any measure, this is a truly beautiful park, with expansive green lawns and promenades, the triangle's dramatically tapered point leading the eye upward to forested green hills. Coal barges and pleasure boats ply the nearby waters, and in summer, sunbathers relax in the wide open area around the great fountain, which sprays an arched plume 30 feet into the air. To commemorate Pittsburgh's 250th anniversary in 2008 the city is renovating Point State Park. Major changes, expected to be completed by 2009, include restoring a promenade bordering the water, creating a bike path, building a dock for small boats, and adding trees, interpretive signage, and lighting.

The park is a National Historic Landmark. The Point is the site of old earthworks and the remains of a wall of **Fort Pitt,** where French and British soldiers contested this strategically important sliver of land in the late 1750s. Artifacts and monuments at **Fort Pitt Museum and Blockhouse** (412/281–9284) bestow much of the credit for Britain's eventual victory on Gen. John Forbes. A Scotsman, Forbes was appointed to his post by British prime minister William Pitt in 1757.

Forbes knew that retaking the fort (then called Fort Duquesne) from the French might require a long siege. To win, he would need to outlast the French and would need a dependable route for provisions and weaponry. His response was to turn his soldiers into road builders—chopping down trees, hauling out boulders, and clearing away brush. Soon the road stretched from the Point east across the Allegheny Mountains. Forbes's strategy was successful, as the Brits established a formidable new outpost.

"I have used the freedom of giving your name to Fort Duquesne," Forbes wrote Prime Minister Pitt in November 1758 after the French deserted it, "as I hope it was in some measure the being actuated by your spirit that now makes us masters of the place." *Point State Park, main entrance at 101 Commonwealth Pl.; 412/471–0235.*

MARKET SQUARE   *map page 232, B-2*

About a third of a mile due east of the Point, between Fourth and Fifth avenues, is **Market Square,** the city center in the years just before the Revolutionary War. The square was a civic gathering place—the Declaration of Independence was read aloud here in 1776. Today, the redbrick paving and antique-style street lamps and clock serve as the backdrop for an outdoor stage for free evening concerts and the occasional protest. Urbanites shop here for locally grown produce and baked goods at the Thursday farmers' market.

HIGH-RISE GRANDEES

Near Market Square rises a structure made almost entirely of plate glass—19,750 pieces, to be precise—called **PPG Place,** the headquarters of PPG Industries, founded in 1883 as the Pittsburgh Plate Glass Company. At sunset, with orange light bouncing off so many glass panes, the effect is pure magic. The building, designed by Philip Johnson and John Burgee, and completed in 1984, remains a spectacular example of postmodern corporate architecture. *Boulevard of the Allies and Stanwix St.*

Pittsburgh's **Allegheny County Courthouse** is a beautiful reminder of the attention paid to detail by architects of another era. Architect Henry Hobson Richardson's 1888 design incorporated Boston-quarried stone, castle-like towers, and an inner courtyard with an impressive circular fountain. The building's rounded arches, rugged stone walls, and Byzantine carvings characterize the architect's style, known as Richardsonian Romanesque. Don't miss the frescoes on the first floor, the grand staircase near the entrance to the old law library, or the "bridge of sighs" connecting the courthouse and former jail (now a court facility). Tours can be arranged through the Pittsburgh History and Landmarks Foundation (412/471–5808). *436 Grant St.*

The 21-story **Frick Building,** erected in 1901 to a design by D.H. Burnham and Company, is a high-class affair that mixes black-and-white marble and mul-

High-rise buildings tower over the sturdy 1883 Allegheny County Courthouse.

ticolored stained glass. The building, bankrolled by coke-and-steel baron Henry Clay Frick, whose bust is displayed in the lobby, is an exceptional example of the beaux-arts style. *437 Grant St., across from the County Courthouse.*

As a former director of U.S. Steel, Frick might just as logically have his bust grace the lobby of the **US Steel Tower,** the 841-foot-high, triangle-shape tower designed by architects Harrison, Abramowitz & Abbe. When completed in 1970, the handsome, rust-color building was the world's tallest skyscraper outside New York and Chicago. *600 Grant St.*

Mellon Square Park provides welcome green respite from the marble, stone, and steel of the Golden Triangle. Noontime concerts often take place here, the music accompanied by the soft gushing of fountains and a waterfall. *William Penn Pl. and Sixth Ave.*

CELEBRATING DIVERSITY

The August Wilson Center for African American Culture—named for the Pittsburgh playwright and two-time Pulitzer Prize winner—celebrates the achievements of African Americans in music, theater, dance, science, sports, and other fields through exhibits and live performances. In an exhibit exploring

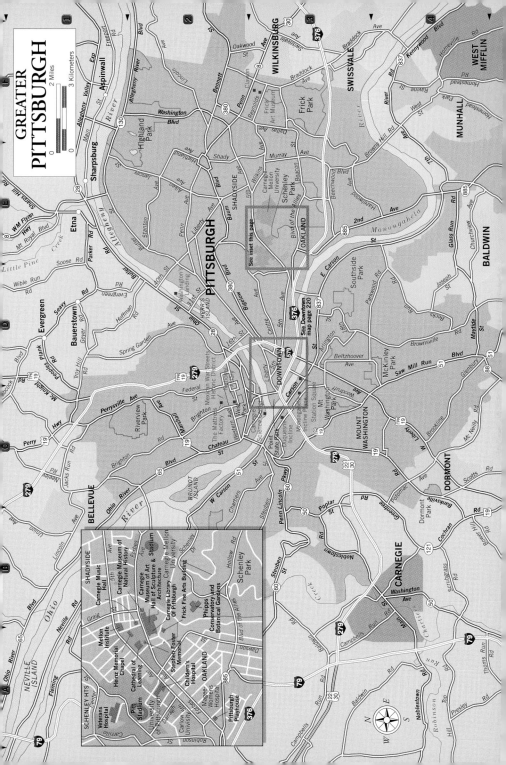

Exhibits at the Wood Street Galleries focus on contemporary art.

the word "soul," female African-American artists analyze manifestations of the term in paintings, ceramics, photographs, collages, and multimedia works. The center's 65,000-square-foot home, slated to open in spring 2009, is a sleek $40 million facility. Its unique bowed design, by African-American architect Allison Wiliams embodies the same sense of movement and energetic force generated inside the space. Conceived with an emphasis on sustainability, it was constructed with locally sourced steel, aluminum, and plate glass. *Liberty Ave. and 10th St., Cultural District; 412/258–7200.*

ARTS SPACES *map page 232, C/2*

One of the city's funkier art spaces, **Wood Street Galleries** is a project of the Cultural Trust, a consortium of arts groups. Conceptual art, multimedia works, and photography are the main attractions, and the long list of notables who have shown work here includes Marina Rosenfeld, Catherine Opie, and Nicole Eisenman. *601 Wood St.; 412/471–5605.*

The performing arts are alive and well throughout the city, but downtown is the headquarters of most major cultural groups. Among the venues of note are the **O'Reilly Theater** (621 Penn Ave.), where the Pittsburgh Public Theater performs; **Heinz Hall** (600 Penn Ave.), which hosts performances by the Pittsburgh Symphony and visiting orchestras; and **Byham Theater** (101 Sixth St.), a handsomely renovated early-20th-century theater that hosts performances by dance and theater companies. A stone's throw from the Byham Theater is **Benedum Center for the Performing Arts** (Seventh St. at Penn Ave.), a 1928 movie palace that was renovated and expanded in 1987 to accommodate the Pittsburgh Ballet, national dance troupes, and touring Broadway musicals.

★ **THE STRIP**   *map page 232, D-1*

Just outside the Golden Triangle and northeast of downtown, the Strip is a 15-block-long, three-block-wide produce and wholesale district where the air is filled with the scent of gourmet coffees, ginger chicken, fresh fish, pastries, breads, cheeses, and other fresh foods. For many years, this area was a factory and warehouse district with a down-at-the-heels reputation. The restaurants lining the streets were geared toward the blue-collar lunchtime crowd. But in the past two decades, the neighborhood has turned into a chic outdoor emporium where local entrepreneurs sell clothing, CDs, art, and ethnic food, and where people from all social classes and walks of life come together.

Some of Pittsburgh's best wholesalers have a shop along the Strip, like **Wholey's Fish Market** (1711 Penn Ave.; 412/391–3737), where you can find dozens of varieties of fresh fish daily, from scrumptious salmon to jumbo Icelandic cod. **Jimmy and Nino Sunseri's** (1906 Penn Ave.; 412/255–1100), a Strip tradition for decades, has mouthwatering Italian sausages, pasta, cheese, and olives. At **Primanti's** (1150 Smallman St.; 412/263–2142) you can devour enormous tuna, steak, or cheese combo sandwiches stuffed with fries and slaw for about $6. To revive yourself, have a cup of joe at **La Prima Espresso Bar** (205 21st St.; 412/281–1922), where regulars play cards and Steelers fans warm up before games. When the sun sets, restaurants and clubs to suit every taste fire up along Penn Avenue and Smallman Street. **Metropol** (1600 Smallman St.), one of the city's trendiest nightspots, frequently hosts concerts by big-name rock artists.

The **Senator John Heinz Pittsburgh Regional History Center,** an impressive redbrick building that looms over Smallman Street, is named after the popular Pennsylvania politician who served in the U.S. Senate from 1977 to 1991. The seven-story building, once owned by the Chautauqua Lake Ice Company, serves today as a center for learning about western Pennsylvania's people, history, and

The *Diplodocus carnegie* in the Carnegie Museum of Natural History.

geography. Among the permanent exhibits is *Points in Time: Building a Life in Western Pennsylvania, 1750–Today,* which includes life-size models of dwellings from three historic periods: a log cabin from 1790, an immigrant worker's home from 1910, and a suburban ranch home from the 1950s. Furniture from several centuries, artifacts, costumes, and live theater provide a historic look at the lives of Pennsylvanians. *1212 Smallman St.; 412/454–6000.*

OAKLAND   *map page 237, D-3*

Oakland is a lively commercial and residential area with art museums, cinemas, shops, prestigious universities, and ethnic restaurants. Lush **Schenley Park** is a playground for adults and children. A four-block, L-shaped complex houses the Carnegie Museum of Art, the Carnegie Museum of Natural History, the Carnegie Library of Pittsburgh, and the Carnegie Music Hall.

CARNEGIE COMPLEX   *map page 237, E-3*

Having made his fortune from Pittsburgh's steel mills, Andrew Carnegie decided to give back to the city, not by paying workers higher wages, but by building

CONTRADICTORY CARNEGIE

As a businessman, Andrew Carnegie was ruthless toward competitors and workers. But upon retirement, he gave most of his wealth away, becoming in the process one of America's greatest philanthropists. His charitable works were not just a guilty afterthought to a life of acquisition. Carnegie wrote in a famous article, the "Gospel of Wealth," that a talented businessman is entitled to great wealth, but has a duty to live without ostentation, provide for his dependents, and help his "poorer brethren, bringing to their service his superior wisdom, experience, and ability to administer." Carnegie's tone is patronizing in titan-of-industry style, but his works have the better of the argument. The wisest fields for philanthropy, he wrote in 1889, are universities, libraries, hospitals, parks, concert halls, swimming pools, and church buildings. Critics may carp that homes should come before swimming pools, and that the "libraries" were just buildings without books. Yet many of the Carnegie libraries endure, as do Carnegie Mellon University in Pittsburgh, the Carnegie Endowment for International Peace and the Carnegie Institution of Washington in Washington, D.C., and New York City's Carnegie Hall— all financed by his $350 million in gifts.

The illustrator of this 1892 cartoon contrasts Carnegie's lavish philanthropy with the low wages he paid his employees. (Library of Congress)

several museums. Some suggest the **Carnegie Museum of Art** was the nation's first modern art museum because early acquisitions included works by Carnegie's contemporaries—artists such as Winslow Homer, James McNeill Whistler, Mary Cassatt, and Camille Pissarro. (Critics contend Carnegie simply didn't want to spend the money for pieces by the old masters.) The painting collection is extensive, stretching from the 1400s to the 1960s and including works by Renaissance artists and European masters Rubens, Goya, van Gogh, and Degas. The museum opens a revealing window on American art with works by John Singer Sargent, Edward Hopper, Andy Warhol, Joan Mitchell, and Jackson Pollock, among many others.

John White Alexander's 1907 mural *The Crowning of Labor,* an ode to industrial workers, graces the entryway to the Hall of Sculpture, a room modeled after the Parthenon. Its double-tiered columns are built with marble from the same quarries. Behind it is the Hall of Architecture, inspired by the Mausoleum at Halicarnassus. Besides decorative arts objects, these rooms contain Carnegie's collection of 69 plaster casts of Egyptian, Greek, and Roman statues and his collection of 144 plaster casts of architectural masterpieces. Copying fragile art works is frowned on today, but it wasn't in Carnegie's time (or earlier—even the Romans made copies of Greek works), and his collection rivals those at museums in Paris and London. Reportedly, Carnegie believed copies were better than nothing for art students who would likely never see the originals. The Heinz Architectural Center contains drawings, photographs, prints, and models, most from the 19th and 20th centuries. *4400 Forbes Ave.; 412/622–3131.*

A walkway connects the art museum to the **Carnegie Museum of Natural History.** Carnegie, a hands-on collector, dispatched one of the earliest teams of paleontologists to unearth fossils and dinosaur bones for reconstruction back in the museum. Aware of the source of their funding, team members named a small dinosaur *Diplodocus carnegie* in his honor. Another large exhibit area is dedicated to gems, the crystals from which they originate, and jewelry designed with these precious stones. One section of the exhibit is dedicated to coal and other minerals historically significant to Pennsylvania's economic development. *4400 Forbes Ave.; 412/622–3131.*

The **Carnegie Library of Pittsburgh** is the mother ship of Andrew Carnegie's network of libraries, which extended first to southwestern Pennsylvania and then to other parts of the country. In all, Carnegie built 2,509 libraries throughout the English-speaking world. Libraries reaped the lion's share of his largesse because of his own experience as an immigrant boy who had benefited from access to a then-

The Cathedral of Learning towers over all on the campus of the University of Pittsburgh.

rare small library to educate himself. Carnegie believed that in a meritocracy like the United States, where effort and ability, not family background, determined success, libraries could provide everyone with an equal opportunity, and allow immigrants to absorb the principles of American democracy.

This library, opened in 1895 and engraved with the words "Free to the People" over its entrance, is an architectural gem that has undergone significant renovation and repair in recent years, thanks to a regional funding system for cultural projects approved by Allegheny County voters. *4400 Forbes Ave.; 412/622–3116.*

The **Carnegie Music Hall** opened in 1895, the same year as the Carnegie Library, to which it is connected. The hall is famous for exceptional acoustics, an intimate environment (it has 788 seats), and grand foyer. Small ensembles such as the Pittsburgh Chamber Music Society perform here. *4400 Forbes Ave.; 412/622–3131.*

Connected to the museum complex and park are the campuses of Carnegie Mellon University and the University of Pittsburgh. The well-endowed CMU is the result of the merger in 1967 of two institutions, the Carnegie Institute of Technology, founded by Andrew Carnegie in 1900 and the Mellon Institute of Industrial Research. The latter had been established in 1911 as a department of the University of Pittsburgh.

Many structures on the University of Pittsburgh campus are historic landmarks. One of the most impressive buildings in the entire city is the **Cathedral of Learning.** Architect Charles Z. Klauder went to town with a Gothic structure, built between 1926 and 1936, that rises 535 feet and is covered with India limestone and Gothic ornaments. Even more famous than the building itself are the 26 impressive Nationality Classrooms (for tours: 412/624–6000) on the first and third floors. Realized over a period of 62 years, each room is uniquely designed and decorated to symbolize the cultural diversity of the immigrant workers who helped build Pittsburgh. *4200 Fifth Ave.; 412/624–4141.*

Across the main plaza and in the shadow of the secular "cathedral" is the French Gothic–style **Heinz Memorial Chapel.** Its ornate spires and detailed stone carvings contrast wonderfully with the smooth lines and mass of the Cathedral of Learning. The Heinz family commissioned this building, with its 73-foot-high stained-glass transept windows, as a memorial to the family patriarch, Henry John, and to his mother, Anna Margareta. Pitt students, employees, and their families have wedding privileges at the chapel, making it a festive place on weekends. *Heinz Memorial Chapel; 412/624–4157.*

Early auto models in the Car and Carriage Museum. (Frick Art & Historical Center)

The **Stephen Foster Memorial** celebrates the life of Pittsburgh native Stephen Foster (1826–64), who composed tunes that have become American classics. "Oh Susanna," "Old Folks at Home," "Jeannie with the Light Brown Hair," and "Camptown Races" are all familiar tunes from the Foster canon. The on-site museum displays thousands of original compositions, articles, and letters written by Foster, as well as his piano. *4301 Forbes Ave.; 412/624–4100.*

The **Frick Fine Arts Building,** across Schenley Drive from the Carnegie Library of Pittsburgh, houses the University of Pittsburgh's History of Art and Architecture Department and the Frick Fine Arts Library. Commissioned by Helen Clay Frick as a memorial to her father, the building draws on the architecture of the Italian Renaissance for inspiration. Its many impressive features include elegant fruitwood paneling in the library and an inner courtyard in an Italian cloister style. The museum houses famous reproductions of 15th-century Florentine Renaissance artworks by Russian Artist Nicholas Lochoff. Helen Clay Frick offered to endow a larger museum, but the university refused to accept her conditions for the bequest: that the museum contain no contemporary art, and that no one of German extraction work on the staff. *Schenley Dr.; 412/648–2400.*

Many varieties of tropical plants thrive at Phipps Conservatory and Botanical Gardens.

CLAYTON AND FRICK ART MUSEUM   *map page 237, F-3*

When University of Pittsburgh officials declined to accept Helen Clay Frick's conditions for building a campus museum, she took her millions back home to the city's Point Breeze neighborhood and set about commissioning a museum of her own.

The result, the **Frick Art Museum,** built in 1969, is a showcase for her collection of paintings, drawings, and decorative arts. The painting collection focuses mostly on Italian Renaissance and 18th-century French works. Highlights include works from the 14th and 15th centuries by Sassetta, Duccio, and Giovanni di Paolo, and a portrait by Peter Paul Rubens. The museum is laid out according to the scion's wishes that works be displayed in an atmosphere of intimacy. Thus, paintings hang next to porcelains, bronzes, and rare examples of 17th- and 18th-century furniture.

The Frick Art Museum sits on the same manicured 5.5-acre stretch of lawn and gardens as the restored family home, **Clayton.** It was an 11-room house when Henry Clay Frick and his wife, Adelaide Howard Childs, bought it in 1882. By the end of the century, however, the industrialist had transformed it into a 23-room mansion. In 1905, the family moved to New York. The couple's daughter,

Helen, returned to Clayton in 1981 and lived there until her death three years later. Since 1990, the house has been open to the public, and retains more than 90% of its original furnishings. Also on the property is the Car and Carriage Museum, where Henry Clay Frick's 1914 Rolls-Royce Silver Ghost is among the vehicles on display. A visit to Clayton sheds light on the lifestyles of Pittsburgh's multimillionaires who lived quite extravagantly compared to the workers who helped make them rich. *7227 Reynolds St., at Homewood Ave., Point Breeze; 412/371–0600.*

PUBLIC PARKS AND BYWAYS   *map page 237, E-3*

Much of the city's East End is covered by a network of gorgeous public parks, but the premier green space is **Schenley Park,** a gift of Mary Schenley, a wealthy expatriate who lived in England. Edward Bigelow, Pittsburgh's director of public works, secured the land for the park, and William Falconer designed it. Schenley Park has 456 acres of rolling hills, woods, and trails. The facilities here include a large botanical conservatory, a swimming pool, tennis courts, a golf course, a nature center, and an ice-skating rink. *Schenley Park Dr. (follow signs from I–376, Exit 5).*

Phipps Conservatory and Botanical Gardens, which opened in 1893, is a stellar example of Victorian "glasshouse" architecture. Under the glass canopy are a dozen rooms containing lush tropical plants—fantastically tall palms, dizzyingly aromatic orchids, and many varieties of exotic flowers. Nearly 3 acres of outdoor gardens surround the complex, including the Japanese Courtyard Garden and its show-stopping bonsai collection. From late April through mid-October, the conservatory's Stove Room becomes a butterfly forest filled with nature's winged wonders. *1 Schenley Park; 412/622–6914.*

NORTH SIDE   *map page 237*

The architecture of Pittsburgh's North Side includes Victorian-era and Craftsman-style row houses along tree-lined streets. The residential sector is separated from the commercial sector, where the former H. J. Heinz plant employed thousands of workers before spinning off its North Side factory to Del Monte Foods in 2002. In 2006, Del Monte sold the operation to TreeHouse Foods, which makes soup in the plant. The landmark factory is adjacent to the leafy, 50-acre West Park.

Andy Warhol's silkscreen *Ladies and Gentlemen* (1975) is part of a series of portraits the artist made of underground drag performers

ANDY WARHOL MUSEUM *map pages 232, B-1, and page 237, C-2*

As soon as Andy Warhol, son of Carpatho-Russian immigrants, graduated from the Carnegie Institute of Technology (now Carnegie Mellon University), the Pittsburgh native headed to New York City to pursue fame and fortune. The quixotic artist-celebrity may have fled Pittsburgh as a youth, but the prodigal son is posthumously the toast of the town. Warhol predicted that "in the future everyone will be famous for fifteen minutes," and his own legacy has far exceeded that time line.

Appropriately, a 1911 industrial warehouse is now the ultramodern shrine to a man who blurred the lines between fine art and pop culture. With seven floors, the ★Andy Warhol Museum is the most comprehensive single-artist museum in the world. Warhol's silkscreen portraits of icons as diverse as Jackie O. and Chairman Mao hang on the walls in full Technicolor. In addition to his most famous works—like sculptures of Brillo pad boxes and Campbell's soup cans—the museum sheds light on Warhol's life outside the spotlight. It houses audio and film interviews with his friends and artistic collaborators, photographs, and magazine articles, as well as memorabilia ranging from Warhol's draft card to his college graduation program. The museum also provides a glimpse into the graphics work Warhol did for New York ad agencies in the 1950s, which planted the seeds for his pop art. And certainly don't leave before getting punchy in the Silver Clouds exhibit, where you can bat at silver Mylar balloons filled with helium, as they gently waft through the air.

At the museum's Weekend Factory, visitors of all ages can create their own silkscreens, à la Warhol. Every Friday after 5 PM the museum slashes the admission price in half and hosts lectures and live music. Many of the Warhol-produced films shown at the museum cannot be viewed anywhere else in the world. *117 Sandusky St.; 412/237–8300.*

MATTRESS FACTORY

The Mattress Factory lives up to its international reputation for pushing the envelope of contemporary art. One of the few museums in the world dedicated to installation art, its room-size works force you to interact with the pieces. The artists experiment with mixed media—a recorded waterfall, incandescent light, even live crickets. The tranquil rock garden by Winifred Lutz incorporates the founda-

Skull conjures up a Warhol saying: "Death can really make you look like a star."

Repetitive Vision, an installation by Yayoi Kusama at the Mattress Factory.

tion and bricks of a building that burned on the site decades ago, fusing art and archeology. *Sampsonia Way; 412/231–3169.*

CULTURAL CENTERS AND STADIUMS
map pages 232, A/B-1, and page 237, C-2

The **National Aviary** is an important center for the breeding and study of exotic and endangered birds. More than 450 birds representing 225 species live here. Some are caged, but many flit around tree-filled aviaries through which you can walk. *Allegheny Commons Park, Arch St. between West North and West Ohio Sts.; 412/323–7235.*

The Pittsburgh Pirates baseball team runs the bases in the 38,000-seat **PNC Park** (Federal St., General Robinson St., and Mazeroski Way). And during home games, nearly 64,500 Pittsburgh Steelers fans wave their "terrible towels" at **Heinz Field** (100 Art Rooney Ave.).

Near the stadiums is the **Carnegie Science Center,** which aims to make science both entertaining and educational. The center has a planetarium and observatory, a theater that typically screens science films, and a huge railroad exhibit that reflects the state's landscape from 1890 to 1930. *1 Allegheny Ave.; 412/237–3400.*

The eight-block **Mexican War Streets** residential district, lined with trees and narrow redbrick houses, was developed in the 1850s. Gen. William Robinson Jr., a Pittsburgh politico and Mexican War veteran, lived here. Later, as mayor of Allegheny, he named many of the streets in this district after well-known battles and generals of that struggle.

Beginning in the 1920s, the community declined. As the middle class started to buy automobiles, they fled to the suburbs. By the 1950s things had deteriorated so badly that city planners talked about razing the neighborhood altogether. But in the 1960s, many homes here—some of them built for craftsmen, others designed for people of means—became the focus of intense renovation. Today, the Mexican War Streets area is something of an architectural wonderland, with styles ranging from Queen Anne to Richardsonian Romanesque to Greek Revival.

Washington's Landing, an island that was once the site of a foul-smelling meatpacking plant, was cleaned up in the '90s. Pittsburgh residents can finally appreciate its commanding bridge and river views, as well as a jogging trail that hugs the shoreline. Hundreds of luxury condos have gone up, plus restaurants, a rowing center, and commercial businesses. *Reached by River Rd. on the North Side and by the 31st St. Bridge in the Strip District.*

PNC Stadium frames dramatic views of downtown Pittsburgh.

MOUNT WASHINGTON   *map page 237, C-3*

Directly across the Monongahela River from downtown is Mount Washington, which, at 367 feet, offers indisputably the best view of Pittsburgh and its rivers. At the foot of Mount Washington, adjacent to the Sheraton Hotel and on the Allegheny riverfront, is **Station Square.** A major renovation in the 1970s developed this site into a commercial tourist destination with chains like the Hard Rock Cafe and the Melting Pot, as well as independent shops.

You can get to the top of Mount Washington by taking one of two inclined planes, the **Monongahela Incline** (412/488–3102) or the **Duquesne Incline** (412/381–1665). Both date from the 1870s and run every few minutes from either the base, along West Carson Street, or the top, along Grandview Avenue. Along the Monongahela River, you'll see the South Side neighborhood, filled with the homes and churches of Ukrainian, Serbian, and Lithuanian immigrants. Surrounding this are wooded hills, and the overall effect is one of space and beauty. The Duquesne Incline, slightly younger than the Monongahela, still has its original cars, with cherry and maple interiors.

GETTING AROUND

I–79 and I–279 are the main roads downtown from the north or south. From the east, take the Pennsylvania Turnpike (I–76), then I–376 to the Grant St. exit. From the west, take I–76 to I–79 south, then follow I–279 to downtown.

Pittsburgh is easily explored on foot and by car, though some streets zigzag up hills that are so steep the sidewalks are stepped, and the streets change names along the way. Major highways disappear into tunnels that run all over the city and ongoing construction often diverts traffic. Parking is not a huge hassle, but you will need to feed meters and even pay for lots near popular museums and stadiums. Although it's not comprehensive, the T Light Rail system (412/442–2000) will get you to most major attractions and the South Hills. Best of all, no digging around your pockets for change—transportation between the four downtown stations is free.

The Point as seen from Mount Washington.

FAVORITE PLACES TO EAT

Café at the Frick. 7227 Reynolds St., Point Breeze; 412/371–0600. $-$$

The sandwiches and salads here are served with almost as much artistic flair as the paintings in the gallery. The menu items change every few months, with seasonal vegetables and herbs plucked from the Frick's garden.

Dish Osteria Bar. 128 S. 17 St., Southside; 412/390–2012. $$$

This intimate Italian restaurant in a corner row home is known for creatively prepared pasta, such as the fettuccine with portobello, shiitake, and cremini mushrooms, as well as shellfish. And even those who hate eating their vegetables will devour the grilled eggplant-and-buffalo-mozzarella appetizer. On a bustling Saturday night, be prepared for secondhand smoke and chatter wafting into the dining room from the bar.

Enrico Biscotti Company. 2022 Penn Ave., the Strip District; 412/281–2602. $$

The wood-burning brick oven here turns out the best biscotti ever, and a box of them makes a great gift. When the café opens on Saturday, then you can also get perfectly baked meals like pizza, chicken, and quiche. If you're too full for dessert, take a cannoli to go.

Grand Concourse Restaurant. 1 Station Square, Downtown; 412/261–1717. $$$

The big draw here is the gorgeous architecture of the former Pittsburgh and Lake Erie Railroad terminal. The restaurant's interior is all brass, wood, and marble, with a glass ceiling. The all-you-can-eat Sunday brunch is especially popular, with carved roast beef, Italian sausage, an omelet bar, and fresh fruit.

La Feria. 5527 Walnut Street, Shadyside; 412/682–4501. $

Tucked into the back of a Latin American crafts gallery, this simple, homey restaurant serves rib-sticking Peruvian comfort food. Start with the camotes frites, homemade sweet potato chips meant to be dipped in a tangy cheese dip. For something lighter, we recommend the house salad, made with lettuce, tomatoes, onions, olives, walnuts, and cheese, topped with a vinaigrette.

FAVORITE PLACES TO STAY

Inn on the Mexican War Streets.
604 W. North Ave., North Side;
412/231–6544. $–$$

*The former home of department store
magnate Russell H. Boggs, this castle-like
bed-and-breakfast is popular with hipsters
and travelers looking to get away from
the hustle and bustle of downtown. Each
room is unique, and all have cozy touches
like loveseats and plants. The Continental
breakfast is best enjoyed on the porch.*

**Marriott's Renaissance Pittsburgh
Hotel.** 107 Sixth St., downtown;
412/562–1200. $$

*For a window into the world of the wealthy
steel barons, stay in this beautifully
restored 1906 theater. The copper
and granite facade gives a clue to the
building's interior: a grand staircase,
mosaic tiles, and marble everywhere.
The cast-iron and glass rotunda dome,
blacked out during World War II, was
cleaned up in 2001 and now sheds bright
sunshine over the entire atrium. The
comfortable rooms offer views of the
Allegheny River and free Internet access.*

Omni William Penn Hotel. 530 William
Penn Pl., downtown; 412/281–7100. $$
*Henry Clay Frick initiated construction
of this Gilded Age building to provide*

*Pittsburgh with a hotel up to New
York City standards. Built in 1916, the
Benno Janssen–designed hotel, ideally
situated between the Allegheny and
Monongahela rivers, is listed on the
National Register of Historic Places.
Many of the rooms are far more spacious
than those found in a typical downtown
hotel, but they could use updating.*

The Parador Inn. 939 Western Ave.,
North Side; 412/231–4800. $$

*Pittsburgh businessman Joshua Rhodes
likely would not recognize the Victorian
mansion he built in 1870. Today, it is a
Caribbean-theme bed-and-breakfast
with a tropical garden and rooms
called African Tulip, Bird of Paradise,
Lady Palm, Oleander, and Hibiscus.*

Sheraton Station Square Hotel.
300 W. Station Square Dr., Downtown;
412/261–2000. $$

*If nightlife and shopping are your thing,
this nonsmoking hotel on the riverfront
is an excellent choice. Walk out the door
to more than 30 shops, restaurants,
and clubs. The walk is a bit far to major
downtown attractions, though. Many
of the simply decorated rooms overlook
the waterfront and stadiums.*

S O U T H W E S T
F A R M L A N D & F A L L I N G W A T E R

Much of southwestern Pennsylvania consists of farm country or forested hills. People here live simply, on isolated produce and dairy farms or in small towns with mom-and-pop businesses. Amish farms prosper near New Castle and Harmony. On the grittier side, some parts of this region still lie in the shadows of abandoned steel mills. Fall is a perfect time to visit the majestic Laurel Highlands, an hour's drive east of Pittsburgh, which offer everything from the architectural masterpiece Fallingwater to white-water rafting. The dramatic mass of ridges folds out in wide pleats like an accordion at the southernmost end of the Allegheny Mountains. By December, snow has cloaked these mountains in white, and skiers flock here for downhill and cross-country thrills. In spring and summer, the countryside is an explosion of buttercups, violets, and white hemlock. Here, visitors find inspiration in nature. But they also find deep meaning in sites dedicated to the cost of conflict. The Flight 93 National Memorial in Shanksville is a profound reminder of those heroes who lost lives when terrorists took—and lost—control of their plane on September 11, 2001. Nearby French and Indian War sites remind us of strategic battles fought more than 250 years ago.

NORTH OF PITTSBURGH

High-end suburbs and wide-open farmland testify to the competing forces at work north of Pittsburgh. Amish farms can be found in and around New Wilmington and New Castle in Lawrence County. In Harmony and Zelienople, the architecture and local crafts reveal German immigrant roots, and in Ellwood, Italian immigrants have influenced the culture. Crossing Interstate 79 about 65 miles north of Pittsburgh is Route 208, a winding backcountry road that traverses the heart of western Pennsylvania's Amish farm country, as evidenced by farmers in wide-brimmed hats tilling their fields with horse-pulled plows.

NEW WILMINGTON *map page 261, A-1*

The peaceful borough of New Wilmington, a Main Street U.S.A. community, is known to many in Lawrence County for Westminster College, whose ivy-covered stone walls date back to 1852. Graceful homes and maple trees line the residential

On the Monongahela (1860), by William Coventry Wall. (Westmoreland Museum of American Art)

streets, and the downtown is busy, with an assortment of shops selling furniture and goods made by Amish families. Most of the Amish who live in the area ride into town in horse-drawn buggies. Amish women come here to shop for sewing supplies, which are used to make quilts sold at auctions around town.

HARMONY *map page 261, A/B-2*

Halfway between Volant and Pittsburgh in Butler County is Harmony, settled in 1804 by Harmonists, a group of pietists. Followers of George Rapp, a German preacher who came to America in 1803, Harmonists believed that the Second Coming of Christ was imminent and that the integrity of their lifestyle—they were celibate, did not indulge in tobacco or drink, and believed in hard work— might warrant a visit and a blessing.

The Harmonists planted orchards and vineyards, built a brewery, a tannery, a general store, a schoolhouse, and an inn. They were admired for their work ethic, their handmade furniture and the elegant simplicity of their quilts. The range of their talents can be sampled at the **Harmony Museum,** which exhibits handmade clothing, furniture, antiques, and other artifacts. The museum's Log House contains early-American chairs and tables and equipment used for spinning, weaving, and rope-making. No descendants of these settlers continue to live in Harmony, a town of about 900. Some are in the western Pennsylvania town of Ambridge. While that town continues to host an annual heritage festival in recognition of the Harmonists who settled there in 1824, community members have long since assimilated into mainstream culture. *218 Mercer St.; 724/452–7341 or 888/821–4822.*

MCCONNELL'S MILL STATE PARK   *map page 261, A-1*

A hidden gem, McConnell's Mill State Park is set in the deep gorge of Slippery Rock Creek. Within this spectacular 400-foot-deep chasm are house-size boulders, waterfalls, and a restored 19th-century gristmill. The park's 7 miles of rugged trails touch only a small portion of its 2,529 acres. Hell's Hollow Trail winds through an area where spectacular wildflowers bloom in spring. Patches of violet and light blue merge into blazing yellows against soft green leaves and tiny white flowers of hemlock. With its multistory rock formations, cascading waterfalls, and abundant wildlife, the park is a magnet for rock climbers, anglers, rafters, and nature lovers. Canoeing, kayaking, and picnicking are permitted. *Rte. 422 off I–79, 40 miles north of Pittsburgh; 724/368–8091.*

WEST OF PITTSBURGH: BEAVER COUNTY

In the 19th and early 20th centuries, the titans of heavy industry built huge mills and factories along the Ohio River in Beaver County. When steel production came to a halt in the late 1970s, many company towns hit on hard times. Since then, some towns have been successful in creating new economic bases and forging new identities. In the borough of New Brighton, for instance, weekenders come to shop and dine. Other communities, though, are still struggling.

Beaver County's population and its aging industrial facilities are concentrated mostly along rivers and creeks, among them Connoquenessing Creek, Slippery Rock Creek, Wolf Creek, and the Ohio River. What's left is mostly rural countryside, with few roads and even fewer signs of modern civilization.

RACCOON CREEK STATE PARK   *map page 261, A-2*

Twenty-five miles west of Pittsburgh on U.S. 30 is Raccoon Creek State Park, which has a lake, bridle and hiking trails, and the remains of a historic mineral spring. The exceptional wildflower reserve, on the park's eastern edge, holds 5

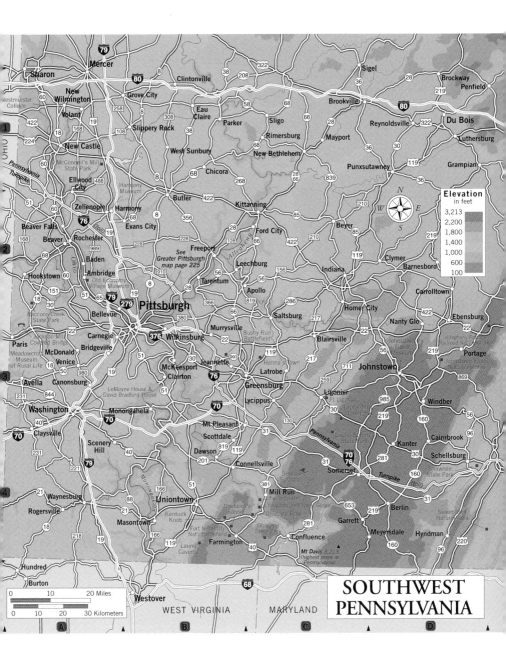

SOUTHWEST PENNSYLVANIA

Elevation
in feet

3,213
2,200
1,800
1,400
1,000
600
100

McConnell's Mill was built in 1852 beside Slippery Rock Creek.

miles of trails that lead through woods containing hickory, elm, black cherry, and a few huge sycamore trees. The peak blooming period for wildflowers is late April through mid-May, when sprays of yellow, white, pink, and purple poke out of the meadow. Information about when different wildflowers bloom is available at the nature center. *Wildflower information: 724/899–3611.*

In the 1800s, the park's **Frankfort Mineral Springs** were part of a well-known health spa. The remains of the spa are visible amid lilies and ancient oak trees, and the nearby footbridge offers an unforgettable view of a waterfall pouring over a broken ledge into a rocky grotto. During winter months, stunning ice formations appear at the springs. *3000 Rte. 18, Hookstown; 724/899–2200.*

MEADOWCROFT MUSEUM OF RURAL LIFE   *map page 261, A-3*

Meadowcroft Village, in Avella, is a 200-acre outdoor museum that re-creates aspects of 19th-century village life. In the 1960s, Albert and Delvin Miller, two Pennsylvania brothers with an interest in history, located structures around the state that were 100 years old or older and moved them to the family farm. The complex includes a log house built by the brothers' great-great-grandfather in 1795, a small schoolhouse, a blacksmith's shop, and a covered bridge.

An ongoing archaeological dig at Meadowcroft Village has uncovered remains dating back 16,000 years, to what may be the earliest human occupation of the Western Hemisphere. The dig area is not open to the public, but hands-on exhibits explain the work. Elsewhere you can try your hand at spinning wool from Merino sheep, candle-dipping, and, during the holidays, taffy-pulling. *Rte. 50, Avella, 35 miles southwest of Pittsburgh; 724/587–3412.*

REBELLIOUS WASHINGTON COUNTY

South of Pittsburgh, the countryside gives way to suburbs sprinkled with upscale homes, the by-product of a burgeoning high-tech industry. Farther south, the landscape alternates between flat farmlands and hills sprinkled with country villages. The pace of life here is mellow.

Historically, people in Washington County have distrusted government, an attitude that can be traced back to the years after the Revolutionary War,

Beaver Falls, Pennsylvania (1854), by Emil Bott. (Westmoreland Museum of American Art)

St. Nicholas Chapel in Beaver County.

when the area figured prominently in the Whiskey Rebellion, a violent campaign to thwart the federal government in its first attempt to tax its citizenry. In 1791, Congress raised excise taxes to help pay off the remaining debts of the Revolutionary War. It instituted a tax of seven cents per gallon on whiskey—which the farmers expected would decrease the amount of whiskey sold and weaken demand for their main cash crop, rye. Farmers who tried to obey the law were ridiculed and threatened, and tax collectors were tarred and feathered.

George Washington, acting on the advice of the Federalist Alexander Hamilton, decided to make an example of the rebels and rode personally into Pittsburgh with 13,000 troops commanded by Gen. Harry "Lighthorse" Lee. Political differences could be tolerated, but open lawlessness could not, and the rebellion was quelled. No one died in the insurrection, although it did get quite violent. One group of resisters disguised themselves as women. Then they attacked a tax collector, snipped off his hair, rolled him in tar and feathers, and took off with this unlucky bureaucrat's horse.

Washington, a 30-minute drive from Pittsburgh, maintains much of the spirited independence that bubbled to the surface during the Whiskey Rebellion. A mid-size city, it has a mixed economy built around light manufacturing, service industries, and education. Decorative gaslights and planters help maintain the historic character of the town's downtown streets. A seasonal farmers' market brings out both locals and tourists, who shop for regionally produced goodies like fresh-baked breads, locally grown fruit, and handmade soap.

Just outside of Washington proper is the **LeMoyne House,** the residence of Dr. John Julius LeMoyne, one of the most courageous visionaries of 19th-century Pennsylvania. He preached the idea of equality between the sexes and races and, as a result, was treated as a pariah in his community. LeMoyne practiced what he preached, helping 25 slaves to freedom on the Underground Railroad. He also started colleges for African-Americans. You can wander through the originally furnished rooms of his stone house, as well as the grounds. A restored 19th-century medicinal herb garden, known as Madeleine's Garden, is a delight to both see and smell. *49 East Maiden St.; 724/225–6740.*

When finished in 2010, the **Washington County Frontier History Center** will display reconstructions of an 18th-century settlers fort—where up to four families could seek protection from Indian raids—a cabin, a blacksmith shop, and a log house filled with rough furniture. The designers of this living history project in Washington Park took pains to incorporate authentic building materials. Both cabins in the stockade area are constructed with 18th-century logs recovered from cabins and barns in Washington and Greene counties. The Washington County Historical Society runs tours as well as demonstrations of blacksmithing, medical procedures, and wood carving. *283 Dunn Ave.; 724/225–6740.*

The **David Bradford House** was the residence of one of the behind-the-scenes leaders of the Whiskey Rebellion. By 1786, when he was 26, David Bradford had earned a fortune from his gristmill and sawmills. He spent the profits to build this house, which became the unofficial headquarters for the plotters of various seditious acts. Enough evidence against Bradford existed for George Washington to sign a warrant for his arrest. Soldiers searching for Bradley nearly caught their man. But as they headed toward his estate, Bradford escaped from the bedroom window to his saddled horse below. He eventually made his way down to the Louisiana Territory, where he resettled and prospered. President John Adams pardoned David Bradford in 1799; he died in 1810.

David Bradford's House, ca. 1794, drawn by J. Howard Iams. (Westmoreland Museum of American Art)

Artifacts from the Whiskey Rebellion days are displayed in Bradford's house, which at $4,500 was the most expensive and talked-about home in the region. The dining room table is set with utensils from the period, and quilts lay atop the wood-frame beds—their feather mattresses supported with ropes. The home's mahogany staircases and marble fireplace mantels themselves are reason to visit. *175 South Main St., Washington; 724/222–6740.*

Several southwestern Pennsylvania communities still have trolleys, but few of these vehicles carry as much nostalgia as those on display at the **Pennsylvania Trolley Museum.** The 9,000-square-foot museum contains nearly four dozen trolley cars, including several prize examples from 1920s-era Philadelphia and a relic that survived the Johnstown flood of 1936—the second-deadliest flood to hit that city. The museum also has archival photos and a film about Pennsylvania's trolley era, which lasted from 1890 to the late 1940s. Price of admission includes trolley rides. *1 Museum Rd., Washington; 724/228–9256.*

By the late 1880s, trolleys had enabled the growth of Pennsylvania's suburbs. (Historical Society of Western Pennsylvania)

BRIDGES OF WASHINGTON COUNTY   *map page 261, A-3*

Spread out across Washington County on backcountry roads are 21 covered bridges, sometimes called "kissing" bridges because they were reputedly the places where young swains took their would-be brides for a covert smooch. The actual reason the bridges are covered, however, is to protect the wood from the harsh Pennsylvania elements. To explore this area, pick up a map at the **Washington County Historical Society** (LeMoyne House, 49 East Maiden St., Washington; 724/225–6740).

EAST OF PITTSBURGH: WESTMORELAND COUNTY

East of Pittsburgh rise the Laurel Highlands, where towns have remained unchanged despite fast and furious resort and condominium development in surrounding communities. Many people who live here are employed in factories, including Sony's large television assembly center near New Stanton. Increasingly, though, outdoor recreation and tourism drive the economy. For a good tour of the region, take any of the smaller roads off I–70 east, most of which wind around small towns and farms.

BUSHY RUN BATTLEFIELD STATE PARK *map page 261, B-3*

In 1763, British general Henry Bouquet was sent to assist the soldiers of Fort Pitt, who'd been under siege by a war party led by Ottawa Chief Pontiac. In addition to the Ottawas, the far-reaching conflict involved more than a dozen Native American tribes. Their members were angry about continued European encroachment on their lands, despite promises made in several treaties. On his trek to the fort, Bouquet camped at what is now Bushy Run State Park, where he was caught in a surprise attack. In retaliation, Bouquet sent half his surviving forces to loop around when the tribes regrouped for a second attack. The maneuver was devastating and the Native Americans retreated. These days, the setting is idyllic, perfect for picnicking and hiking. Three miles of historic hiking trails run along the battlefield, and guided tours led by park rangers explore the battlefield's history. *Rte. 993, 3 miles west of intersection with Rte. 66, Jeanette; 724/527–5584.*

GREENSBURG *map page 261, B/C-3*

Greensburg, the oldest county seat west of the Alleghenies, is a hilly, midsize town with a beauty of a courthouse and the **Westmoreland Museum of American Art.** Greensburg resident Mary Marchand Woods, who cherished the arts but had no personal collection—nor any heirs—bequeathed her entire estate to fund the museum's building in 1949. The museum opened a decade later and quickly gained a stellar reputation for its American and southwestern Pennsylvania art. The permanent collection includes works by artists such as Norman Rockwell, William Michael Harnett, Paul Manship, Winslow Homer, and John Singer Sargent. The museum also displays early-19th-century furniture, and during the Christmas holidays you can view a 2,000-piece toy exhibit. *221 North Main St.; 724/837–1500.*

LAUREL HIGHLANDS *map page 261, C-3/4*

East of Greensburg, gentle slopes rise toward the arching foothills of Laurel Ridge and the beginning of the Allegheny Mountains. The Pennsylvania Turnpike (I–76) and secondary roads cross forests of oak and hemlock and trout-filled mountain streams. This is the Laurel Highlands region, a place of spectacular valleys and ridges and the 1,700-foot-deep Youghiogheny River Gorge. The highlands area has been a magnet for city dwellers from Pittsburgh and surrounding communities since the early 1900s. Today, vacation homes, ski resorts, condo communities, and rustic backwoods hideaways can all be found here. The largest ski resort in Pennsylvania is **Seven Springs** (777 Waterwheel Dr., Seven Springs; 814/352–7777), which has downhill and cross-country skiing, and plenty of accommodations. Snowboarders will have a blast here—all 31 slopes and trails are open to them, along with a terrain park and half-pipe.

LIGONIER   *map page 261, C-3*

Ligonier is the playground of the old-money crowd from Pittsburgh, some of whom keep horse farms nearby. Country clubs and bridle trails can be found throughout the region.

This area was the last outpost of the British in Pennsylvania during the French and Indian War. The main route to the Laurel Mountains extends east to Ligonier from Greensburg. Fort Ligonier, today the town's main tourist attraction, was built in 1758 when British Gen. John Forbes, ordered to take Fort Duquesne from the French, needed a staging area for his forces. He called the fort Loyalhanna, later renamed Ligonier. Though attacked numerous times, the fort was never taken by an enemy. It became inactive in 1766, and was rebuilt and turned into a museum in the 1950s.

On display in Fort Ligonier are weapons, documents, and several noteworthy paintings, including one by society portraitist Sir Joshua Reynolds (1723–92). A 1,600-foot-long outer retrenchment encompasses the fort. Inside are the officers' quarters and mess hall, barracks, quartermaster, guardroom, underground magazine, and commissary. Outside the barrier are additional symbols of daily life during Colonial times—a hospital, a smokehouse, a sawmill, and bake ovens. *Rte. 30 West, Ligonier; 724/238–9701.*

In 1878, Ligonier Valley Railroad magnate Judge Thomas Mellon donated 350 acres of his own estate as a park. There was one stipulation to the creation of **Idlewild Amusement Park,** however: no trees or other plants could be disturbed. Ranked among the state's most scenic parks, Idlewild's attractions include a carousel, a steam train, a roller coaster, water rides, and the Mister Rogers' Neighborhood of Make-Believe. *Rte. 30, off Rte. 711; 724/238–3666.*

A truss bridge spans
the Monongahela River
in Brownsville.

Johnstown is surrounded by high hills that once contained a precious resource: coal. It was a prosperous industrial town in the 19th century, with jobs aplenty in steelmaking, river transport, and mining—which attracted immigrants from nearly every country of Europe. Even today, Johnstown's many unique neighborhoods reflect the ethnic character of their early settlers. High-tech and healthcare companies have set up shop here in recent years, breathing life back into a long-dormant economy. Arts and culture are certainly alive and well here. The Pasquerilla Performing Arts Center is a popular venue for concerts and plays, while the Johnstown Symphony Orchestra can fulfill your craving for classical music. The Bottleworks Ethnic Arts Center hosts classes and exhibits, while some of Johnstown's architecturally significant but vacant industrial buildings are now a cluster of studios called "ART WORKS In Johnstown!"

The event that will forever haunt Johnstown is its Memorial Day flood of 1889. Bad luck, the wrath of nature, and scandalous indifference to safety on the part of public officials and mill owners combined to make the calamity that hit the city one of the worst preventable disasters in American history.

Johnstown's historic district, a three-block-long stretch that survived the flood, is interesting to explore on foot. The **Johnstown Flood National Memorial** (Lake Rd. off Rte. 869; 814/495–4643) overlooks the ruins of the dam, whose failure caused the death of 2,209 people. The **Johnstown Flood Museum** (304 Washington St.; 814/539–1889) reveals the tragedy through vivid archival photographs and a 26-minute Academy Award–winning documentary, *The Johnstown Flood,* which identifies the culprits and causes of the disaster. For an untrammeled view of the town and the route the floodwaters took through the valley, travel up Yoder Hill via the **Johnstown Incline** (711 Edgehill Dr.; 814/536–1816). A kiosk on the observation deck traces the town's history and recounts the flood.

★ FLIGHT 93 NATIONAL MEMORIAL

A long section of fence blanketed with flowers, handwritten notes, artwork, and flags serves as a temporary memorial to the 40 passengers and crew members aboard Flight 93 credited with thwarting a terrorist attack on our nation's capital on September 11, 2001. The horror of what happened at this crash site in Shanksville, just south of Johnstown, is in stark contrast to the tranquil landscape of fields and rolling hills that surround it. A jury of family members, local leaders, and design professionals chose a permanent memorial design by architect Paul Murdoch from more than 1,000 submissions. When completed in 2011, a

JOHNSTOWN FLOOD DISASTER

High above Johnstown, at the head of the Little Conemaugh River, stood the South Fork Fishing and Hunting Club, known locally as the "Bosses Club" because its membership included Andrew Carnegie, Andrew Mellon, and Henry Clay Frick. The club owned a reservoir encircled by summer mansions. The 72-foot-high South Fork Dam had been built in 1853 to create a reservoir for the Main Line Canal. But the canal system was abandoned by the time the dam was completed and the dam went through several owners before being purchased by the sporting club in 1879.

When the dam showed signs of age, club officers ordered it repaired but failed to authorize an engineer to oversee the work. To prevent the loss of the black bass that had been stocked in the lake, a screen was placed across the spillway. Meanwhile, the hillsides around Johnstown had been stripped of timber, creating the potential for a dangerous erosion problem.

Years of complaints about the decrepit condition of the dam, 14 miles upriver from Johnstown, fell on deaf ears. On Memorial Day 1889, a storm dropped 7 inches of rain on the area, and the runoff rushed down the denuded hillsides and filled the reservoir. The fish screen quickly became clogged and the dam burst with a thunderous roar. More than 20 million tons of water raced through the narrow valley, creating a wall of water 35 to 75 feet high. The force, powerful enough to carry houses, train locomotives, and boulders, destroyed Johnstown and killed 2,209 people in what remains America's deadliest flood. The disaster initiated the first relief effort organized by Clara Barton's American Red Cross. About half the members of the Bosses Club made hefty contributions to the relief efforts, and Carnegie built a new library for the town.

The Johnstown Flood Museum, formerly the Johnstown Library, was built with funds supplied by Andrew Carnegie. In the background is the Johnstown Incline. (Johnstown Area Heritage Association)

Of the many homes Frank Lloyd Wright designed, Fallingwater is generally considered his masterpiece.

Tower of Voices housing 40 metallic wind chimes—one for each victim—will welcome visitors to the site. Murdoch says the memorial, which will incorporate a bowl-shaped plot surrounded by wetlands and a grove of maple trees, is meant to reflect "the spirit of truth and freedom of expression that the passengers and crew fought to defend." *From Johnstown, take Rte. 219 South. Exit onto Rte. 30 East at Stoystown/Jennerstown. From the Lincoln Hwy (U.S. 30), turn right onto Lambertsville Rd. Turn left onto Skyline Rd. to reach the memorial. 814/443–4557.*

★ FALLINGWATER   map page 261, C-4

Fallingwater, built as a private residence improbably suspended over a waterfall, is unquestionably a masterpiece of one of America's most important architects.

Edgar J. Kaufmann, who had made a fortune as owner of Kaufmann's, Pittsburgh's premier department store, hired Frank Lloyd Wright to design a weekend retreat for his family on a piece of land in Mill Run. Battles of will between Kaufmann and Wright over the details of the design became legendary. In September 1935, when Frank Lloyd Wright was beginning to sketch out the blueprints for Fallingwater, Kaufmann stared at the drawing. "I thought you would place the house near the waterfall, not over it," he commented. In a soft voice, Wright replied, "E.J., I want you to live with the waterfall, not just to look at it, but for it to become an integral part of your lives." And this exchange perfectly embodies the spirit of Fallingwater, a design so fragile skeptics expected the building to hold up for a decade at most.

Wright's design integrated both the tangible and visual landscape. For instance, a massive rock already on the property is part of the home's foundation, and it's incorporated into the stone floor of the great room. Fallingwater's cantilevers dramatically stretch out over Bear Run Creek, reflecting the natural ridges of the rocky land. The surging creek provides background music for every space in the house, especially when its unique corner windows are pushed open. Wright designed the home's modern-yet-rustic built-in sofas, shelves and dressers—his effort to "client-proof" the interior design of the house. Tours, run by the Western Pennsylvania Conservancy, are essential not just for witnessing the home's stunning architectural details but also for the stories about Wright and the eccentric Kaufman family. As many as 900 visitors walk through Fallingwater on a summer day, so reserve tickets well ahead of time. *Take the Pennsylvania Turnpike to Donegal Exit, then take Rte. 31 east to Rte. 381 south and look for signs; 724/329–8501.*

KENTUCK KNOB   *map page 261, B-4*

Seven miles southwest of Fallingwater is another spectacular, though far less famous, example of Frank Lloyd Wright's trademark organic architecture. Impressed by Wright's Fallingwater, Pittsburgh businessman Isaac Newton Hagan hired the architect in 1953 to design a more modest home for his family at Kentuck Knob. Built on a hexagonal grid, geometry defines this house—from the triangular stone pillars out front, to hexagonal skylights carved into the overhang, to drawers that open on a diagonal. Typical of the Usonian style, the design for Kentuck Knob emphasizes openness with a single-floor plan without basement or attic.

The exterior of the house, like Fallingwater, was designed to blend in with its natural setting. To this end, the only building materials Wright used are tidewater red cypress, glass and native fieldstone, which local laborers cut by hand. The copper roof mimics colors of nearby brush, one of the many reasons Kentuck Knob blends in seamlessly with its setting. Simply step out onto the terrace for a sweeping view of the Youghiogheny River Gorge. A traipse through Kentuck Knob's grounds takes you past 35 wood, metal, and stone sculptures by artists such as Andy Goldsworthy and Ray Smith. Two sections of the Berlin wall acquired by current Kentuck Knob owner Lord Peter Palumbo are also on display in the garden. Tours are conducted year-round, weather permitting. *Chalk Hill/Ohiopyle Rd., off Rte. 381; 724/329–1901.*

OHIOPYLE STATE PARK   *map page 261, C-4*

Nearly 19,000 acres surrounding one section of the **Youghiogheny River Gorge** have been preserved as Ohiopyle State Park. A testament to the restorative powers of nature, the Yough, or the "Yawk," as natives know it, was for years considered a dead waterway after being polluted by a century of pit and strip mining. A concerted cleanup effort in the 1980s, however, has restored the ecosystem. Several white-water rafting companies operate in the area and the park is popular with mountain bikers, swimmers, and hikers. *Ohiopyle State Park, Rte. 381, 6 miles north of U.S. 40; 724/329–8591.*

FORT NECESSITY NATIONAL BATTLEFIELD   *map page 261, B-4*

Young George Washington's first military campaign—one of the events that sparked the French and Indian War—took place here in 1754, when the 22-year-old lieutenant colonel was sent by Virginia's governor to force the French out of the Ohio Valley. After Washington and about 300 Virginia volunteers stumbled

FAVORITE PLACES TO EAT

Highwaters Grill & BBQ. 1856 Mill Run Rd., Mill Run; 724/329–4669. $

Just outside the town of Ohiopyle, the grill specializes in slow-cooked baby back ribs, pulled pork, and corn on the cob, though you'll also find pizza and sandwiches.

Stonehouse Restaurant. 3023 National Pike, Farmington; 800/274–7138. $–$$

When this spot in the Laurel Highlands opened in 1822, it initially served travelers chasing renewed health in nearby Fayette Springs. Today, it serves hungry tourists seeking a bowl of creamy crab bisque or Caeser salad.

Tavern on the Square. 108 North Market St., New Wilmington; 724/946–2020. $$

In the mid-1800s, this former house was a refuge for escaped slaves following the Underground Railroad. In 1933, two graduates of Westminster College converted the house into a restaurant known for creamed chicken on a biscuit, grilled pork chops, ham steaks, and delicious sticky buns.

across 33 French soldiers, Washington ordered a surprise attack at dawn and 10 French soldiers were killed, including the commander, Ensign Jumonville. Within 10 minutes the survivors had surrendered, but one soldier escaped and made his way to Fort Duquesne in what is now Pittsburgh.

Flush with his first victory, Washington camped at Great Meadows to regroup and ordered his men to build a slap-dash fort "of necessity" to protect them from a possible French counterattack. In July 1754, a French force, led by the brother of the fallen Jumonville, did return—and, outnumbered, Washington surrendered after an eight-hour siege. In return for being allowed to march from the fort with swords and weapons, Washington signed a document of surrender written in French. Either deliberately or inadvertently, the English translation omitted a line in which Washington acknowledged that Jumonville's death was the result of an assassination instead of legitimate combat. Later, the French used the assassination of Jumonville as propaganda, accusing Washington and the British of war crimes. Not surprisingly, Washington took serious flack for the incident. British statesman Horace Walpole characterized the controversy surrounding Jumonville's death as "a volley fired by a young Virginian in the backwoods of America [that] set the world on fire."

The reconstructed fort contains the **Mount Washington Tavern,** a rebuilt stagecoach stop from the early 1800s. Although it's open for tours and furnished similarly to how it looked when pioneers traveling the National Road stopped in, the tavern no longer serves meals. Trails lead through forest and meadows around Fort Necessity and **Braddocks Grave,** where a monument marks the final resting place of British Gen. Edward Braddock. He was fatally shot in the chest while battling French and Native American soldiers in 1755. The British Army buried Braddock in the middle of the road near Fort Necessity to prevent the Native Americans from detecting his body. *U.S. 40, 11 miles southeast of Uniontown; 724/329–5512.*

GETTING AROUND

From Philadelphia, the most direct route to Pittsburgh and other points southwest is I–76 (the Pennsylvania Turnpike), which travels through Harrisburg and Bedford County, skirting Shanksville and Somerset before moving north to Monroeville and the I–376 connector to Pittsburgh. Route 381 south, off I–76, leads to Mill Run and Fallingwater, Ohiopyle State Park, Braddock's Grave, and Fort Necessity National Battlefield. Interstate 79, starting in Washington, travels north, brushing the outskirts of Pittsburgh and traveling near Harmony, Zelienople, and McConnell's Mill State Park. Route 208, off I–79, offers direct access to Volant and New Wilmington. Route 50 east, off I–79, leads through tranquil countryside to Hickory and Avella.

FAVORITE PLACES TO STAY

The Century Inn. Route 40, Scenery Hill; 724/945–5180. $

Instigators of the Whiskey Rebellion supposedly met here to drink and plot their next moves. A National Historic Landmark, the inn is the oldest continuously operating hostelry along the National Road. The stone structure has five dining rooms and nine bedrooms with antique furniture.

Frank Lloyd Wright's Duncan House. 1 Usonian Dr., Acme; 877/833–7829. $$$$

Within 30 miles of Fallingwater and Kentuck Knob, this classic Usonian-style home was moved from a Chicago suburb, then reassembled in Laurel Heights in 2007. The horizontal board-and-batten construction and the cathedral ceiling will be familiar to Wright fans. Duncan House sits on a 125-acre resort, adjacent to miles of hiking trails. But none of these features beats the thrill of boasting that you slept in a building designed by the architectural genius.

Grammy Rose's Bed & Breakfast. 405 E. Maiden St., Washington; 724/228–1508. $

Relax on the wraparound front porch of this cozy B&B run by a florist and a tavern owner. The pretty guest rooms are filled with antiques, and the beds are covered in soft linens. It's also near the LeMoyne House, Meadows Racetrack, and Pennsylvania Trolley Museum.

Summit Inn. 101 Skyline Dr., Farmington; 724/438–8594. $$–$$$$

This mountaintop resort is among the accommodations closest to Fallingwater. Built in 1907, it has managed to retain a leisurely feel of yesteryear. Open April to November only, the resort has 94 rooms, indoor and outdoor pools, restaurants, and a golf course.

THE QUIET NORTHWEST

Northwestern Pennsylvania is the least-visited corner of the state, but in many ways this is what gives it its unique character. In Erie, its largest city, the lake effect is felt in both the climate and the history of the shipping and fishing industries. East of Erie is an agricultural region where vintners are gaining a national reputation for their distinct reds and whites. Farther east is the Allegheny Forest. A hike through the dense sea of white pines will quickly convince you little has changed since Pennsylvania was known as "Penn's Woods." And before Texas there was Titusville—a fascinating place to learn about the nation's first oil wells.

EARLY HISTORY

Erie—the city, the county, and the lake—was named for the Erie Indians, whose history became obscured following their conquest and assimilation in the early 1600s by the Senecas, one of the powerful five nations of the Iroquois Confederacy. (The others were the Mohawks, Oneidas, Onondagas, and Cayugas.) French explorers and trappers working their way down from Canada were the first Europeans to set foot on Seneca land. The French, however, were allied with the Huron and Algonquin nations, archenemies of the Iroquois, and fierce battles were waged until 1696, when the French finally prevailed.

In the early 1700s, the French sought to control a direct route via the Ohio River south to the Mississippi River and the French colonies in Louisiana. When English settlers began flooding into Iroquois land, the Iroquois turned on them. Capitalizing on their anger, the French recruited the Iroquois to help fight the British, initiating what came to be known as the French and Indian War. The French built defensive forts on Presque Isle and other key lakeside points, abandoning and burning them after a wave of British attacks forced them to retreat.

Fort Presque Isle and Fort Le Boeuf were rebuilt by the British, but lost again to the Indians, led by Chief Pontiac. The forts were in Indian hands for several years until the 1768 treaty of Fort Stanwix returned the northwestern Pennsylvania territory to British control. The treaty also opened Indian land to settlement, and by the end of the decade, immigrants were moving westward. The second treaty of Fort Stanwix, in 1784, effectively ended the reign of the Iroquois Confederacy.

Throughout the 19th century, Lake Erie was of tremendous economic importance to the fledgling United States, as freight crossed from the interior into the port of Erie and on to other cities on the lake, such as Cleveland and Buffalo.

When it was built in 1882, Kinzua Bridge was the highest railroad bridge in the world.

During the War of 1812, Commodore Oliver Hazard Perry, aboard the brig US *Niagara,* defeated the British at the Battle of Lake Erie, thus securing American control of that trade route. It wasn't until after the Civil War that cities like Erie began to expand, and smaller outlying communities sprang up to link the port city to other areas of the state and to New York City. In 1859, an area on the outskirts of Titusville became the site of the nation's first oil well, and for a time the region rode the prosperity of an oil boom.

MODERN TIMES

While the economy across the United States boomed during the 1990s, the northwestern region continued to lose population and industry at a slow but steady rate. Many factories closed in this area, and farms ceased production. The shrinkage of manufacturing has allowed nature to reclaim land that was originally part of the vast Eastern forest. Great herds of elk and other animals that used to roam the region have been reintroduced, birds of prey have returned, and formerly distressed habitats now thrive with living creatures.

Tioga County is full of Norman Rockwell–esque sights.

WOODED HILLS, SMALL TOWNS

There is no mistaking the towns of northwestern Pennsylvania for the suburbs of Pittsburgh. Places like Mercer and Franklin are the kind of communities Americans envision when they talk about wanting to have a simpler life. These are Norman Rockwell–type hamlets, often with a town square and a bandstand, a majestic courthouse, big Victorian homes, and broad, tree-lined streets.

For a taste of the countryside, take a drive through the small villages, lakefronts, and country lanes that characterize Mercer County. Start in the borough of Grove City and follow Route 173 toward Sandy Lake then on to the small town of Midgeville, home to the legendary Indian Graveyard. Continue on the Route 173 to Stoneboro. If it's a warm day, take a dip at Lakeside Park. A right turn on Route 358 will take you past Amish farms and a series of rough roads. When you make your way back to District Road, turn left on Route 58 and head toward Mercer. Along the way, you'll pass a one-room schoolhouse and farms. Before heading out, download a road map from mercercountypa.org.

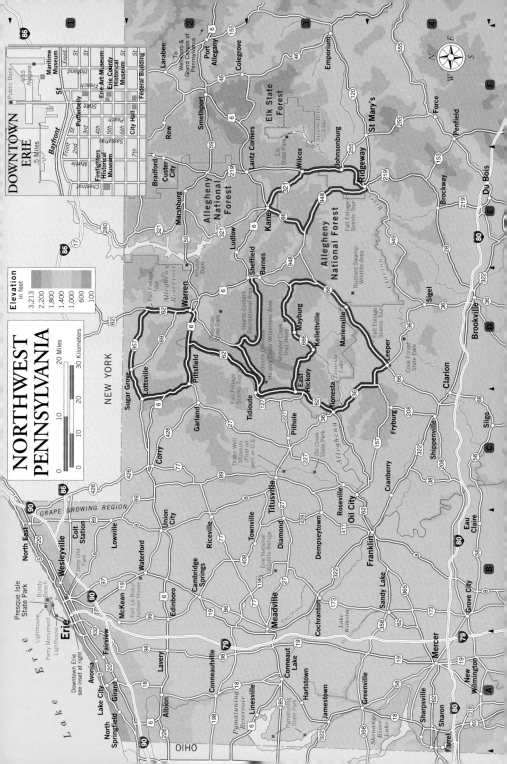

A farm in Nauvoo, in Tioga County.

MERCER   *map page 283, A-4*

With a population of 2,300, Mercer is typical of the picturesque small towns in this area. Its courthouse is built on the highest elevation in the county and can be seen for miles around. There are many stately old homes here and the town puts on a Victorian festival (724/662–4185) on the last weekend in July.

PYMATUNING STATE PARK   *map page 283, A-3*

To control flooding and reclaim swampland, the Pymatuning Dam was completed in 1934, creating in the process Pymatuning Lake, one of the largest man-made lakes in the eastern United States (it's 17 miles long, with 70 miles of shoreline). It is now part of one of Pennsylvania's largest state parks.

The name Pymatuning is derived from the Seneca phrase meaning "crooked-mouthed man's dwelling place"—a reference to the Erie tribe that lived here, and to its queen, known to the Senecas for her crooked dealings. The lake provides ample opportunities for swimming, boating, and camping. Fishing from the causeway is forbidden, but there are plenty of other places to cast a line. The park is open year-round but is especially pleasant in summer, when cool breezes take the edge off the summer heat, and in fall when the pine, maple, and birch trees are splashed in autumn's colors. *2660 Williamsfield Rd., Jamestown; 724/932–3141.*

LAKE ERIE   *map page 283, A/B-1*

The Great Lakes, including Lake Erie (the fourth largest and shallowest of the five), were formed by the final expansions and contractions of the Wisconsin Glacier about 15,000 years ago. Much of the land was scraped to bedrock by glaciers, and in some cases gouged into deep craters. When the ice melted, water filled the craters and the Great Lakes were formed.

In the early 1800s, Erie became one of the busiest inland ports in the United States. The great sailing ships eventually gave way to steam-powered vessels, and by 1850 Lake Erie and the other Great Lakes were bustling with hundreds of 300-foot-long steamers, popular with travelers because of their speed and comfort. Unfortunately, not all of them made it safely to their destinations. About 1,700 shipwrecks in Lake Erie have been documented, but the locations of only about 277 of them are known. (Some researchers suspect as many as 3,000 ships rest on the lake floor.) Since the United States and Canada began investing billions of dollars on cleanup in the late '60s, Lake Erie has become a popular for spot for scuba divers, who explore the sunken ships. Pollution garnered national attention in June 1969, when petrochemicals from Cleveland and other Ohio cities contaminated the Cuyahoga River so badly that it actually caught fire. A positive outcome of the incident is that it prompted the U.S. Congress to pass the Clean Water Act of 1972.

Transport businesses continued to search for a more efficient way to move goods from vessels docking in Erie to inland Pennsylvania. They found it in the Erie Extension Canal, a man-made waterway connecting Erie to the Ohio River at Beaver, about 30 miles northwest of Pittsburgh. The canal was built between 1838 and 1844, with stops at Conneaut Lake, Franklin, and Meadville along an eastern route. A western extension covered New Castle and points along the Beaver River.

By 1853, water transportation was supplanted by the railroad lines connecting Erie to Pittsburgh and Pittsburgh to the East Coast. The town of Erie survived the resulting economic U-turn by specializing in ship repair and fishing, but its boom era was drawing to a close.

Today the town draws beach bums in summer, when the waters of Lake Erie temper the heat, making this a great place for swimming and water-skiing. Winter can be very cold, though, and some restaurants and tourist attractions operate "in season" only. From November through January, intense snow squalls often blow off the lake, making travel hazardous.

CITY OF ERIE *map page 283, B-1*

Downtown Erie is level and major streets are unusually broad, having been designed for horse- and ox-drawn wagons to make wide turns. State Street, which bisects the area, has plenty of excellent coffee shops and boutiques. Finding your way around town is easy because the cross-streets are numbered, starting at the lake. The higher the number, the farther you are from the lake. Whether you walk or drive, check out the restored Victorian mansions on West Sixth Street, once known as Millionaire's Row.

At the foot of State Street, on the city's bayfront, stands the 187-foot-high **Bicentennial Tower** (Dobbins Landing; 814/455–6055), built in 1995 to celebrate Erie's 200th birthday. The tower's two observation decks provide spectacular lake views. To take a ride on Lake Erie, catch a water taxi (814/881–2502) at Dobbins Landing, Liberty Park, or the East Avenue Boat Launch.

Farther up on State Street is the **Warner Theater,** a glamorous 1930s movie palace, with a grand lobby filled with art deco details and gold- and silver leaf. The theater presents touring Broadway shows and performances of the Erie Philharmonic. *811 State St.; 814/452–4857.*

The **Erie County History Center** has a superb photographic archive stocked with images that trace Erie history from the late 1800s through the early 1900s. You'll see photos of old gristmills and sawmills, remnants of Erie County's agricultural past, and other photo exhibits of bicycles, automobiles, and planes, built in the county's glory days as a manufacturing hub during the 19th and early-20th centuries. The history center is also where you can pick up excellent driving-tour maps of the area's many back roads. A walkway in the building leads directly to the **Cashier's House,** an 1839 Greek Revival town house that served as the residence of Peter Benson, chief executive of the Erie branch of the U.S. Bank of Pennsylvania. Noted Philadelphia architect William Kelly designed the house. Its no-nonsense exterior hiding an ornate interior of wood carvings and marble fireplace mantels is typical of those built by Erie's wealthier citizens in the mid- and late 1800s. *419 State St., off the Bayfront Pkwy.; 814/454–1813.*

The showpiece of the **Erie Maritime Museum** is a reconstruction of the US Brig *Niagara,* which figured prominently in the War of 1812 when, under the

This print shows Commodore Oliver Hazard Perry being rowed to the US Brig *Niagara* after the *Lawrence* was sunk.

command of Commodore Oliver Hazard Perry, it won the Battle of Lake Erie. On September 10, 1813, Perry's flagship, the *Lawrence,* had endured two hours of cannon fire from the British, which crippled the vessel and either killed or wounded more than 80 percent of his crew. Reestablishing himself aboard the nearby US Brig *Niagara* and bearing his signature flag with the words "Don't Give Up the Ship," Perry daringly re-engaged the enemy and emerged victorious. Following his conquest, he sent the famous message: "We have met the enemy and he is ours."

Perry's victory won the War of 1812, but in 1820, the US Brig *Niagara* was "scuttled" by the navy—a practice in which boats were sunk and then scavenged for useful material. In 1913, the ship was resurrected and restored as part of the centennial celebration of the 1813 battle. Though restored again in the 1930s, the ship was in a dismal state by the 1980s. This time, the Erie County Historical Society came to the rescue, building a new boat from original plans and including 100 pieces of the original vessel. The reconstructed craft is berthed on the bayfront. The museum also has exhibits about the War of 1812 and other famous warships and sea battles. *150 East Front St.; 814/452–2744.*

Erie County history is movingly told through paintings, documents, and artifacts at the **Watson-Curtze Mansion and Planetarium.** Built in 1891, the mansion suggests the good life enjoyed by some residents of Millionaire's Row in the late 19th century. Handsome friezes, stained-glass windows, paintings, and antiques dazzle the eye. The planetarium, in the carriage house, has regular slide shows and lectures. *356 West Sixth St.; 814/871–5790.*

The imposing Old Custom House, a Greek Revival structure built in 1839, houses the **Erie Art Museum.** Ceramics, Japanese prints, Indian bronzes, Chinese porcelains, and Tibetan art objects are among the thousands of objects on display. *411 State St.; 814/459–5477.*

The **Firefighters' Historical Museum,** which occupies a once busy Erie firehouse, has more than 1,300 fire-fighting artifacts, including a horse-pulled water wagon, fire call boxes, uniforms, a hand-pulled pumper, a horse-drawn fire engine, and a vintage fire truck from the 1920s. The enthusiastic guides, who are all connected to firefighting in some way or another, know the stories behind every object on display. *428 Chestnut St.; 814/456–5969.*

★ PRESQUE ISLE STATE PARK *map page 283, B-1*

More a peninsula than an island, Presque Isle is fringed by sandy beaches and favored by several varieties of sandpipers. Wetland areas on the southern-facing inner shore are a breeding ground for blue herons, which strut majestically through the reeds. The song of a whippoorwill sometimes provides background music for an afternoon stroll. A National Natural Landmark, Presque Isle is one of the world's premier venues for the study of the ecological succession of plants. More than 500 plant species grow here, in habitats that reflect the progression of development from dune stage to pond stage to final forest stage. *Birder's World* magazine calls Presque Isle one of the top birding spots in the country, with more than 320 species spotted. Forty-seven species of mammals live here as well.

Presque Isle can be visited at any time of year, although it's awfully cold in winter. An 1872 lighthouse overlooks the lakeshore, and a 14-mile loop road provides excellent opportunities to view autumn foliage. Misery Bay is where the US Brig *Niagara* was scuttled in 1820. A monument to Oliver Hazard Perry can be found at Crystal Point. *Take I–90, Exit 5 and follow Rte. 832 North to Sterrettania Rd., which becomes Peninsula Dr. and leads into the park; 814/833–7424.*

Before the entrance to Presque Isle State Park you'll come upon **Waldameer Park & Water World,** a family park with some of the longest and steepest water

The Presque Isle Lighthouse was built in 1872.

Locals often fly kites on the wide, sandy beaches at Presque Isle State Park.

slides in the country. The park's giant Ferris wheel twirls riders 100 feet in the air, while the Ravine Flyer II roller coaster gives thrill-seekers a truly breathtaking glimpse of Lake Erie. *220 Peninsula Dr.; 814/838–3591.*

★ GRAPE-GROWING REGION   *map page 283, B/C-1*

About 15 miles east of Erie is grape-growing country. Most of the grapes in this region are of the sweet Concord variety, and likely to end up in jams and jellies, but some are wine varietals. All the wineries listed below are in the town of North East. To bicycle through the area, drop by **Lake Country Bike** (21 East Main St., North East; 814/725–1338) for maps and rentals.

WINERIES

Run by six generations of the Bostwick family, **Heritage Wine Cellars** has the largest tasting room in the area and an astonishing variety of Pennsylvania reds, whites, and sparkling wines. More than 50 varieties can be sampled for free. *12160 East Main Rd. (U.S. 20), North East; 814/725–8015.*

Since 1998 Nick and Kathy Mobilia have been growing grapes and producing red, white, and blush wines for **Arrowhead Wine Cellars.** Adjacent to the winery, you can pick your own seasonal fruits and purchase homemade jams and jellies. *12073 East Main Rd., North East; 814/725–5509.*

Mazza Vineyards, on a hilly estate overlooking Lake Erie, has sweet dessert wines, champagnes, and chardonnays in addition to a merlot, a cabernet sauvignon, and a French hybrid, Vidal Blanc. *11815 East Lake Rd. (Rte. 5), North East; 814/725–8695.*

Its wine- and cheese-tasting parties have made **Penn Shore Vineyards** a popular destination. Kir, a dessert wine made from black currants, is the specialty, but the winery has a full range of whites, reds, and French hybrids. *10225 East Lake Rd. (Rte. 5), North East; 814/725–8688.*

The merlots and cabernets at **Presque Isle Wine Cellars** are celebrated, as are the late-harvest Vignoles. The winery is located alongside scenic Twelve Mile Creek. *9440 West Main Rd. (U.S. 20), North East; 814/725–1314.*

SOUTH FROM ERIE   *map page 283, B-1/2*

South from Erie, U.S. 19 quickly leaves the strip malls behind and enters rolling farm country sparsely dotted with farm equipment dealers, modest homes on endless lawns, and the occasional tackle shop.

WATERFORD   *map page 283, B-2*

Picturesque Waterford can take you quite by surprise. Looming over most of the town is the **Eagle Hotel,** which is no longer a hotel but a historical exhibit operated by the Fort Le Boeuf Museum. The upper floors are jammed with interesting bric-a-brac and period furniture. Although Waterford offers little in the way of shops, the taxidermy studio keeps its door open, and the proprietors are friendly. Don't be surprised if you smell a strange aroma in the place—the head of a bear or some other animal part might be boiling on the stove in the back room. *32 High St.; 814/796–0060.*

CAMBRIDGE SPRINGS   *map page 283, B-2*

In the late 19th century, Cambridge Springs hosted 10,000 people at a time who hoped to benefit from the supposed healing properties of the mineral waters that flowed from local springs.

Most of the magnificent old hotels that once lined the streets here are long gone, as are the spas that drew people to them. Still standing on U.S. 19, however, is an octagonal house—a popular, if now rare, style of early-American design. Advocates of eight-sided dwellings argued that such houses were healthier than standard four-sided homes as they had better ventilation and more natural light.

Many of the springs in this region are fed by French Creek, which was a major waterway for Native Americans and French fur traders. It remained the primary access to the area until the emergence of the railway. Because the bed of French Creek is especially deep near Cambridge Springs, this is a terrific place for canoeing. Public access points along the creek make it easy to drop in a canoe or kayak, if you've got one. And the **Crawford County Conservation District** sponsors an annual canoe sojourn along French Creek each summer. *Woodcock Creek Nature Center, 21742 German Rd., Meadville; 814/763–5269.*

OIL COUNTRY   *map page 283*

Pennsylvania's Oil Heritage Region is not as bleak as visitors from other oil regions might expect. This is a hilly, wooded area south and west of the Allegheny National Forest, sprinkled with small towns and surrounded by areas of great natural beauty. You can access the region from U.S. 6, the Commonwealth's longest highway and one of the nation's most scenic routes.

The country's first oil well was drilled near Titusville in 1859, and the region was soon pockmarked with "black gold" wells. Scores of small businessmen from towns such as Franklin, Oil City, and Pithole became millionaires overnight. The boom continued until the early 1900s, when more efficient extraction methods made backyard oil wells obsolete.

Small-town charm mixes with history in far northern Custer City, near Bradford (along Route 219). Exhibits at the town's **Penn-Brad Oil Museum** showcase the tools of the oil trade and shed light on the "miracle molecule." Professionals who have had first-hand experience working on oil rigs lead guided tours of the oil fields, where you'll see a 72-foot-tall drilling rig left over from the oil-rich 1880s. It's open Memorial Day to Labor Day. *50 Parkway La.; 814/362–1955.*

(above) Drake Well Museum, south of Titusville. (below) During Pennsylvania's oil boom, derricks were a common sight. (Pennsylvania Historical & Museum Commission)

The late-19th-century oil boom in this area made possible the mansions lining the streets of even the very small towns in Oil Country.

THE DRAKE WELL MUSEUM   map page 283, C-3

The museum, south of Titusville, provides a detailed history of the late 19th century, when oil was Pennsylvania's most valuable commodity. Exhibits tell the story of New York lawyer and entrepreneur George Bissell, who was fascinated by petroleum, then viewed as a messy substitute for kerosene. Working with a Yale University chemistry professor, Bissell developed uses for the product—but in order to get his petroleum products to market, he had to get it out of the ground in a way that would assure sufficient quantities to cover his extraction costs.

Bissell hired a retired railroad conductor, Edwin Drake, to investigate the oil seeps on land owned by his company, Seneca Oil. Drake, who was paid $1,000 a year, built the first successful oil well in the United States on Bissell's country estate near Titusville. A month after Drake perfected the oil well machinery, a *New York Times* reporter wrote about the "excitement attendant on the discovery of this vast source of oil." Soon, well operations were chugging throughout the region and the refined petroleum was selling well. Some oil products that came from the region were rather dubious, though. One example: "Rock Oil," a medicine that promised "wonderful curative powers." *East Bless St. (Rte. 8), south of Titusville; 814/827–2797.*

OIL CREEK STATE PARK   *map page 283, C-3*

Paralleling both sides of Oil Creek, between the Drake Well Museum to the north and the main park entrance at Petroleum Center, a 37-mile loop has both a walking and a biking trail, with a 500-foot elevation change along the Westside trail. In the 1860s, oil wells, hamlets, and refineries lined this 13-mile stretch of the creek. Today you can camp in one of the park's 12 shelters, which are equipped with water and toilet facilities. Exhibits at the visitors center, housed in a historic train station, tell the story of the park's changing landscape. Once polluted during the oil boom, the streams are now pristine and filled with trout. *Off Rte. 8 (follow signs) 1 mile north of Rouseville in Oil City; 814/676–5915.*

FRANKLIN   *map page 283, B-3/4*

Few of the prospectors who came to this area in search of oil realized their dreams. But many who rode the oil wave successfully hailed from the little town

Downtown Franklin.

ALLEGHENY RIVER map page 283, C/D-2/3

From Oil City north to Kinzua Dam, the Allegheny River has been designated a Recreational Waterway under the federal Wild and Scenic Rivers Act.

Along U.S. 62 from Franklin to Tionesta and north past Warren, the Allegheny River is slow-moving and tranquil. Many people go north to Warren and canoe down the Allegheny, camping on islands along the way. Canoe outfitters advertise their services here, and there are several places downstream to rest or be picked up and brought back to your car. Among the outfitters are **Eagle Rock** (814/755–4444) and **Outback Adventures** (814/755–3658), both near Tionesta; **Allegheny Outfitters** (814/723–1203), in Warren; and **Indian Waters** (814/484–3252), north of Tionesta in Tidioute.

of Franklin, which became a trading and management center for the oil industry following Drake's discovery.

In the heart of Venango County, Franklin has an imposing, white-topped courthouse, plenty of wide, tree-lined streets, and stately homes. Redbrick exteriors with white stone lintels characterize the downtown buildings, and two adjacent parks make this town unique.

Clusters of handsome mansions can be found in the Liberty, Miller Park, and Adelaide neighborhoods. Most were built between 1860 and 1890—the styles range from Queen Anne to Victorian to Arts and Crafts. Many are private residences, but one is open to the public: the **Venango County Historical Society House Museum,** which contains period furniture, paintings, antiques, and other finery of the era. *301 South Park St.; 814/437–2275.*

St. John's Episcopal Church has 30 stained-glass windows from the studios of Louis Comfort Tiffany. The most beautiful of these, the Rose Window, is made of *favrile* glass, a favorite medium of the decorator-designer. Call ahead for hours. *1141 Buffalo St.; 814/432–5161.*

The Grand Canyon of Pennsylvania.

U.S. 62 ABOVE OIL CITY *map page 283, C/D-2/3*

Above Oil City, U.S. 62 meanders through hills covered with aged trees that turn magnificent colors in fall. As you near McPhearson Road and the Allegheny General Store (814/676–5769) you'll see signs along the road advertising old-fashioned ring bologna, slab bacon, and Amish baked goods. Step inside the store for a sandwich, or sample the excellent cookies, breads, jams, and maple syrup.

As you continue north, the hardwood forest is replaced by conifers. By Tionesta Lake, the Allegheny River is wide and beautiful.

★ ALLEGHENY NATIONAL FOREST *map page 283, E-2/3*

The Allegheny National Forest is known for its rugged beauty and status as one of the few remnants of the ancient forest that used to cover most of the eastern United States. There is something primordial about this forest. Track marks in the dirt tell you where wild critters have searched for food, the animal kingdom here including white-tail deer, raccoons, skunks, wolves, and plenty of bears. Elk roam free and the bald eagle is a frequent guest. This is among the most majestic

Allegheny National Forest is one of the last ancient forests in the eastern U.S.

spots in Pennsylvania, a place of still-unspoiled natural beauty. It's obvious why outdoor enthusiasts swarm here for hiking, kayaking, swimming, fly-fishing, and camping. The Allegheny National Forest Visitors Bureau operates visitors centers in Bradford (80 E. Corydon St., Suite 114), Lantz (3183 Rte. 219), and Marshburg (Intersection of Rtes. 321 and 59)—all of which can be reached by calling 800/473–9370. *Allegheny National Forest Headquarters, 222 Liberty St., Warren; 814/723–5150.*

COUNTRY ROUTE 666   *map page 283, D-3*

Don't be in a hurry if you want to travel Route 666, which heads east from the Allegheny River to the town of Barnes. The road sharply twists and turns, with only a few straight-ahead stretches. The views are spectacular as the route cuts through wooded valleys, past small farms with red barns and silos, and past small white houses backed by forest. Route 666 starts in East Hickory and moves east through Kelletville and Porkey, before ending in Barnes. It's easy to get lost on side roads, but that's one of the pleasures of traveling through this serene territory.

COOK FOREST STATE PARK   *map page 283, D-4*

South of the Allegheny National Forest is Cook Forest State Park, established by a private landowner who wanted to save 8,500 acres of forest land from logging. The old-growth forests here are among the most beautiful forests in the state. Some of the white pine and hemlock are more than 300 years old and more than 200 feet tall. Climb the old fire tower for the view, and take time to relax by the Clarion River and contemplate its deep green waters. *Rte. 66 or Rte. 36, north from I–80. 814/744–8407.*

ELK COUNTY   *map page 265, F-3/4*

East of the Allegheny National Forest is **Elk State Forest** (Rte. 120), where elk have been reintroduced to the region. The plan is controversial, however: it introduced elk from western states to encourage the development of local herds, but because the imported elk were larger than the indigenous variety, the cross-breeding produced a strain of voracious eaters with enormous antlers. To placate local farmers, crops have been planted especially for the elk. **St. Mary's,** west of Elk State Forest on Route 120, is the largest town in Elk County and a good place to seek advice on where the elk with the largest racks might be hanging out.

GRAND CANYON OF PENNSYLVANIA   *map page 283, F-2*

Nestled in 158,000 acres of Tioga State Forest is the Grand Canyon of Pennsylvania, a 45-mile gorge that runs a zig-zag course through one of the most densely forested regions of the state. In some places, the cliffs of the gorge rise well over 1,300 feet above fast-flowing Pine Creek, giving way to jaw-droppingly gorgeous views of Tioga County. Canoeists, kayakers, and white-water rafters all come here to enjoy their sports, and there's a "rail trail" that follows the east bank of Pine Creek into the Grand Canyon (the trailhead is found 7 miles southwest of Wellsboro). Along the way you can fish for trout and small-mouth bass. In spring, wildflowers are abundant, and in fall the hills are bright with the color of autumn leaves. Bird-watching is popular here, as bald eagles, osprey, and hawks frequent the skies over the gorge. The northern end of the Grand Canyon is reached by Route 6, the southern end by Route 414. *For maps and information, contact the Tioga State Forest District Office at 1 Nessnuk Lane, Wellsboro; 570/724–2868. For canoe and kayak rentals, contact Pine Creek Outfitters, Wellsboro; 570/724–3003.*

FAVORITE PLACES TO EAT

Barbato's Italian Restaurant.
1707 State St., Erie; 814/459–2158. $

You can't visit Erie without trying the pepperoni balls, a local specialty. These deep-fried spheres of dough, about the size of a golf ball, surround a chunk of pepperoni. Purists eschew adding cheese to the filling, but they're extra-decadent with it. Barbato's is happy to "get creative" by adding cheese, mushrooms, sauce, or anything else to the center of your pepperoni ball upon request.

Presque Isle Downs and Casino. 8199 Perry Hwy., Erie; 866/374–3386. $–$$$

Try your luck at any of the three restaurants in this sprawling complex. They range from casual (the Clubhouse and the Triple Crown Buffet) to fine dining (La Bonne Vie). Four lounges in the casino serve until 2 A.M. and host jazz and rock bands on the weekends.

Pufferbelly. 414 French St., Erie; 814/454–1557. $$

This unusual eatery is in a former Erie firehouse built in 1907. The walls are covered with old firefighting equipment and pictures from the late 1800s, when firefighters used steam pumps and engines (or "pufferbellies"). Firehouse chili is a specialty.

Sugar N Spice. 32 High St., Waterford; 814/796–0060. $

This lively restaurant is in the former Eagle Hotel, now part of the Fort Le Boeuf Museum. At lunchtime, it swarms with local businesspeople and grandmothers, but few tourists. Comfort foods like juicy roast beef, mashed potatoes, and creamy coleslaw are mainstays here.

GETTING AROUND

The quickest route north to Erie from Pittsburgh is I–273 to I–79, which skirts Harmony, Zelienople, Volant, and Meadville on its way to Lake Erie. From the northeast, scenic U.S. 6 shows the region to its best advantage, passing through Warren, Youngsville, Columbus, and Albion before ending at I–90 near the Ohio border. From southeastern Pennsylvania, the quickest route to the northwest is I–80, connecting from Route 476 if you're coming from Philadelphia, and connecting from Route 81 from Harrisburg.

FAVORITE PLACES TO STAY

Allegheny National Forest campgrounds. 877/444–6777. $

The U.S. Forest Service maintains campsites throughout the Allegheny forest. Campgrounds range from "developed" sites with hot showers and flush toilets to "primitive" sites accessible only by hiking or boat, with hand-pumped water. The Willow Bay Recreation Area, just south of the New York border, offers five rustic cabins adjacent to bath houses.

Kane Manor. 230 Clay St., Kane; 814/837–6522. $

This bed-and-breakfast is in a turn-of-the-19th-century mansion commissioned by Civil War Gen. Thomas L. Kane. Its 10 rooms, many with private baths, are furnished with antiques. The mansion has a cozy wood-burning fireplace in the rotunda, which overlooks the sprawling forest.

Riverside Inn. 1 Fountain Ave., Cambridge Springs; 814/398–4645. $

This former spa on the banks of French Creek continues to pamper, even if its fountain of youth no longer runs. The white clapboard structure, built in 1885, is surrounded by pretty gardens. The somewhat dated rooms, which don't have TVs or phones, are furnished with antiques. But if the weather cooperates, you'll be hanging out on the wraparound porch, anyway. It's open April through Thanksgiving.

PRACTICAL INFORMATION

BUSINESS HOURS

Stores open around 10 and close at 6 or 7 on weekdays, an hour or two later on weekends. In Philadelphia's Center City, stores stay open later on Wednesday nights, and the galleries in Old City are open late on the first Friday of every month. Though the state no longer enforces Blue Laws, only a few liquor stores are open Sunday. All alcohol except beer is sold through the Liquor Control Board's wine and spirit stores. Most museums are closed on Monday, but call to check hours.

CLIMATE

Cloudy days are common in western Pennsylvania throughout the year. Spring starts in early April in most of Pennsylvania (May in the northern regions), and fall comes gradually in October, with temperatures dropping dramatically all around the state by the end of the month. Ski areas in the mountain ranges generally have snow from December through March. Winter in Pennsylvania can be forbiddingly cold, with heavy snow squalls between November and February.

BEST TIMES TO VISIT

Each season has something different to offer in each region of Pennsylvania—skiing in winter, river tubing in summer, hiking in fall and spring. The very touristy areas in the Dutch Country and Philadelphia are much more congested during school holidays and in summer. You'll get better deals on hotels and enjoy some breathing room at attractions like Independence Hall and Kitchen Kettle Village during other times of year. Fall is ideal for leaf-peeping and antiquing. There are also some wonderful arts festivals around the state during the temperate months.

An Amish hat shop.

GETTING THERE AND AROUND

BY AIR

Philadelphia International Airport (PHL) is 8 miles southwest of downtown and is accessible from I–76, I–95, and I–476. [sc]septa[esc]'s R1 regional rail line runs between the airport and downtown, *8900 Essington Ave., off I–95; 215/937–6937; www.phl.org.*

Pittsburgh International Airport (PIT) is the northeastern hub for US Airways. The airport is accessible to downtown via Route 60 and I–279 South. *1000 Airport Blvd.; 412/472–3525; www.pitairport.com.*

BY BUS

Greyhound has the greatest number of scheduled bus routes in the state and has long-distance service to New York, Boston, Washington, D.C., and beyond. *800/231–2222; www.greyhound.com.*

PATransit. Port Authority Transit has bus routes throughout the Allegheny County region, many beginning in Pittsburgh. *412/566–5500; www.portauthority.org.*

BY CAR

The main driving routes through Pennsylvania are I–79, running between West Virginia and Erie in the western portion of the state; and I–80, running between the Ohio border and New Jersey. The Pennsylvania Turnpike (I–76) runs between New Jersey and Ohio, passing through Philadelphia and into some of the state's most beautiful territory. I–81 enters from New York and runs through Scranton, Wilkes-Barre, Hershey, and continues south into Maryland. All of the freeways are in good condition. In rural areas, once you exit the freeways, the roads can be narrow and winding, and lacking signage. Bring good maps and a cell phone while exploring. You can turn right on red unless a sign reads otherwise. All gas stations are self-serve. For more regionally specific driving information, see the Getting Around sections at the end of the preceding chapters.

BY TRAIN

Amtrak. Philadelphia is one of the cities on Amtrak's Northeast Corridor route; trains arrive here from New York, Boston, Baltimore, Washington, D.C., and other cities. Amtrak also provides service to Pittsburgh, Harrisburg, and other cities in central and western Pennsylvania. *800/872–7245; www.amtrak.com.*

FESTIVALS AND EVENTS

Check with the Pennsylvania Tourism Board at www.visitpa.com to get the full rundown on what's happening where and when.

JANUARY

Mummers Parade, Philadelphia. The festive Mummers strut their stuff through Center City on New Year's Day. *215/336–3050.*

FEBRUARY

Groundhog Day Celebration. An old-fashioned four-day festival full of hay rides, tours of pretty Punxsutawney, food, and, of course, Phil, the famous groundhog who got his star turn in the Bill Murray and Andie McDowell film, *Groundhog Day.* Gobbler's Knob, Punxsutawney. *800/752–7445.*

MARCH

Charter Day. On the second Sunday in March, free admission to the Natural History Museum in Ambridge and tours of Hope Lodge in Fort Washington commemorate the granting of Pennsylvania's charter to William Penn in 1681. Ambridge (724/266–4500); Fort Washington (215/591–5250).

Philadelphia Flower Show. Ten acres of floral displays, contests, and demos make up the largest indoor flower show in the world, which takes place over a week in early March. Every year has a different theme, such as Irish gardens. *215/988–8888.*

APRIL

New Wilmington Quilt Auction, Wilmington Grange. Held the third Saturday in April and October, the auction is a tradition more than two decades old, with quiltmakers and buyers coming from all over the country. *724/946–2425.*

The Philadelphia Antiques Show. The crème de la crème of suppliers sell at this show benefiting the U. of Penn's hospital. There are usually one or two other, more reasonable, shows in town that weekend. *610/902–2109.*

World International Beer Festival, Lake Harmony. Around 30 breweries plus live music and international food and craft vendors, at a Poconos resort. *570/722–9111.*

MAY

City of Pittsburgh Marathon. Point State Park. *412/647–7866.*

Pennsylvania Arts & Crafts Country Festival, Fayette County Fairgrounds. Memorial Day weekend. *724/863–4577.*

JUNE

Kutztown Festival. A 10-day Dutch folklife fest with arts, crafts, and Pennsylvania Dutch cooking. *888/674–6136.*

Manayunk Arts Festival. One weekend in June, Main Street is a sea of booths selling arts, crafts, and food from local boutiques, restaurants, and artisans. *215/842–9565.*

Three Rivers Arts Festival, Pittsburgh. Two weeks of music and dance concerts, exhibits, and festivals in downtown Pittsburgh. *412/281–8723.*

Welcome America, Philadelphia. A 10-day festival celebrating America's birthday in America's birthplace, running before and through the July 4th holiday.

Includes classical and pop concerts, an outdoor movie series, and arts and food fairs. *800/770–5883.*

JULY

Fourth of July at the Point, Pittsburgh. Fireworks and concert. *412/255–2493.*
July 4 in Washington Crossing Historic Park, Philadelphia. Military re-creations, a mock trial of a British spy, open-hearth cooking. *215/493–4076.*

AUGUST

Gettysburg Bluegrass Festival. Four days of concerts. *717/642–8749.*
Johnstown Folkfest, Cambria County. Burgers and bluegrass. *814/539–1889.*
Philadelphia Folk Festival, Schwenksville. Three days of concerts. Come for the day or camp overnight. *800/556–3655.*

SEPTEMBER

Covered Bridge Festival, Washington County. Country-style foods, arts and crafts. *724/228–5520.*
Eisenhower World War II Weekend, Eisenhower National Historic Site, Gettysburg. See Allied tanks and hear war veterans' stories. *717/338–9114.*
Mushroom Festival, Kennett Square. Music, arts, and mushrooms. *888/440–9920.*
North East Wine Fest, Erie County. A long weekend of wine tastings, demos, and food. *814/725–4262.*

OCTOBER

Fort Ligonier Days, Ligonier. Commemorates the battle at the fort. *724/238–4200.*
Great Pumpkin Event, Chadds Ford. Artists carve pumpkins. *610/388–7376.*

NOVEMBER

Clayton Holiday Tours, Pittsburgh. Frick house tours. *412/371–0600.*
Overly's Country Christmas, Westmoreland Fairgrounds. Through December, see 2.4 million lights blaze away at this drive-through display. *800/968–3759.*

DECEMBER

Christmas at Old Economy Village, Ambridge. The Beaver County home of the Harmonists holds a two-day event in early December. *724/266–1803.*

Reenactment of Washington's Crossing, Washington Crossing. *215/493–4076.*
Christkindlmark, Bethlehem. A week-long holiday fair modeled after Germany's traditional open-air holiday markets. Crafts, ice sculpting, holiday edibles, and, of course, Santa Claus. *610/332–1300.*

VISITOR INFORMATION

Allegheny Mountains. *800/842–5866; www.alleghenymountains.com.*
Armstrong County. 800/265–9954; www.armstrongcounty.com.
Beaver County. 800/342–8192; www.co.beaver.pa.us.
Brandywine. 800/343–3983; www.brandywinecvb.org.
Butler County. 800/741–6772; www.butlercountychamber.com.
Erie Area. 800/542–3743; www.eriepa.com.
Gettysburg. 800/337–5015; www.gettysburg.com.
Laurel Highlands. 800/925–7669; www.laurelhighlands.org.
Lehigh Valley. 800/747–0561; www.lehighvalleypa.org.
Mercer County. 800/637–2370; www.mercercountypa.org.
Penn State Country. 800/358–5466; www.visitpennstate.org.
Pennsylvania Dutch. 800/723–8824; www.padutchcountry.com.
Pennsylvania Tourism. 800/847–4872; www.visitpa.com.
Philadelphia. 800/575–7676; www.gophila.com.
Pittsburgh. 800/366–0093; www.visitpittsburgh.com.
Pocono Mountains. 800/762–6667; www.800poconos.com.
Washington County. 800/531–4114; www.washpatourism.org.

OTHER USEFUL WEB SITES

City Papers. Philadelphia and Pittsburgh weeklies have news, features, and events listings. *www.pghcitypaper.com, www.citypaper.net, www.philadelphia weekly.com.*
Philadelphia blogs. Written by locals: *www.uwishunu.com.* Restaurant news and reviews: *www.foobooz.com.* Events and listings: *www.phillyist.com.*
Factory Tours in Pennsylvania. *www.factorytoursinpa.com.*
Pennsylvania Hunting & Fishing. *www.pahuntandfish.com.*
Philadelphia. Check out the "Best of" lists. *www.phillymag.com*
Philadelphia History. Informative site highlights city history with stories about people, neighborhoods, and events at *www.ushistory.org/philadelphia.* Also see Independence National Park's Web site at *www.nps.gov/inde.*

Philadelphia Inquirer. Site of city's biggest daily newspaper. *www.philly.com.*
Pittsburgh. Monthly magazine has features about the town, plus arts, dining, and other listings. *www.wqed.org/mag*
Pittsburgh Post-Gazette. Daily newspaper's site. *www.post-gazette.com.*
Pittsburgh Regional History Center. History and culture of western Pennsylvania. *www.pghhistory.org.*
Western Pennsylvania Museum Council. *www.westernpamuseums.org.*

INDEX

ACKNOWLEDGMENTS

PUBLISHER'S ACKNOWLEDGMENTS

All photographs in this book are by Jerry Irwin unless noted below. Compass American Guides would like to thank the following individuals or institutions (from Pennsylvania unless noted otherwise) for the use of their photographs, illustrations, or both: **Abby Aldrich Rockefeller Folk Art Center**, p. 104; **Allegheny Forest National Vacation Bureau**, p. 281; **Atwater Kent Museum of Philadelphia, Historical Society of Pennsylvania Collection**, p. 17; **Justina C. Barrett**, p. 178; **Bucks County Visitors Bureau**, p. 121; **Carnegie Library of Pittsburgh**, p. 32; **Cumberland County Historical Society, Carlisle**, p. 176; **Fallingwater Western Pennsylvania Conservancy** p. 274; **Family Communications, Inc.**, p. 231 (photo by Walter Seng); **Fonthill Library**, p. 115 (Barry Halkin); **Free Library of Philadelphia Rare Book Department**, p. 19; **Frick Art and Historical Center**, p. 245 (Ken Love); **Granger Collection, New York**, p. 224; **Greater Philadelphia Tourism Marketing Corporation**, pp. 46, 75 (Bob Krist); **Heritage Center Museum, Lancaster**, pp. 132, 133; **Hershey Entertainment and Resorts**, p. 141; **Historical Society of Western Pennsylvania, Library and Archives Division, Pittsburgh**, pp. 225, 226, 267; **Independence Seaport Museum**, p. 67 (John F. Williams); **Johnstown Area Heritage Association**, p. 273; **Kimmel Center for the Performing Arts**, pp. 48–49 (Jeff Goldberg), 76 and 78 (Roman Viñoly); **Kittochitinny Historical Society**, p. 200; **Library of Congress**, pp. 27, 31, 89, 227, 228, 241; **Library of Congress, Geography and Map Division**, pp. 39; **Library of Congress, Prints and Photographs Division**, p. 24 (LC-USZ62–112159); **Library of Congress Prints and Photographs Division, Farm Security Administration–Office of War Information Photograph Collection**, p. 21 (LC-USF34-082411E); **Library of Congress Rare Book and Special Collections Division**, p. 171; **Laurence Loewy**, p. 171; **Daniel Mangin**, p. 56; **Mattress Factory**, p. 252; **National Archives**, p. 189 (220-TMI-42-2785-29); **National Center for the American Revolution/Valley Forge Historical Society**, p. 26; **National Museum of American History**, p. 230; **New York Public Library**, pp. 22, 45; **Old Print Shop, New York**, p. 214; **Penn's Cave**, p. 287; **Pennsylvania Dutch Convention and Visitors Bureau**, pp. 127, 131, 141 (Keith Baum);

ABOUT THE AUTHORS

A graduate of Pennsylvania State University, **DOUGLAS ROOT** has written for several newspapers, including *The Pittsburgh Press.* He received an Alicia Patterson Foundation fellowship for documentary journalism, and he has written for *Time,* the *Washington Post,* the *Washingtonian,* the *Philadelphia Inquirer,* and *Mother Jones.*

GWEN SHAFFER moved to Philadelphia for a reporting job in 1998, intending to stay for just a year. Instead, she was charmed by the city's cobblestone streets and its lively cultural scene. For this edition, she revised the chapters on Central Pennsylvania, Pittsburgh, the Southwest, and the Northwest. Shaffer has worked as a journalist for 14 years. She is a former staff writer for *Philadelphia Weekly,* and her work has appeared in the *New Republic,* the *Columbia Journalism Review,* the *Nation, Philadelphia* magazine, the *Philadelphia Inquirer,* and *Two.One.Five* magazine. Her favorite way to start the day is with a vigorous row on the Schuylkill River, and whenever she gets the chance

Shaffer goes hiking in the nearby Poconos or raptor-watching at Hawk Mountain.

CAROLINE TIGER is a freelance journalist and author, and a former managing editor of *Philadelphia* magazine. Her byline has appeared in *Departures, Town & Country, Fortune Small Business, National Geographic Traveler,* and the *Washington Post.* She writes frequently about travel, design, business, and the culinary arts. Tiger has also authored books on the Battle of Germantown, Philadelphia architecture, and modern manners. She grew up in New Jersey but has lived in Center City Philadelphia since graduating from the University of Pennsylvania in 1996. For this edition, she revised the chapters on Pennsylvania's culture and history, Philadelphia, the Southeast, the Northeast and the Poconos, and Practical Information.

ABOUT THE

PHOTOGRAPHER

A Lancaster County resident, **JERRY IRWIN** is a nationally recognized photographer known especially for his images of the Amish. His photo essays have appeared in *National Geographic, Life, Country Journal,* German and French *GEO* and numerous other publications. A former locomotive engineer with the old Pennsylvania Railroad, Irwin has also been an active skydiver for three decades.